THE PLANET CONSTRUCTION KIT

The Planet Construction Kit

by Mark Rosenfelder

☰♀ YONAGU BOOKS

www.yonagu.com • Chicago • 2010

Contents

Introduction

What we're going to do here is create worlds. You want a world for your epic novel, or a movie or video game, or an RPG session, or as an artistic creation. Or you are a mad scientist with an army of nanites who will construct your world from the atoms up. Whatever, we'll talk about how to make a plausible, interesting constructed world— a conworld.

The companion volume, *The Language Construction Kit*, explained how to create languages, so I won't cover that that here. This book covers everything else:

- Stars and planets
- Alien creatures
- Economics and history
- Daily life
- Religions
- Magic
- Technology and war

And more. We'll also cover some of the technical details of creation:

- Storytelling
- Drawing
- Making maps
- Making 3-D models

I've tried to answer all the immediate questions you'll have while conworlding, from how to calculate the year (p. 42) to how far a horse can run in a day (p. 142) to how early you can have iron weapons (p. 228).

Sources and extra reading

The *Language Construction Kit* served as an introduction to one subject, linguistics. This book is an introduction to all kinds of stuff, and I'm not an expert in all of them. And in some areas, no one is: magic or alien biology, for instance.

On the bright side, one advantage of conworlding is that *everything* is source material. Anything in the physical sciences could be relevant. Anything historical or religious can go into fantasy; anything you learn about foreign cultures can help you create new ones.

In some ways I should have written five books instead of one. But it's useful, and a lot cheaper for you, to have all of this material in one place. Plus, if any subject interests you, you can always pursue it more. I've included an **reading list** at the end with books I've found particularly helpful. These will also supply the details and nuances I haven't had room for.

You can be inspired by fiction, of course, but make sure you read real-world sources as well. You may be able to write a convincing battle scene merely by reading Tolkien, but you'd do better to read some military history. Or join the army.

Websites: URLs rot too quickly to list in a book. I'll list some useful pages on this page of my own site:

> http://www.zompist.com/resources/pck.html

The dire consequences of failure

What happens if you don't follow the recommendations in this book? Well, not to be too alarming, but that could well be part of a process which ends in *the heat death of the universe*. But in the short term, the advantages of the book are these:

- **More options**. All too often fantasy books are retreads of medieval Europe, and s.f. books of contemporary America. It's like a painter who's restricted to using yellow and orange.

- Greater **accuracy** and **immersion**. If you don't know much, you're bound to write vaguely. If you write about a swordfight, you want to go beyond just knowing that the combatants swing pointy things at each other.

- **Depth** and **allusion**. As an example, my novel *In the Land of Babblers* occasionally quotes the Cuzeian holy book, *the Count of Years*. This isn't just a made-up name; this book exists and people can go read it. Or people who've read it as an aspect of my conworld will recognize the reference when they read *Babblers*. This is part of Tolkien's secret; we sense while reading that his world is larger than the books before us.

- **Memorability**. A well constructed world is fascinating in its own right; we want to go there. The underground London of Neil Gaiman's *Neverwhere*, for instance, is as much of an enticement as the characters or the plot.

- **Avoidance of distractions** for the reader. You want the reader following your story, not snickering at the cheesy or implausible bits.

Getting started

How do you start creating a culture?

There's no obvious or necessary order, but I'd suggest something like this:

- Choose the **big picture** elements, if any, that have the biggest impact on the world. If your people have three sexes, or live on a gas giant, or all use magic, or live a thousand years, those things will affect everything else you do.

- Look over the **E-Z Fantasy World** chapter (p. 15) to make some basic decisions. This can give you a brief overview of your culture.

- Make a **map**. Don't worry too much about names. It just helps to know the geographical situation for your people: is it an island? is it big or small? is it hemmed in by threatening neighbors?

- Write a **culture test** (p. 118). This is an easy way to cover many aspects of what it's like, day to day, to live in your invented culture, and how it's different from your own.

- Create a **naming language**— for how, see the *Language Construction Kit*. You're going to want names for characters and places anyway.

- Write a **biography** of a characteristic person from your culture (p. 30)— not the protagonist of your epic story or game, but an ordinary shmo. You'll have to think about their childhood, what their village looks like, how they make a living, how families and marriages work, what rites they follow and what games they play.

  If you created some unusual Big Picture elements, this is your chance to see how they actually work. If they don't really affect the character's story, they're either not so major after all, or you didn't fully work out their consequences.

- Write an **outline history**. Don't worry about lists of kings. Ideally, the place used to be quite different, and there's a story about how it changed. E.g.

It used to be...	*and now it's...*
a vast empire	a motley collection of states
ruled by elves	dominated by humans
two separate nations	united, with cultural remnants of the former independent countries
a rich and prosperous planet	nearly destroyed
underwater	reclaimed bit by bit into a prosperous nation
a nation of bold warriors	a bunch of pedantic bureaucrats
full of magic	mundane, with a few exceptions
mundane	transformed by magic

- **Read this book**, applying what you've learned chapter by chapter. That is, systematically cover the astronomy, geology, biology, culture, and religion of your culture.

Expect to have to **revise** as you work out details. You may toss in a reference to "the gods" in your culture test and then discover that the people actually worship ancestors and spirit animals.

Don't worry if your first attempts are crappy. It's always good to get something down, and revising is easier than writing from scratch. Put the crappy piece aside for awhile; then take it out and identify specific problems— not "it sucks" but "the king is talking like a teenager" or "no reasons are given for any of these events". Then address those.

How to present it

Creating a language, there's an obvious end product: a grammar. What do you do with a conculture?

- One possible answer: **nothing**, it's all background material for a story or game, and once you've created that, you have no further use for the background materials.

- Or you write **appendixes**, as in *Lord of the Rings*. These days, you can post as much supplementary material as you want on the web.

- In some media you can use it as **supplementary creations**. The games made by Bethesda (*Oblivion*, *Fallout 3*) and Bioware (*Jade Empire*, *Dragon Age Origins*, *Mass Effect*) are great examples: they contain quite a bit of material players can find and explore if they like.

- A natural format for concultures is the **wiki**. For my conworld Almea I've created the Almeopedia. You can post everything you've created in such a format, and readers can explore it as much as they like and in any order. Wookieepedia, the fan-created *Star Wars* wiki, has over 75,000 articles.

  The web resources page includes instructions on how to set up a wiki.

- Conworld materials may make a good **RPG scenario**, especially if you have a strong focus on specific locations. Add some monsters and loot and it becomes a playable game!

- You can publish your material as a **supplementary text**. François Bourgeon and Claude Lacroix, after creating two s.f. graphic novels, *Le cycle de Cyann*, released a third volume which simply documented the amazing world they'd created. *Star Wars* has generated a whole array of reference works.

- Some authors have created **pseudo-nonfiction** where a book about the world is the main event. One example is the Italian artist Luigi Serafini's *Codex Seraphinianus*, a brilliant and thoroughly weird encyclopedia from an alien culture, profusely illustrated, with a text in an unreadable alphabet. Another is Dougal Dixon's *After Man,* a gallery of animals from 50 million years in the future.

- With modern tools it doesn't take a huge company to make a **video game**. *Zeno Clash*, a game that shows off an impressively bizarre conworld, was created by a team of ten people. A quality mod for an existing game can be made by a single person.

One of the best ways of making a culture come alive is **visually**. Maps, character portraits, and 3-D models help immensely in showing what your culture is like. We'll cover all of that in later chapters.

When am I done?

This question is also harder to answer for conworlds. Here too the most honest answer is **never**. One individual can never fully work out all the cultures of a planet, much less a galaxy full. There's always more to do.

Or more usefully: you're done when you have **just enough** material for the uses you're going to put it to. If you're writing a short story, a brief sketch will do. For a novel you might end up with pages and pages of notes. For a series of works, you may easily end up with a book's worth of supplementary material.

A basic rule of thumb might be: you have enough material when you can answer all the questions that come up when writing your story.

A warning: **this stuff is addictive**. Especially if you have another main goal in mind— like writing a novel— you can overdo the conworlding. Eventually you have to put aside the royal genealogies and the table of currency conversions and write the damn story.

Skipping and faking

As with the LCK, **you don't have to read** everything, much less work out everything I talk about. I hope it's all useful, but I realize that it can be daunting.

Go back and forth between this book, the LCK, your own background materials, and your stories. It's fine to write a paragraph about your conreligion now and flesh it out later. Or let the demands of the story drive the process. If a character dies, think about your culture's treatment of death.

Here and there I'll give tips on **faking it**. The biggest tip: if you refer to fine-grained details, it looks like you've worked everything out even if you haven't. Take the famous speech at the end of *Blade Runner*:

> *I've seen things you people wouldn't believe. Attack ships on fire off the shoulder of Orion. I've watched C-beams glitter in the dark near the Tannhauser Gate. All those moments will be lost in time, like tears in the rain. Time to die.*

It's specific and memorable even if neither viewer nor screenwriter knows what the fighting in Orion was about, nor what C-beams are, nor where the Tannhauser Gate leads to.

But I like it implausible!

I'm going to talk a lot about plausibility— how to make realistic planets, animals, aliens, cultures, and religions. To save space, I'll give you blanket permission here to ignore all the guidelines.

We're making art here; art can take liberties. And of course you can always fall back on magic, or engineering by highly advanced intelligences, or new physical laws.

I talk about how things work on our planet for two reasons. First, you might want to keep things realistic. And second, it broadens your options. The real world is highly inventive.

Plus, if you know how things generally go, you know what to change or reverse to create strangeness and fantasy. Take a general rule mentioned here— e.g., humans posit supernatural beings they can ask favors of— then twist it around. What about a culture where the spirits ask favors of us? Even the rules of drawing can be purposely violated in order to create misshapen monsters (p. 302).

Date conventions

For brevity I often write 5C for "the 5th century AD", i.e. the 400s, and likewise -13C is "the 13th century BC", i.e. the 1200s BC.

Acknowledgments

Many thanks to those who read and made comments on drafts of this book: James Miers, Samuel Lereah, Dave Townsend, Benjamin Buckley, Geoff Eddy, Richard Weatherby, Carlos Verrecchia, Ugo Lachapelle, Michele Moss, and Ian Samuels. Thanks to Richard Seal for help on Almean climates, to Ken Hite and Mike Schiffer for a long alternate history lunch, and to Samwise for the use of his head. And to my wife Lida who has been incredibly supportive.

Mark Rosenfelder

September 2010

E-Z Fantasy World

Fantasy worlds in particular often seem all the same— usually, medieval Europe minus Christianity plus magic.

Let's take a pop quiz on your culture. For each item, choose one option. As each is independent of the others, there are over 438 trillion possible cultures— enough for every conworld to be different, and for each to have a full set of differing cultures.

And there's even more, of course, if you blend the options or come up with new ones.

This alone isn't enough to give a country a strong character of its own, of course. We'll get to that later. But the quiz is designed to break the habit of *always* creating Standard Fantasy Kingdoms.

Government

- Absolute monarch
- King and council
- Oligarchy
- Theocracy (for any belief system)
- Elite democracy (a large electorate but still a minority)
- Full democracy (universal electorate)
- Warlord
- Clan leaders only, perhaps a king in wartime
- None at all

How is the **leader** chosen?

- Heredity
- By family council

15

- By the secondary powers (council, priests, voters— see previous item)
- By contests of skill, strength, and/or intelligence
- By the military
- By divine powers
- Randomly
- By a secret cabal

How **unified** is the country?

- Completely centralized
- Nobles govern their own lands but king is powerful
- The center has few uncontested powers
- No central power

How **tolerant** are people?

- No dissent allowed!
- Best to follow convention
- Eccentricity is mocked but permitted
- Do as you please

How do most people get their **food**?

- Hunting and gathering
- Fishing
- Garden agriculture (plots cleared, cultivated awhile, then abandoned)
- Rainfall agriculture
- Irrigation agriculture
- Animal herds (pastoralism)
- Magic
- Algae vats and slabs of mutant ever-growing chicken meat

What's the **climate**?

- Temperate
- Tropical
- Extreme— desert, mountains, tundra
- Unusual— the sea, outer space, the spirit realm

What kind of **economy** is there?

- Communities are self-sufficient except for luxuries
- Command economy— industry controlled by the state
- Nationwide market economy
- The nation is part of a sophisticated international trade network

How does the **army** work?

- Professional standing army
- The powers that be each have their own army
- The citizens as a whole form the army
- There's nothing we'd call an army

What's the most-used **weapon**?

- Bow and arrow
- Sword
- Spears or pikes
- Guns
- Antimatter propulsors
- One's own body
- Magic

What's the **literacy** level?

- Nearly universal
- Only the elite
- None
- Writing is superseded by telepathy or high technology

How prevalent is **magic**?

- Almost everyone can use it
- Restricted to a small, secretive class
- Rare— there are only a few wizards
- Nonexistent

What's the essence of magic?

- A biological ability
- A natural power that can be harnessed like technology
- A natural resource (e.g. mana) which may be exhausted
- Communing with supernatural beings
- Accessing a separate dimension
- Special properties of some herbs or minerals
- Superstition and chicanery

What's the overall **technology**?

- Tribal
- Bronze age (looms, kilns, chariots, spears)
- Classical (sailing ships, aqueducts, water mills, swords)
- Renaissance (telescopes, watches, windmills, artillery)
- Early modern (science, rifles, sailing ships, factories)
- Age of steam
- Contemporary
- Futuristic
- Godlike

What do people **worship** or invoke?

- God
- The gods
- Spirit animals
- Their ancestors

- Another species
- Minor spiritual beings
- Nothing

What is the most admired **class**? Or to put it another way, whose values and interests are paramount?

- Nobles and kings
- Priests and clerics
- The military
- Merchants or manufacturers
- Scholars or magicians
- Another species

What's the **lowest class**?

- Slaves
- Serfs
- A motley collection of poor people
- Castes devoted to unpleasant jobs (e.g. gravediggers)
- A foreign community or racial minority
- Another species

How are **women** treated?

- Equally with men
- Men are completely dominant
- Men are usually the leaders, but there are powerful women and some female-run institutions
- The sexes divide up work and control different institutions in society
- Women are in control

What's the attitude toward **sex**?

- Restricted to marriage
- Marriage is one thing, romance/sex is another

- There are some accepted outlets besides marriage
- Freely indulged
- Restricted to an elite

What are the major **species**?

- Just humans
- Just humanoid cats
- Several species, but separated by region or habitat
- Several species, fairly intermingled
- Several species, separated by class or profession (e.g. one forms the servant class)

What's the most pressing **problem**?

- Other nations (barbarians or civilized states)
- Demons
- Another species
- Rebellion or civil war
- Tyranny
- A dangerous secret cabal
- Ecological collapse
- Just ordinary cussedness

Storytelling

Many conworlds are intended to be background for a story. So it's worth looking at how conworlding can serve storytelling.

The basics of story

Stories involve conflict and failure.

As my improv-trained friend Michele puts it, "Stories begin when things go wrong. *How I flew from Boston to Chicago* isn't a story. *How I got to Chicago when the plane never took off* is a story."

Once you get past the basics— this planet is 1.04 Earth masses, the elves have pointy ears and the elven kings have pointy hair— conworlding is a series of little stories too, and they need conflict and failure.

Bad!	*Good!*
Ervëa was the greatest emperor of Caðinas, who conquered the ktuvok empire.	Ervëa was the rightful emperor of Caðinas, but deposed as a boy by his usurping uncle Sevurias. He was saved by the local garrison, who defeated the force Sevurias sent to arrest him. The realm plunged into civil war. Ervëa finally defeated Sevurias, only to be faced with a massive invasion by the ktuvoks...
Morgan is the greatest agent of the Terran Incatena, who was responsible for ending the dictatorship on Okura.	Morgan arrived on Okura, only to be intercepted by agents of the dictatorship posing as tourist guides. The canny agent evaded them and began to organize a resistance. Just when the resistance broke out into all-out war, Morgan was betrayed...

21

David Mamet has memorably explained the basic formula for drama: Someone has a problem. They take action to solve it, and it's going well. At the last minute it fails. The bad guys advance— they're about to win! They're stopped just in time. Then the pattern repeats.

Of course, we like heroes with extraordinary abilities, and we like to see them walloping mundane challengers (muggers, tiny hunters with speech impediments). But to keep the story interesting, extraordinary heroes need to encounter extraordinary challengers.

You know this— it's taught by every blockbuster epic and movie. But it can still be tempting to have your main conculture the most advanced civilization on the planet, happy and well-ordered, united under their noble monarch. If it's that well ordered, there's few stories to be told there... your heroes will have to light out for the wilderness to have any adventures.

Nick Hornby stated it nicely: as a reader, I want to read about the worst time of your characters' lives. If it's only the second worst time, I'm going to feel cheated.

That isn't to say that all stories must be violent. A romance, like *Pride and Prejudice*, is largely the story of obstacles that must be overcome before the match can proceed.

Overexplaining

The easiest vice for a conworlder to fall into is **overexplaining**. You have all this beautiful material to use; why not put it in?

Now, I'm a huge fan of detailed worldbuilding; but the best practitioners are also great storytellers, and they never let exposition get in the way of the story. And they know when *not* to explain things.

Tolkien is a good and bad example. A huge amount of his worldbuilding is only alluded to in *LOTR*— you have to look elsewhere to understand what exactly Gandalf is, how the Númenoreans fell, even what happened to God. At the same time he can't resist beginning with an explanatory anthropological (hobbitological?) sketch, and the first book is filled with people explaining things to each other.

Science fiction can be much worse. I wrote a little sketch to show what the same approach would be like if applied to the contemporary world:

If most stories were written like s.f.

Roger and Ann needed to meet Sergey in San Francisco.

"Should we take a train, or a steamship, or a plane?" asked Ann.

"Trains are too slow, and the trip by steamship through the Panama Canal would take months," replied Roger. "We'll take a plane."

He logged onto the central network using his personal computer, and waited while the system verified his identity. With a few keystrokes he entered an electronic ticketing system, and entered the codes for his point of departure and his destination. In moments the computer displayed a list of possible flights, and he picked the earliest one. Dollars were automatically deducted from his personal account to pay for the transaction.

The planes left from the city airport, which they reached using the city bi-rail. Ann had changed into her travelling outfit, which consisted of a light shirt in polycarbon-derived artificial fabric, which showed off her pert figure, without genetic enhancements, and dark blue pants made of natural textiles. Her attractive brown hair was uncovered.

At the airport Roger presented their identification cards to a representative of the airline company, who used her own computer system to check his identity and retrieve his itinerary. She entered a confirmation number, and gave him two passes which gave them access to the boarding area. They now underwent a security inspection, which was required for all airline flights. They handed their luggage to another representative; it would be transported in a separate, unpressurized chamber on the aircraft.

"Do you think we'll be flying on a propeller plane? Or one of the newer jets?" asked Ann.

"I'm sure it will be a jet," said Roger. "Propeller planes are almost entirely out of date, after all. On the other hand, rocket engines are still experimental. It's said that when they're in general use, trips like this will take an hour at most. This one will take up to four hours."

After a short wait, they were ushered onto the plane with the other passengers. The plane was an enormous steel cylinder at least a hundred meters long, with sleek backswept wings on which four jet engines were mounted. They glanced into the front cabin and saw the two pilots, consulting a bank of equipment needed to fly the plane. Roger was glad that he did not need to fly the plane himself; it was a difficult profession which required years of training.

The surprisingly large passenger area was equipped with soft benches, and windows through which they could look down at the countryside as they flew 11 km high at more than 800 km/h. There were nozzles for the pressurized air which kept the atmosphere in the cabin warm and comfortable despite the coldness of the stratosphere.

"I'm a little nervous," Ann said, before the plane took off.

"There's nothing to worry about," he assured her. "These flights are entirely routine. You're safer than you are in our ground transport cars!"

Despite his calm words, Roger had to admit to some anxiety as the pilot took off, and the land dropped away below them. He and the other passengers watched out the windows for a long time. With difficulty, he could make out houses and farms and moving vehicles far below.

"There are more people going to San Francisco today than I would have expected," he remarked.

"Some of them may in fact be going elsewhere," she answered. "As you know, it's expensive to provide airplane links between all possible locations. We employ a hub system, and people from smaller cities travel first to the hub, and then to their final destination. Fortunately, you found us a flight that takes us straight to San Francisco."

When they arrived at the San Francisco airport, agents of the airline company helped them out of their seats and retrieved their luggage, checking the numeric tags to ensure that they were given to the right people.

"I can hardly believe we're already in another city," said Ann. "Just four hours ago we were in Chicago."

"We're not quite there!" corrected Roger. "We're in the airport, which is some distance from the city, since it requires a good deal of space on the ground, and because of occasional accidents. From here we'll take a smaller vehicle into the city."

They selected one of the hydrocarbon-powered ground transports from the queue which waited outside the airport. The fee was small enough that it was not paid electronically, but using portable dollar tokens. The driver conducted his car unit into the city; though he drove only at 100 km/hr, it felt much faster since they were only a meter from the concrete road surface. He looked over at Ann, concerned that the speed might alarm her; but she seemed to be enjoying the ride. A game girl, and intelligent as well!

At last the driver stopped his car, and they had arrived. Electronic self-opening doors welcomed them to Sergey's building. The entire trip had taken less than seven hours.

Some rules of thumb

So what should you do and not do?

- The big no-no: characters **explaining things** to each other that they **already know**. You have several alternatives:

  ○ Show, don't explain. Is your transportation system bus-sized angry yaks? Fine, describe what they look like, how big they are, show them nearly biting someone's head off. If any aspect really doesn't affect the story, leave it out.

  ○ Have a viewpoint character that's not from the culture. Then you have an excuse to describe all the things that are as novel to them as to the reader.

  ○ Put all the fancy details in an appendix or web page.

  ○ If your ideas are highly visual, illustrate them instead. Comics, movies, and video games can easily show off an exotic world. You can't spend much time *describing* your huge yaks, but in visual media the reader can directly experience them.

- If you have a really neat bit of conworlding, **tailor the plot** to show it off.

  ○ This is the essence of s.f.— the story is *about* the details of the setting as much as it is about the characters and their conflicts. Asimov's robot stories, for instance, are explorations of robot nature and the relationship between robots and humans. If your world is permeated by magic, your story had better have magician characters and plot situations that can only be solved by magic.

  ○ The classic means of exploring a world is a quest. It just happens that to solve her problems, your heroine needs to visit a rogue in the slums, a princess in the capital, a magician in the Purple Forest, and the cultists in the elven ruins.

    °   Another natural story form for exploration, and one that isn't as exploited in fantasy and s.f., is the detective story. Again, you have an excuse to visit many locations and people of every class.

- Use just a few telling details. In an S.F. story, to get the characters from point A to point B as in the above passage, all we need is "Roger and Ann took the next shuttle to Lowell City." But you can certainly make it more flavorful:

> *Roger and Ann took the first shuttle they saw. The pilot was a huge and malodorous Mollostoman, whose tentacles seemed to fill the cabin and had to be constantly swatted away. Even worse was his conversation, a mumbled rant about the amoebizoids who'd forced him to seek employment among the mammals. It was a relief to step out of the shuttle in Lowell City.*

- Just to please me, avoid this pet peeve of mine: characters who face some aspect of their daily reality unfamiliar to us as if they've never seen it before. E.g. a character in one of the Culture novels spends multiple pages trying to get useful, human-tailored data out of a massive AI. In this world humans and AIs have interacted for *centuries*; this would be an old solved problem.

Evil and Eeeevil

I blame Tolkien for one of the hoariest clichés in fantasy and adventure stories: the eeeevil warlord. Tolkien's heroes have their failings, but his villains are pure evil. Sauron never has any regrets, his agents never come close to making you see their point of view, you never see a cute orc or wonder at the morality of slaughtering them. They're pure sword fodder.

This bugs me because the real world is never like this. Take the most evil leader you can think of, and I guarantee he has his good points and could make a case for himself. His supporters very likely consider themselves good and *your* side to be wrong.

Chris Livingston puts it well:

> *Question: if the monsters ever did take over, what the hell would they do then? Stand around roaring? Do they have other marketable skills besides stabbing villagers and operating catapults? Can any of them grow crops or improve roads or manage an inn?*

It's always safe to write about these dudes— all your readers can be assumed to hate eeeevil. But it's also a huge missed opportunity. Moral dilemmas are a lot more interesting and involving than just fighting.

We can do better. A neat example is the video game *Bioshock*, whose villains are a twisted form of Ayn Rand Objectivists. Using a recognizable real-world philosophy allows the game to serve as satire, and also allows the main culprit, Andrew Ryan, to be a charismatic figure who has a good deal to say for himself. His philosophy is dubious, but his determination and creativity are admirable.

Bad luck for the Objectivists, of course, who will have to console themselves with their positive press in Heinlein novels. No wonder most writers choose eeeevil as a target: eeeevil has no constituency that might lose you sales or send hate mail.

Perhaps authors worry that if the villain isn't eeeevil, people might take his side instead of the hero's? But the open secret is, people *love* villains anyway. Who's the most iconic character from *Star Wars*? Darth Vader, of course, with his creepy mask and elegant robes. Create the most evil creatures you can think up, and I guarantee you that teenage boys will be naming themselves after them in online games.

It's probably a form of the escapism that fuels much of literature: we like to vicariously experience lives of greater adventure than our own. Heroes get to do things we can't, but it's villains who have the ultimate freedom, the freedom from morality. *We* can't choke the snotty guy in the suit using the power of our minds— believe me, I've tried— but Darth Vader can.

As an exercise in making rounded beings, write a speech where your main villain justifies himself as clearly as possible. Why is he doing these terrible things? No one is purely destructive for the hell of it; even revenge is in service to a virtue— justice or honor. If he wants power, what does he want it for? If he's creating orcs, why does he prefer them to humans?

A cute example from Rich Burlew's online comic *The Order of the Stick*: a girl allied with the bad guys explains why she hangs out with the undead:

> *Look, everyone knows that the undead are the antithesis of life, right? Except people are jerks. Lying, untrustworthy jackasses, every one of them. Everyone knows this, too. So logically, undead must be the opposite of that: caring, sensitive honest souls who are oppressed by the living majority and their negative stereotypes.*

It's not deep— she *is* a comic strip character— but she has a reasonable motivation, something we can sympathize with.

Really using your ideas

In Mary Gentle's *Rats and Gargoyles*, one of the characters has a tail. In most fantasy books this would be noted and then forgotten, much like the hobbits' hairy feet. But Gentle tells us on almost every page what the character is doing with her tail. This is the difference between world-building and bringing a world alive.

Another example is the daemons in Philip Pullman's *His Dark Materials*. I confess I don't understand the connection to the idea of souls, but the idea of a double consciousness, one manifested in an animal companion, is fascinating, and Pullman leverages our knowledge of animals without making the daemons into mere pets.

Know your genre

Before you get too far on your world it's good to know what the goals and conventions of your genre are. Fantasy isn't just swords and dragons and wizards; s.f. isn't just robots and spaceships and rayguns.

What both have in common is the importance of the **setting**— that is, the world we're building, what this book is about. Both are an excuse to explore a very different world than the one we live in. And both pay the price of giving up the reader's familiarity with our own world; the easy realism and recognition gained by setting the story in contemporary times.

And in both cases, if there's nothing about the world that differs interestingly from ours, why is it genre at all? If you just want to write a novel of intrigue among the "berons and dux" of "Ferrance and Ingilland", you'd might as well write historical fiction.

In general science fiction plays with the physical, fantasy with the metaphysical. The quintessential s.f. story is about a **neat idea**— teleportation, first contact, robotic intelligence, time travel, psychohistory, telepathy, tesseracts— and rings the changes on it. The quintessential fantasy story is a **spiritual exploration**: an everyman stumbles into a strange and perilous world and has to develop to meet its challenges.

You can mix and match, of course. *Star Wars* is essentially fantasy with s.f. trappings. Many a fantasy game treats magic exactly like technology, with fixed and predictable rules.

Genre conventions are tools to use, not rigid laws; but you need never apologize for following them. For instance, fantasy typically takes place on **earthlike worlds**, with main characters who are human. I emphasize this because making a world more realistic, as I've done with Almea, sometimes raises questions: if it's a different planet, why are the humans nearly identical to Earth's?

The answer is that Almea is fantasy, not s.f. It's informed by astronomy and biology but it's not an attempt to create a science-fictional planet with a thoroughly alien flora and fauna. It's more like an alternative version of Earth.

The genres have different attitudes toward **realism**. Both can cheerfully violate physical laws, but s.f. expects a greater bow toward science. You can invent a new physical law for each short story or episode, but you're expected to treat it consistently. If you've established that blasters can cut through metal, you can never imprison a blaster-wielding character in a metal cell. It's more acceptable in fantasy that (say) a newly introduced villain has previously unmentioned powers that counteract the hero's.

But even in fantasy, **don't cheat the reader**. Magic can be unreliable, but don't let it get out of hand. If you can always invent a spell to get out of any difficult situation, the reader's involvement drops, because there's no real danger. Supernatural powers should be limited, and the reader should generally know what those limits are. There's a reason Gandalf casts fewer spells per day than the lowest-level wizard in a D&D game.

Biography as worldbuilding

A great way to help you figure out your culture and make it come alive is to write a biography of a typical resident.

In this case you'll ignore some of the usual restraints on stories: there's no character arc; the events don't have to be notable— indeed, quite the opposite, since you're telling *everyone's* story: the background condition in your society.

Here's the biography I wrote of a **Lé** peasant named **Múr**.

Birth and infancy

Múr was born in the house belonging to her *jɔ* (family): a large circular structure that was mostly thatched roof, supported by wooden beams. Hammocks were strung here and there for sleeping; dried meat and other stored food hung from the ceiling. She was washed and handed to her mother in a hammock for feeding.

The household seemed to ignore her for three days, not even speaking of her; then it exploded into a storm of activity, culminating in a huge celebration with many rituals, gifts, and blessings. The birth of a daughter was a big event, but only once it was clear she was healthy.

Her infancy was a sort modern developmental psychologists can only dream about: plenty of contact with everyone in the family, nursing on demand, attention as soon as she cried, almost no punishment. She started receiving masticated food early, at six months or so, and wasn't fully weaned till four.

She wore no clothes; she was taken outside the house to relieve herself, and was able to do this on her own before the age of two.

Childhood

When she was four her mother had another child; this was a huge and unwelcome change in Múr's life, since she saw her mother much less and wasn't allowed to nurse. She was hardly ignored, though; she was looked after by almost the whole family, though most often by her father, her older sister, and her grandfather.

Her family farmed in a plot (*brɔ̀ŋ*) cleared from the jungle, adjoining a little stream. It was a quarter hour's walk to the nearest neighbors— though this and longer walks were routine; there were frequent visits for business and pleasure, enough that she soon had friends in other settlements. She learned how the farm worked and began to help out with cleaning, weeding, removing stripcorn and tengbean husks, gathering eggs from the gallenes, watching babies.

The whole family was about 20 people in all; all the females were descendants of Grandmother Lâ, who had died before Múr was born. Her older daughter Prèn, Múr's grandmother, was the new matriarch (*háɔ*). Prèn's younger sister Trâo and her descendants were still part of the *jɔ* as it wasn't large enough to split.

The family had a number of amusements: music, dancing, storytelling, games played with a wooden board and a set of tokens. The children also had toys, often carved for them by the adults: wooden animals, or small representations of adult tools or weapons.

Múr still went about naked, except for various decorations— earrings, beaded necklaces or bracelets. She wore a braided leather band around her waist that was useful for hanging things from, such as her prized possession, a knife. When she was eight, the family dog had puppies, and for some time she carried a puppy around in a sling, the way women carried babies.

By this time she was trusted to go about in the jungle by herself or with other children. They explored quite a bit, sometimes finding a clearing to create their own miniature *brɔ̀ŋ*, complete with a flimsy but serviceable house; or they might walk to another settlement and spend the night with friends. They were safe so long as they didn't stray too far from established trails. Large animals rarely came close to human settlements, and the minor dangers of the jungle (from poisonous slugs to stinging vines to army ants) they had long ago learned to recognize and avoid.

Adolescence

Múr's life changed when she was eleven. First, Prèn and Trâo decided it was time to move. A *brɔ̀ŋ* could only be cultivated for ten years or so. This involved a lot of exciting novelties: hiring a geomancer (*insùŋdlán*) to consult on the right spot; asking the neighboring families for help; trips to the market town for supplies; building the new house; hiring a pair of nawr oxen— frighteningly large and fierce-looking animals— to clear the land.

Secondly, this year marked Múr's transition from girl (*rɛ̀*) to maiden (*dǎr*). In part this meant that she had to work a lot more. Unlike her brothers and male cousins, she'd always be part of this *jɔ*, so she had to know how to do everything from midwifery to horticulture to trading to knowing a hundred or more local plants and what they were good for.

She also began to wear skirts, at first truca fronds hung from her belt, and later a petay loincloth. She continued to wear decorations: bracelets, large earrings, flowers, bright feathers.

There were also family traditions to learn and genealogies and stories to memorize. There were religious practices, so diverse that it's hard to consider them one thing:

- Various taboos, superstitions, cantrips, and rituals, passed on without much rationalization. Why was it forbidden to eat brains? No one really knew (though the practice prevented the spread of certain diseases, and preserved the supply of brains for tanning).

- Stories about goddesses and gods, as well as rituals of appeasement or supplication. People mostly gravitated toward a deity whose personality matched their own; Múr chose the cheerful and helpful Ɖisú.

- Several times Múr was awakened in the middle of the night, dressed in a robe (an uncomfortable sensation), blindfolded, and taken into the jungle, where she was given secret instruction (*sârpáɔ*) that she was not allowed to repeat to males or children. Sometimes this was cosmological tales, or information about sex or the afterlife; sometimes she was given drugs and experienced strange visions.

- Shamans had access to the *nɔŋă*, the spirit realm. They were consulted on grave occasions, such as when someone was sick and ordinary herblore and rituals failed, or when it was necessary to speak to the late Grandmother Lâ.

Múr and her friends indulged in some amount of sexual play— generally when they were alone, as adults discouraged it if they saw it. It wasn't considered very serious before menstruation; once this began, when Múr was about fifteen, she was strongly discouraged from actually having sex. This was the subject of one of the more frightening *sârpáɔ*, and Múr was careful to follow the prescription. (The boys she played with were younger and followed her lead.)

Marriage

When she was eighteen, the family began to seriously look around for a potential husband. Everyone older than Múr had advice or had a candidate to propose. There were a number of rather awkward visits to neighboring families or to the market town. Múr knew many of the boys already, but it was one thing to play or talk with them, quite another to be evaluating them as husbands. Nonetheless she made her opinions clear to her family afterwards, especially negative ones.

The final choice, after nearly a year of looking, was a boy named Nàŋ— an old playmate and a cheerful fellow who got along well enough with the family. He was about three years younger than Múr.

The marriage started with a big meal in Nàŋ's *bròŋ*. A priestess offered rituals and blessings, and Múr's family gave generous gifts to Nàŋ's. Then the whole party walked to Múr's *bròŋ* for another meal, lubricated with plenty of heady *bǎɔsa* wine and milky *ŋássa*. There were many embarrassing jokes, till finally, at sunset— with the whole family watching and laughing— the two newlyweds removed their loincloths and got into a hammock together.

Fortunately, they weren't expected to perform for the onlookers. Without lights, people didn't stay up long after dark; soon most everyone was asleep except for Múr and Nàŋ. Lying naked together in the darkness, the couple found it not so difficult to have sex for the first time.

The first few weeks were fun; it was like an extended sleepover with the added novelty of sex. Then it sank in that Nàŋ was here for good; for a time he missed his family and she missed her freedom. After a quarrel, Nàŋ set up his own hammock.

She was upset to learn, a few months later, that Nàŋ was sleeping with her cousin. Her mother and her sister were sympathetic, but pointed out that that was just how men were. This alerted Múr to observe more carefully what happened after dark, or who disappeared into the bush during the day, and she realized that almost no one stuck to their spouse, though they did keep to their age group. She looked at her own father with new eyes, wondering if he was really her biological father. She decided she'd rather not know.

She was embarrassed now when the newer men in the family— her sister's and cousins' husbands— looked at her frankly and even flirted with her. But finally she realized that nothing would happen unless she showed interest back. Perhaps inevitably, she ended up sleeping with her cousin's husband— the partner of the cousin Nàŋ had slept with. He was older and stronger than Nàŋ and had a beard, which fascinated her for some reason.

Just a week after this she found she was pregnant. When she confessed her worries to her mother, she asked for some details, then laughed; the baby could only be Nàŋ's. Even if that weren't the case, social custom dictated that he was the father.

The pregnancy and birth repaired her relationship with Nàŋ. He was a comfortable presence and helpful with the baby, while her cousin's husband was clearly just a fling.

Adult life

Múr was now a *lɔ*, a married woman, a full member of the family. It wasn't appropriate to wear flowers and feathers any more— those were for unmarried girls. Instead she wore jewelry, made of metals, gems, or shells— all things that couldn't be found locally and had to be acquired in trade, thus emblems of wealth.

She nursed her baby, often carried it around in a sling, and slept with it, but in a short time the baby spent more than half its time with other people: Nàŋ, Múr's sister and younger brother, older relatives.

Múr welcomed this, as there was plenty to do. Tending the plot wasn't that laborious, but preparing food was an endless chore, and there were other things to make: pots, baskets, rope, mats, hammocks, loincloths, sandals, musical instruments, toys for the children. The heaviest work, such as cutting trees and erecting the pillars and beams for houses, was done by the men.

Both sexes could go fishing, or hunting for small game, using bow and arrow. Occasionally there was a large predator around— mostly boars or jaguars— and the men gleefully took the lead in hunting these. This could take a few days, and often more jugs of *ŋássa* than animals were disposed of.

Periodically there were trips to the market town, a welcome change of pace. There was always something to sell— extra petay cloth, yams, keng oil, *ŋássa*, dried fish, herbs and spices, gallene eggs— and there were things to buy as well, from leather to cheese to salt to medicine to metal tools. There were people to see, novelties to watch, sometimes specialists to consult.

The major crops— sorghum, stripcorn, and tengbeans— were sold here too, but this was more complex, not only because they were harder to transport (often a wagon had to be hired), but because they were taxed. The family's land wasn't their own; it belonged to a *jinlɔ* or noblewoman, and she was entitled to a tenth of the produce. She had a representative at the grain merchant's who accepted this share and gave out tokens indicating compliance.

In Múr's region, the usual currencies were salt, seashells, or glass beads— easily transported and hoarded items not produced locally. But many transactions were more easily handled with barter.

Elderhood

Life wasn't always calm; one year the *lè* or monsoon didn't come and most of the crops failed. The family subsisted mostly on dried food and hardroot; half a dozen children and two adults died.

Sometimes family life flared up as well. While she was bearing children Múr mostly stayed with Nàŋ, but in later years they drifted apart; he bonded most closely with the cousin he had slept with years ago. Múr didn't really replace him, but when she wanted sex she often ended up with her sister's husband. But this was minor compared to the problems of one of Trâo's daughters: her husband couldn't get along with her or with anyone and he ended up leaving the family. That was traumatic enough, but it also offended his birth family, and that was a problem because it was their nawr ox that Múr's family usually hired.

Grandmother Prèn finally died, in her late sixties. She was buried quickly— bodies don't last long in the jungle— and a few days later there was a funeral service attended by a large crowd.

After a decent interval, it was decided that the *jo* should split. Prèn's and Trâo's lineages felt a little more distant now that Prèn was gone; and the acrimony over the departed husband didn't help. But the main reason was the size of the family. There were five women in Múr's generation (Múr and her sister, and Trâo's three granddaughters), and all had children— there were more than thirty people in the family, more than the house and plot could easily support.

The split was a major undertaking, as two new *bròŋs* had to be established; it was also necessary to get approval from the goddesses, deceased Grandmother Lâ, and the landlady. The family had to go into debt to cover its expenses, though this was partly offset by a gift from the *jinlo*.

It was difficult for Múr to move away from people she had known all her life. Nàŋ faced an even harder decision, whether to live with Múr (and his children), or the cousin he had bonded to. He ended up choosing the cousin; fortunately, another cousin-in-law made the opposite switch as he preferred Múr's sister to his original wife. The two new families could easily visit— they were just a half-hour's walk away— but further sexual mixing was discouraged.

Múr's mother was now the *háo* of the new *jo*. In some ways this was the most enjoyable phase of Múr's life. She and her sister were respected elders and religious authorities; the hard work could be left to younger people; she could relax as much as she wanted, and spend more time with the young children.

There was no retirement in Lé life: Múr remained active, and grew only more important with age, especially after her mother died and she was the second-ranking family member after her sister. She grew arthritic, and hard of hearing, which simply meant that she could give up tedious tasks like husking tengbeans, and could continually insist that the youngsters repeat themselves.

She started to complain about pains in the abdomen; some medicinal herbs helped with the pain, but the blood in her stool showed that she wasn't cured. She died a few months later, nearly sixty.

She was buried just outside the house, and while the family lived there they would greet her or leave small offerings for her; but after the brɔŋ was next moved she existed only in memories.

Notes

A lot of things are covered here: sustenance, clothing, sex, family life, technological level, even something of the larger society (the market town, the local noblewoman).

It should be clear that the Lé live in the rain forest, with a typical garden agriculture system of clearing a plot, cultivating it for awhile, then moving on (see p. 89).

The most striking difference from earthly societies is that Lé society is female-dominant (for more see p. 158). The Almeopedia contains a detailed explanation of how this works; but Múr's story shows it in action. Hopefully it gives an idea of *what it's like* to live in such a society.

As this is background material, it can indulge in a certain amount of exposition. Still, I tried to show rather than tell as much as possible— e.g. instead of saying "Lé marriages are arranged by the family", I describe how Múr's family found her a husband and how it worked out for her.

You don't have to stop with a typical peasant's lifestyle. To help work out the continent of Arcél on Almea, where the Lé live, I wrote biographies of an isolated fisherman, an evangelistic shaman, a barbarian lord, a grandiose architect, a eunuch dictator, a magician defending his land, a sleazy entrepreneur, a tea merchant, a couple of thief adventurers, a pirate queen, and a princess who became a major philosopher. These are more like miniature short stories— they're individuals rather than generic types, they make mistakes, they have reverses, not all their stories end well. (You can find them all on the Almeopedia in the People category.)

This not only makes your planet feel like a populated, interesting place, but it's great practice for writing longer stories.

Astronomy and Geology

Conphysics

Most of this chapter is going to be about applying the known laws of physics to your world. But of course you can create your own physics.

My favorite example along these lines is A.K. Dewdney's *The Planiverse*, a rigorous exploration of a two-dimensional world, from its quantum mechanics on up. Another example is Stephen Baxter's *Raft*, set in a universe with a force of gravity far stronger than ours. For teaching purposes George Gamow wrote about a world where the speed of light is just 15 km/h.

Sadly, much of the science in s.f. is outmoded or unlikely: faster-than-light travel, time travel, new types of radiation. But these can still make great worlds and stories. It's tacky to simply *invent* all the consequences as in a comic book; the elegant approach is to vary one or a few parameters and work out the results consistently— a feat that requires good knowledge of existing science.

Another approach is to adopt some previous level of science— Aristotelian physics, for instance. The definitive s.f. treatment of phlogiston has perhaps yet to be written.

Stars

In a hurry? Your star is "sun-like"; see you in the geology section. S.f. writers may not be happy without a stellar class— fine, the sun's is G2; vary the last digit if you like.

Stellar classifications

Stellar class is essentially a scale of surface temperature. Here's a table of the classes, showing surface temperature in kilokelvins (degrees above absolute zero; for comparison it's 0.3 kK outside right now), color, mass compared to the sun, and the fraction of all main sequence stars.

Class	Temperature	Color	Mass	Main sequence
O	≥ 33	blue	≥ 16+	0.00003%
B	10-30	blue-white	2.1-16	0.13%
A	7.5-10	bluish white	1.4-2.1	0.6%
F	6-7.5	white	1.04-1.4	3%
G	5.2-6	yellowish white	0.8-1.04	7.6%
K	3.7-5.2	yellow orange	0.45-0.8	12.1%
M	≤ 3.7	orange red	≤ 0.45	76.45%

As a G2 star, the sun is near the top of the G class and its color is white. That is, the range of colors it produces is largely restricted to our visual spectrum, without skewing to any one color. This isn't coincidence; our eyes are adapted to the light from the sun. The sun appears yellow from the earth's surface for the same reason the sky is blue— blue light is scattered more by the atmosphere; in space it looks white.

You were probably told at some point that the sun is an average, unremarkable star. Not true; as you can see from the chart, it's hotter and bigger than 90% of all stars. Of the 50 nearest stars, only one is hotter than the sun— Sirius A. (Alpha Centauri A is also a G2 star, very much like the sun. The only other G star in the lot is Tau Ceti, thus its popularity in science fiction.)

Stars are also classed by **luminosity class**, expressed as a Roman numeral; these may be of any stellar class. The vast majority of stars lie either along the main sequence (V), like the sun, or are giants (III).

Class	Type	Abs magnitude	Lifetime
0	hypergiants	-8	millions of years
I	supergiants	-5 to -7	< 30 million
II	bright giants	-3 to -5	
III	normal giants	0 to -5	
IV	subgiants	+3 to 0	billions
V	main sequence	+20 to -5	depends on mass
VI	subdwarfs	+10 to +5	
VII	white dwarfs	+15 to +10	billions

Absolute magnitude measures brightness; negative is brighter. The scale is logarithmic: each magnitude is 2.5 times brighter than the next higher one.

Luminosity and hotness can be plotted on a Hertzsprung-Russell diagram, which allows us to see that the luminosity classes are really clumps in this two-dimensional space.

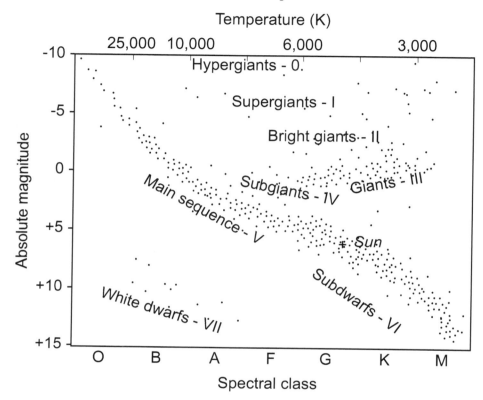

Suitability for life

So which are the good ones? You're welcome to imagine beings living in Jupiter's gases or the hell-hothouse of Venus, but most of us would prefer an earthlike planet, and the type of star you choose affects that. Let's look through some relevant criteria.

- **Stellar lifetime.** Intelligent life took 4.5 billion years to evolve. If a star is more than 1.4 times the sun's mass— that is, classes O, B, A— its lifetime is likely to be measured in millions of years; even F stars only last two billion or so.

- Stars have a **habitable zone** based on distance and stellar mass. For the weakest and commonest stars— M class—this is so close to the star that the planet is likely to be tidally locked, and this would probably destroy its atmosphere. Stellar flares could also be a problem.

The habitable zone is where water and a greenhouse effect both exist. Closer to the star, stellar radiation breaks water up into hydrogen and oxygen; farther from the star you lose the greenhouse warming effect. Venus and Mars are each just outside the habitable zone.

Main sequence stars brighten as they age. It's expected that the earth may be too hot for life in 500 to 900 million years— which means that we evolved just in time, and terrestrial real estate is not a good long-term investment.

- **Number of stars**. More than half of all stellar systems are multiple, and this plays havoc with planetary orbits. Dust disks— regions where asteroids and planets may form— have been observed in binary systems, but mostly when the stars are either closer than 3 AU or farther than 50 AU. (1 AU is the distance from the earth to the sun, 149.6×10^6 km.)

  If the stars are far apart, it's best to have your planet orbit just one of them (and just use that star's mass M for the calculations below). If they're very close it might orbit both, and M should be the total of both stellar masses.

- Distance from the **galactic core**. It may not be coincidence that we're 30,000 light years out: if your star gets too close it may be fried by supernovas, which are more common toward the core.

Calculating the habitable zone

There are numerous formulas for calculating the habitable zone; here's a simple one that depends merely on the amount of light.

Start with the mass M relative to the sun, which you can take from the stellar classification (p. 38). Derive the luminosity L (also relative to the sun) with the formula

$$L = M^3$$

Now the orbit in AU (earth-sun distances) where the luminosity is the same as the earth receives is

$$d = \sqrt{L}$$

The edges of the habitable zone may be calculated as 95% to 137% of this distance.

Calculating the year

While we're at it, let's calculate the length of the year p, given the size of the orbit d in AU. For planets orbiting the sun, we use Kepler's third law $p^2 = d^3$ to derive the period:

$$p = d^{1.5}$$

(That's easy to do on a calculator, but $\sqrt{d^3}$ may be easier to grasp.)

For instance, a planet at 1.524 AU has an orbit of $1.524^{1.5} = 1.88$ Earth year— which in fact is the distance and year of Mars.

The general formula for an orbiting body is $p = \sqrt{\dfrac{d^3}{M}}$ where M is the total mass of the two bodies in solar masses. This works for other stellar systems, for binary stars, or for moons orbiting planets; but the units are still Earth years, AU, and solar masses; convert as necessary.

Planetary orbits are actually ellipses. The earth's eccentricity is minimal (0.0167); that of Mars is ten times larger, so that its distance from the sun varies from 1.38 to 1.67 AU. The formula is $\sqrt{\dfrac{a^2 - b^2}{a^2}}$ where b is half of the smaller axis and a is half the larger axis.

All the planets orbit counter-clockwise, as viewed from the Sun's north pole, and orbit in roughly the same plane— a relic of their common origin in the flattened spinning gas cloud of the early solar system.

One planet to go, side order of moons

There's a few basic decisions to make about your planet:

- **Size.** The Earth has a radius of 6371 km, and a meridional circumference of 40,008 km. (The near-roundness of this number is no accident; the meter was supposed to be

1/10,000,000 of the distance from the equator to the pole, but they didn't quite get it right.)

In case you've forgotten basic geometry:

circumference $= 2\pi r$

area $= 4\pi r^2$

volume $= 4/3 \; \pi r^3$

The Earth is a little flattened of course— the polar radius is 6357 km, the equatorial radius 6378 km.

- **Mass.** The Earth's is 5.9736 x 10^{24} kg. As a rough estimate we may say that mass varies with volume; comparing it to Earth's, this reduces to comparing r^3. For instance, for Venus $r = .9499$, so its mass should be $(.9499^3) = .857$ of Earth's. In fact it's .815— Venus is slightly less dense than Earth.

Given the mass you can find the surface **gravity**

$$g = m/r^2$$

where the values are again are proportions of Earth's. E.g. for Venus we get $.815/(.9499^2) = 0.903$ Earth gravity. To get an absolute figure, multiply by the value for Earth, 9.78 m/s^2.

- **Rotation**, the time it takes for the planet to turn on its axis— this gets tricky, so I'll come back to it below.

- **Magnetism.** Earth is unusual among the inner planets in having a relatively strong magnetic field. (The gas giants have stronger ones than ours.) The magnetic field deflects parts of the solar wind, which is part of why Earth has kept its oceans. Some animals can sense the magnetic field and use it for navigation.

More importantly, the magnetic field seems to be associated with movements in the Earth's molten core that also produce continental drift. Venus and Mars therefore lack this phenomenon.

The poles of the magnetic field don't quite align with the axis of rotation, and moreover move at up to 15 km per year. For unknown reasons their polarity sometimes switches, the last reversal being 780,000 years ago.

- **Axial tilt.** Earth's is 23.5° and produces a nice range of seasons. This varies widely for the other planets, from nearly 0° for Mercury to 98° for Uranus, which thus rolls on its side: at the solstices, one pole or the other faces the sun nearly head-on.

- Number of **moons.** Outer planets are richly supplied with moons; Jupiter has over 60. Earth's relatively large moon is unusual— Mars just has a couple piddly ex-asteroids orbiting it— though Pluto also has a large moon, Charon.

  Our large moon (0.0123 Earth mass) has a profound effect. Earth's day was once 6 hours long; it has lengthened to 24 through the moon's tidal effect. The slowing of the planet's rotation also affects its wind patterns, allowing more north/south winds as well as east/west.

One consequence of all this is that there are three ways to determine **north** on your world:

- According to the planet's rotation: the pole that's moving counter-clockwise is north; the sun rises in the east.

- According to the *sun's* rotation. In our case there's no difference, but Venus rotates clockwise compared to the sun.

- According to its magnetic field: the magnetic pole that attracts the north end of a magnet is north. (But again, the polarity can flip.)

Neil Comins's *What if the moon didn't exist?* explores in much greater detail the probable consequences of various astronomical factors on an earthlike planet: no moon, closer moons, a vastly greater mass, and so on.

Rotation

The time it takes a planet to rotate with respect to the stars— i.e. the time from when a star is on the horizon to the time it's on the horizon again— is the rotation period or **sidereal** day. The rotation time with respect to

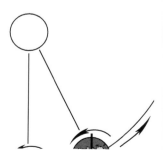

the sun— the time from sunrise to sunrise— is the **solar** day.

Like most of the sun's planets, the earth rotates counter-clockwise, matching its orbit (it's **prograde**). As the diagram shows, after it's rotated once with respect to the stars (thick line), it has to rotate a bit more to line up with the sun (thin line). Thus our sidereal day is 23.93 hours, while the solar day is 24 hours.

For a prograde planet, the lengths of the sidereal day T, the solar day d, and the year y are related as follows:

$$d = \frac{y}{\dfrac{y}{T} - 1} \qquad\qquad T = \frac{y}{1 + \dfrac{y}{d}}$$

Mercury's rotation period is 58.64 Earth days, its year 87.97 days, so its solar day is 175.88 days— three times its rotation period!

Venus rotates clockwise, opposite its orbit— it's **retrograde**. The sun rises in the west on Venus. For such planets the formulas are:

$$d = \frac{y}{\dfrac{y}{T} + 1} \qquad\qquad T = \frac{y}{\dfrac{y}{d} - 1}$$

For Venus $y = 224.70$, $T = 243.02$, $d = 116.75$, all measured in Earth days. Thus its solar day is half its year.

Close orbits tend to produce **synchronous** rotation by tidal locking; i.e. the rotation period is equal to the year, as in our moon and in fact all the major moons in the solar system. This is also why Venus and Mercury have such long rotation periods. Earth escapes this effect, and Mars's day is very close to ours.

Some s.f. writers have exploited the exotic worlds created by synchronous rotation: the side of the planet facing the sun being blistering hot, the opposite side freezing cold, with a habitable strip in between. But this seems to presuppose an otherwise Earthlike atmosphere, which is hard to picture developing on such a world.

On the moons

For a moon, this formula takes the orbit's semi-major axis in kilometers and the planet's mass in kilograms, and gives the period in Earth days. (The constant is the result of changing the units.)

$$p = 281539\sqrt{\frac{d^3}{m}}$$

E.g. for Callisto, with d = 1,882,700 km and (Jupiter's) m = 1.8986×10²⁷ kg, we get a period of 16.69 Earth days.

As noted, the known moons are tidally locked to their planets. By moving closer, you can get a fairly nice day— e.g. Io, at 421,800 km, has a period of 1.77 Earth days.

Making a moon habitable may be problematic— after all, our own is firmly within the Sun's habitable zone and is lifeless and airless. On the other hand, some moons are intriguing, if not hospitable:

- Europa seems to have an icy crust over 10 km thick, then a liquid ocean 100 km deep, containing twice the water of our oceans. The water may be heated by tidal forces.

- Titan is the only moon with a dense atmosphere— indeed, its surface pressure is 1.45 times that of the earth. Don't break your helmet, though; it's mostly nitrogen and methane. Plus the surface temperature is -179 °C, and there's methane rain.

No planets for me, *mater*

Planets are so vulgar. Natural alternatives are hard to come by— stars and deep space are challenging environments. But there are some interesting engineered habitats:

- Ringworlds, memorably explored by Larry Niven. These are enormous rings with a radius of 1 AU, rotating around the sun to provide gravity, with an inner ring of shadow squares producing a day/night cycle and high walls to contain an atmosphere. Niven's ring had a surface area of 3 million earths.

  There are technical problems. There's no known material that can handle the tensile forces to hold the ring together, and the orbit isn't stable.

- A Dyson sphere is an arrangement of structures that capture all or most of a sun's energy. The simplest conceptually is a single huge sphere, but we run into the same technical troubles as ringworlds and don't get gravity. A huge number of satellites, or stationary sails, would be more practical.

- Or just build ships— either huge asteroid-sized ones, as in Iain M. Banks's Culture, or an enormous fleet, as in *Mass Effect* or the French comic series *Sillage*. These have the advantage that you can travel the galaxy, but they require some portable source of energy.

Banks also posits Orbitals, miniature ringworlds with a radius of merely 2 million km or so. They still require unobtainium to hold together.

Plate tectonics

The Earth's crust is broken into tectonic plates, moving on top of the semi-solid mantle. There are seven major plates— North America, Eurasia, Pacific, Australia, Africa, South America, and Antarctica— plus a number of smaller plates.

Oceanic crust is about 6 km thick, continental crust about 35 km; oceanic crust is denser, which is why it's submerged under the ocean. Beneath the crust is a brittle layer of lithospheric mantle at least 100 km thick. A single plate will be a mixture of oceanic and continental crust— The Pacific plate is notable for being the only one without a continent on it.

The plates are all moving with respect to each other, which means there are three basic types of boundaries:

- The plates are diverging. New crust is created at the boundary; in the oceans this creates the mid-ocean ridges; within continents it creates rift valleys.

- The plates are colliding. In this case one plate will slide beneath the other— a subduction zone. If there's a continent involved it'll be pushed up by the subducting plate, forming mountains; in the ocean volcanoes can form into island chains. The Marianas and other ocean trenches are subduction zones.

- The plates are sliding past each other; the San Andreas fault is an example.

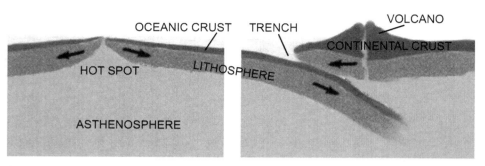

As we're talking about huge plates of rock, the movement is really a matter of increasing pressure punctuated by earthquakes and volcanoes. As a comparison, the Mid-Atlantic ridge averages 2.5 cm of new crust per year, while the 2010 earthquake in Chile moved some areas 10 feet in a few hours.

Volcanoes can also form from plumes of molten rock anywhere in a plate; the Hawaiian islands were formed by one— as the plate moves the hot spot creates new islands.

As we have only one planet to inspect— a regrettable state of affairs that will plague our conworlding in many ways— we can't say how much variation there is in plate size and shape. Earth's plates seem to be a good deal less irregular than its continents, and many are roughly square; there are a couple of odd protrusions though, such as the salient of the Eurasian plate between Kamchatka and Japan.

Our plates can be traced back in time to a single super-continent Pangea, about 250 million years ago. But Pangea wasn't primeval; rather, there's been a cycle of continents forming supercontinents and then breaking up, at least three different times. Such earlier events formed older mountain ranges such as the Appalachians and the Urals.

The underlying mechanisms of plate tectonics— and why we don't see it on Venus and Mars— are controversial. Possible culprits include the size and composition of the Earth, its magnetic field, its oceans, and the fact that we have a large moon.

Creating your own plates

When a divergence zone pulls a continental mass apart, the resulting continental edges will retain a similar shape; the usual example is the curve of South America which fits neatly into the bow of western Africa. Similarly eastern North America fits the northwestern coast of Africa. Note that it's the continental shelf, not the shoreline, that actually has to match.

For Almea, I drew the continents on a ball, which allowed me to create shapes matching this process, without the distortions caused by projecting the spherical surface onto a flat map. Once I had continental shapes I liked, I copied them by eye onto a world map.

There's a low-tech method for this you may not be aware of: draw a grid on the globe, and one on your paper. Then look at the squares one by one and copy what's in them. Even if you can't draw well, it's easy enough to draw the simple blobs within a grid square— if they're still too complicated, make the grid finer.

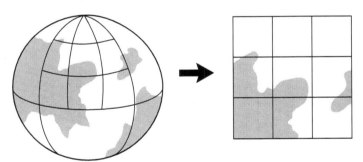

These days you might work instead with a computer modeling program... though I doubt it'll be as direct or easy as drawing on a ball! But see p. 293 for how to create a CGI model of a globe.

If you're ambitious, you could simulate the last billion years or so of plate tectonics and draw maps of the various supercontinents and how they divided. This would give you a very realistic set of old and new mountains. I'll be the first to admire your perfectionism, but it's overkill for most conworlders.

Drawing your continents, think about how separated they are. On continents isolated for millions of years, like Australia, evolution diverges from the rest of the world. They may also be take longer for humanoids to settle, especially if a long sea voyage is needed.

If you create an entire planet, you'll avoid the silliness noted by Not the Net: "All fantasy worlds are roughly *square*, i.e. the shape of the double page of a paperback." And that in turn is because the author started with a single sheet of paper, and drew just the part of the world that interested him. This isn't the worst sin in the world, but it's going to distort your world if you don't know what's beyond the edge of the paper. The natural tendency is to forget it and make the area of the map implausibly self-contained.

Climate zones

Once you've got your continents, you'll want to know what the prevailing climate is. These can be divided in three overall regions:

- Tropical, near the equator— the zone we evolved in

- Temperate, farther from the equator, not so hot in the summer but experiencing unpleasant winters

- Arctic, near the poles— very inhospitable to humans and thus the last region settled

Plants and animals that evolved within each zone are unlikely to thrive in the others, which creates ecological boundaries between civilizations. This is one reason Europeans preferred to settle the temperate rather than the tropical zones in each hemisphere.

For largely this reason, Jared Diamond suggested that a continent extending largely east-west, like Eurasia, is more conducive to developing advanced cultures: it provides a very large zone where people can share crops and domestic animals— and also acclimate to each others' diseases. The Americas, by contrast, are oriented largely north-south; crops that developed in Mexico or Peru couldn't as easily diffuse to the other zone through the tropical areas in between.

But such barriers are not absolute; e.g. maize did diffuse from Mexico south to Peru and north to Canada. Perhaps the Old World did better just because it was larger.

The "not enough planets" problem rears its ugly head here as well. Although I'll suggest modifications for earthlike worlds, like where you should put your Mediterranean climates, the details would certainly vary on other planets, especially if you've chosen any of the more dramatic options (such as high axial tilt, much smaller world, no moons).

Still, there's reason to avoid one cheap s.f. effect: assigning a single climate to an entire world: a jungle planet, a forest planet, a desert planet. Planets should have a lot more diversity than that.

The atmospheric engine

The tropical/temperate/arctic division just deals with heat; we need to consider rainfall as well. This also depends on heat, but indirectly, by means of the atmospheric engine.[1]

The lower atmosphere can be divided into three convection cells between equator and pole: the Hadley, Ferrel, and polar cells.

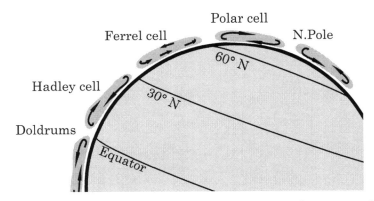

- **Hadley** cell: Warm air rises at the equator (more precisely, in between the equator and where the sun is highest), moves at a height of 12-15 km toward the poles and eastward, becomes cooler and turbulent and sinks at a latitude of about 30°, and returns along the surface toward the equator and westward.

---

[1] This section assumes that "north" is the pole that revolves counter-clockwise (p. 44), which makes "east" where the sun rises.

The air is very moist at the equator and dry when it sinks down— so the overall pattern is rain forest on the equatorial side of the cell and desert on the poleward side.

- **Ferrel** cell: The overall movement is opposite the Hadley cell: poleward and eastward along the surface. This cell is weaker and more turbulent: the overall pattern is frequently interrupted, leading to the fickle winds and weather of the temperate zone.

On either side of the cell there are high-velocity eastward winds high up— the jet streams. At any one time these are not straight but meander north and south.

- **Polar** cell: relatively warm air rises at about 60°, move poleward and eastward at a height of 8 km, sinks at the pole, and moves equatorward and westward along the surface. The air is dry so that the whole area has little rainfall.

The 30°/60° values are not constants; a faster-rotating planet, or a hotter one, will have a larger Hadley cell. (Venus, whose surface temperature is a balmy 467° C, has a Hadley cell reaching 60°.)

The bands of Jupiter's atmosphere may derive from a similar mechanism, with light zones marking upwelling and dark belts marking downwelling; there are at least four cells.

Winds

The prevailing winds within the Hadley cell— **trade winds**— blow towards the **west**. To be precise, they also blow somewhat toward the equator. You're likely to get a rainshadow on the west side of continents if the wind is blocked by mountains; thus the arid west coasts of Mexico, Peru, and Australia.

The surface winds in the Ferrel cell go in the opposite direction— towards the **east**. Winds are named for their origin, so these are called **westerlies**. One consequence is that there's a natural cycle in the North Atlantic: you can go west from Europe in the southern latitudes, and go home using a more northern route. Winds are more variable here, but there can be a rainshadow on the eastern coast— Patagonia is an example.

The black arrows show prevailing surface winds in January; the grey arrows, where different, indicate winds in June.

There are some areas where the trade winds reverse direction part of the year; the best known are India and Indonesia, where winds blow northeast in the summer, bringing the **monsoon**. They depend on the differing heat capacity of oceans and continents; so they're likely where you have ocean at the equator and a continent to the north or south occupying the 30° line. The only region in the southern hemisphere that fits this configuration is the northeast coast of Australia.

Currents

In the tropical and temperate zones, each ocean largely has warm **currents** (shown in black) flowing in a circle: clockwise in the northern hemisphere and counter-clockwise in the southern hemisphere. The Gulf Stream is an example, giving a pleasant warm bath to northern Europe.

Cold water (shown in white) flows in from the poles. In the southern hemisphere, where there's a lot more ocean, the effect is important. Major cold currents cool the western coasts of South America, Africa, and Australia. In the former two continents, the cold current colludes with the coastal mountains to reduce rainfall.

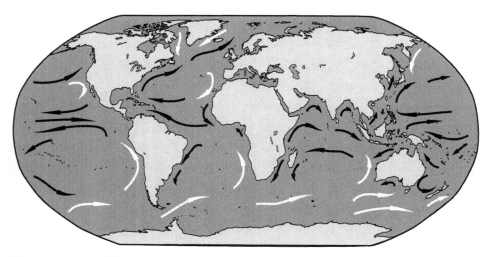

The great swirling currents in the northern hemisphere turn cold in their eastern portion, as cool northern waters are pulled south and cold water is drawn up from the depths. When these hit the mountainous southwestern coast of North America they create a similar low-rainfall zone.

There's not much room for big cold currents in the north, though small ones come down to say hello to New England and Hokkaido.

Köppen classification

The Köppen climate classification system is widely used; it has five overall categories:

A	Tropical moist	0 to 20° from equator
B	Dry climates	15 to 35°
C	Subtropical	20 to 55°
D	Continental	40 to 70°
E	Arctic climates	70 to 90°

If you look at the climate map on the next page, these areas make fairly nice bands in the big low flat areas of continents, as suggested by the last column. There's a **color version** of this map on the web resources page (and on the back cover).

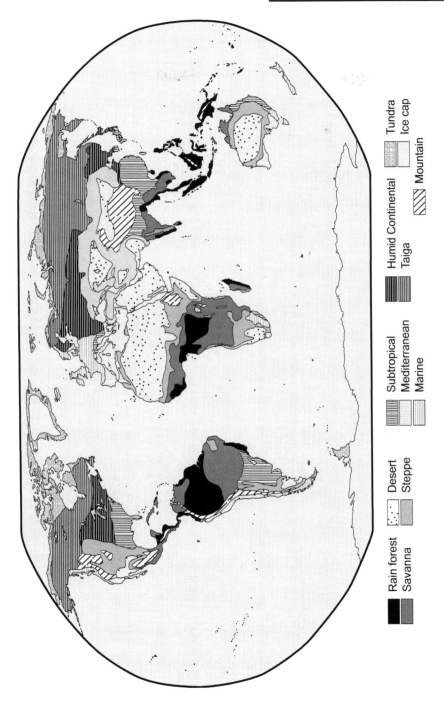

Rain forest
Savanna

Desert
Steppe

Subtropical
Mediterranean
Marine

Humid Continental
Taiga

Tundra
Ice cap
Mountain

The **latitudes** discussed here apply to present-day Earth. On a warmer planet (e.g. closer to the sun, or Earth when it's not in an ice age) the tropical and dry bands will extend farther north; on a colder one the continental and arctic ones will extend farther south.

These zones are subdivided according to their seasonal variation. Here's an overview:

Temp	Code	Temp	Rainfall	Typical flora	Prototype
Tropical					
Rain forest	Af	27 °C	heavy all year	very dense forest	Amazon
Monsoon	Am	20 - 27	long wet season	dense forest	India
Savanna	Aw	24 - 28	short wet season	scrub	East Africa
Dry					
Desert	Bwh	13 - 35	almost none	cactus, shrubs	Sahara
Cold desert	Bwk	-6 - 28	almost none		Gobi
Steppe	Bs	2 - 25	minimal	grassland	Central Asia
Subtropical					
Subtropical	Cfa	10 - 26	all seasons	deciduous forest	southern US
Mediterranean	Cs	11 - 25	wet winters	forest or shrubs	S Europe
Marine	Cfb	6 - 18	wet summers	deciduous forest	NW Europe
Continental					
Humid	Da/b	-4 - 24	all seasons	forest, prairie	northern US
Taiga	Dc	-20 - 18	low	conifer forest	Siberia
Arctic					
Tundra	ET	-28 - 12	minimal	no trees	Arctic fringe
Ice caps	EF	-80 - 15	almost none	almost none	Antarctica

The temperature column gives the seasonal variation; it was calculated by averaging several different locations within the region.

These finer distinctions aren't the ecological barriers of the major zones. Mediterranean crops, for instance, grow quite nicely in Marine or Humid Continental climates. (On the other hand, rice, which requires a good deal of water to germinate, isn't suited to semi-arid climates.) The zones do help determine what crops and animals are available. Grains are characteristic of grasslands or scrub; horses evolved on the steppe; pigs in forests.

The map shows high mountains— the Rockies and Andes, the Himalayas, Ethiopia— as a separate zone; you can take these as cold and arid in general, but divided into a plethora of sub-zones. High mountains are also important because they block rain-bearing winds.

Below I'll give brief descriptions of each zone and suggestions on where to put it.

A – Tropical

These hot, largely wet climates occur in the equatorward half of the Hadley cell.

Rain forests (Af) have heavy rain all year long, and little variation in temperature. There's not much underbrush, and poor soil. These are the areas of greatest biodiversity— no one type of tree or animal predominates.

> *Location*: Low continental areas along the equator, out to about 10°, excluding the monsoon zone.

Monsoon (Am) areas have a long wet season and a short dry season; this is determined by the reversing wind pattern described above (p. 53). The forest is not quite as dense, and there's more ground cover.

> *Location*: Low continental areas off equatorial ocean, out to about 20°.

Savannas (Aw) have a long dry season and a short wet season. The typical vegetation is scrub, with isolated trees. This should sound homey, because it's our ancestral environment— we still prefer its average temperature.

> *Location*: Bands on either side of the rain forests and monsoon areas, out to 15 or 20°, or as far as 30° on the east side of continents.

B – Dry

Deserts (Bwh) are areas of minimal rainfall; plants are cactus, shrubs, and ephemerals that bloom during rare showers. Temperatures may become quite cold at night.

> *Location*: The poleward side of the Hadley cell. Storms travel west in this region and deposit rain when they go from sea to land, so the eastern coast of a continent won't be desert.

If the continent is thin at this point (as in South America and Africa), only the western coast will be desert, and of a milder sort with fog.

Cold deserts (Bwk) are those in the temperate zone; they're not quite as hot in the summer and can get very cold, below freezing.

Location: In the temperate zone, shielded from rain by high mountains to the west or toward the equator.

Steppes (Bs) receive a little more rain; they're usually grassland or scrub. They really come in two variants, hot (e.g. Damascus, Laredo, or Mogadishu) and cold (e.g. Denver, Kabul, or Zaragoza).

Location: A thin transitional band between tropical and desert areas, and between cold deserts and more temperate regions. Also the eastern coast of continents in the desert zone.

C – Subtropical

These are climates in the equatorward portion of the Ferrel cell.

Subtropical (Cfa) areas have hot muggy summers and cool winters. The typical vegetation is forest with some grasslands. The southern U.S. and southern China are examples.

Location: On the eastern sides of continents between about 30° and 45°. They may also, as in eastern Europe, form a transitional zone between Mediterranean and Continental.

Mediterranean (Cs) areas have dry summers and mild, rainy winters. The vegetation includes evergreens and deciduous trees, fruit trees such as olives and citrus, shrubs and grasses, all adapted to survive summer droughts. Large parts of the southwestern US and southern Australian coasts have Mediterranean climates.

Mediterranean climates are particularly important in the development of agriculture; many of the world's major crops were developed in the Middle East. These crops adapted to the summer drought: their seeds were resistant, and thus easy to store, and annuals, which meant they put their energy into producing seeds rather than inedible stalks.

In a wetter world— e.g. during the Pleistocene— these regions had a different climate, **humid subtropical** or laurisilvan, without the summer drought. The typical vegetation was evergreen hardwoods. This climate is still found on the Azores and Canary Islands.

> *Location*: On the western sides of continents between about 30° and 45°.

Marine temperate (Cfb) areas have mild and rainy summers and relatively warm winters; they're typically covered by forest. Britain and Northern Europe are the prototypical case, though they're so modified by agriculture that only portions of the primeval forest remain. The Pacific Northwest is another example.

Next to strong polar currents, a variation called Magellanic may occur, with frigid winters; an example is the southern tip of South America.

> *Location*: On the western sides of continents, poleward of the Mediterranean climates to about 55°. On the eastern side as well, on continents too narrow for Continental climates.

> Some tropical highlands are cool enough to fall into this zone; in these areas (e.g. Mexico City) winters are very dry.

Note that all of these areas are blocked by high mountains, which is why the examples from the Americas are narrow, as opposed to Europe where the region extends thousands of miles inland.

D - Continental

Humid continental areas are characterized by warm humid summers and very cold winters. The vegetation is largely deciduous forest, giving way to grassland in some areas. The area may be subdivided into hot summer (Da) and warm summer (Db) regions.

> *Location*: the eastern lowlands of large continents, poleward of the subtropical, up to about 55°; the band trends a bit southward.

Taiga (Dc) has a brief mild muggy summer and very cold winters. It's mostly covered by conifer forest, though there are some deciduous trees such as birch and aspen. Soils are poor and there is little undergrowth.

Location: Between the humid continental areas and the tundra.

Parts of Siberia are classified as Dd with extremely severe winters, even colder than the tundra; e.g. winter temperatures in Verkhoyansk average -46° C.

There's no suitable areas for continental climates in the southern hemisphere on our planet. The only area at about the right latitude is Patagonia, which however is a desert with little rainfall, perhaps due to the cold currents offshore.

E - Polar

Tundra (ET) is defined by permafrost— i.e. the soil is permanently frozen— and by the absence of trees. Vegetation consists of shrubs, grasses, mosses, and lichens. Winters are cold and dark; in the summer the top layer of soil melts, forming bogs and lakes.

Location: Along the poleward coast of continents above 60°. High mountains also have tundra conditions.

Ice caps (EF) are areas covered permanently by ice. Vegetation is limited to lichens and mosses.

Location: Polar oceans and continents, and the interior of large islands above 60° (on our planet that means Greenland).

Ice ages

Before you get too excited about the descriptions and rules above, remember that they're **quite wrong** about at least one earthlike planet... namely ours, 20,000 years ago, during the last glacial maximum.

At that time the continents were in virtually the same position, but ice sheets covered Canada and Northern Europe as well as the Andes. The southern US and central Europe were taiga, like parts of Siberia today; northern China was steppe; much of today's rain forest was arid grassland instead.

Ice sheets have geological effects: they depress the terrain, which takes millennia to spring back during the interglacial— Scandinavia is still depressed, which is why it has those lovely fjords, which are essentially sunken river valleys. Retreating glaciers leave moraines, rounded hills formed from rocky debris carried by the glacier. The larger lakes, such as the Great Lakes, are also the results of glaciation.

During a glaciation the amount of water locked up in the ice sheets greatly lowers sea level, exposing parts of what is now continental shelf.

Technically we're still in an ice age, meaning an alternation of glaciations and interglacials. It started about three million years ago; before then the planet was ice-free, with a correspondingly different pattern of climates— generally warmer and wetter.

The distribution of continents may affect ice ages, if they prevent the flow of water from the equator to the poles— e.g. a continent resting on the poles, or a polar sea being land-locked, both conditions that obtain today.

Land and sea imbalances

What if your planet is mostly ocean, or mostly land?

A mostly oceanic planet should be, well, awfully wet. You're unlikely to have very arid regions, unless you have an island big enough and with appropriately placed mountains to produce a large rainshadow.

If there's not much ocean, there's also not going to be much rainfall. Look at your major bodies of water and follow the prevailing winds to see where the rain will go. Everything else will be dry.

An example: Almea

Here's a map of Almea which attempts to follow the above rules, with one major change: the planet is warmer than Earth, so I extended the Hadley cell to 35° and the Ferrel cell to 70°.

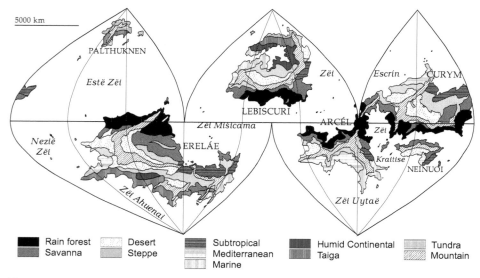

■ Rain forest	░ Desert	▤ Subtropical	▨ Humid Continental	▦ Tundra
▦ Savanna	░ Steppe	▤ Mediterranean	▨ Taiga	▨ Mountain
		░ Marine		

Almea doesn't have much land above 55° north or south, so there's little room for continental zones. There's not a lot of land along the equator, and what there is tends to be mountainous, so rain forest is limited. There's also a good deal less desert; Almea doesn't have the large rain-blocking land masses that produce the Sahara desert.

In the southern hemisphere, the east coast of both Erelâe and Arcél proceeds from subtropical to marine. Usually we see marine climates on the *west* coast in the Ferrel cell, but these are relatively small continental regions facing a large ocean; a terrestrial analog is the east coast of Australia which has the same progression. In the far south of Erelâe we'd get Magellanic climate.

The southern coast of Arcél would be Mediterranean according to the rules given, but since it's next to ocean I've made it Laurisilvan instead, largely meaning that summers are dry rather than parched.

I actually worked out the above map while writing this book, and it differs significantly from earlier versions of Almea. That's typical of conworlding: as you learn more, you find things that you want to redo. However, you need to balance two opposing tendencies:

- Impatience— the urge to get it all done in an hour. If this describes you, slow down and accept that good work takes time.

- Perfectionism— the urge to tinker with it forever. If that's your besetting sin, learn to recognize when you're thrashing, making changes without improvements. Instead of remaking something, make a variant: e.g. rather than redoing your main language, make a sister language.

Rivers

Rivers flow from the mountains downward to the sea. You know that, but I've seen plenty of amateur maps where the water flow just doesn't make sense— rivers cross high regions, there's no high ground between separate river basins, rivers wander down the middle of a peninsula.

Let's look at an actual example. Here's a map of Borneo, with rivers and relief indicated; darker shades are higher.

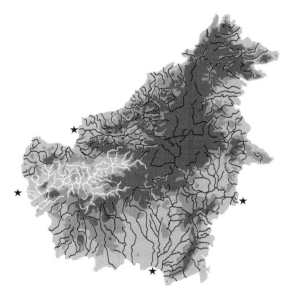

Some things to note:

- There's a lot more rivers than most conworlders would care to supply. Rivers are roughly 10 km apart. You don't need to provide this level of detail, but don't assume that the only rivers are the ones you've drawn.

- There's 70 separate river basins, though most of them are quite small. Four basins (their mouths are starred on the map) are pretty large; the largest of them, the Kapuas, is shown in white. The largest rivers will drain the largest area.

- The smallest rivers run perpendicular to the mountains, feeding into the big rivers that lie along the valleys.

- If two river basins are separate, the ground in between must be higher.

Biology

Now that you've got a world, let's populate it.

Sapients

Sapients, the class to which so many of my readers belong, are egotists— they want to read about other sapients. Let's review your options.

Humans

Your default. You can stop right there if you like.

If you add others, it's fun to show what humans look like to them. You can use this in a backwards way to help define the other species. E.g. the elves might see us as volatile, bulky, terribly serious, and pitifully short-lived. Many alien races see us as dinner.

It's a common trope of s.f. that humans are special in some way— they somehow disturb the interstellar order. This strikes me as conceited or even speciesist on the part of these human authors... though we're going to be galactic noobs at first, and new elements can trigger change.

Humanoids

These are humans with minor changes... a somewhat cheesy way of adding additional flavor. It's completely hopeless from a scientific point of view; its respectability comes entirely from convention, and *that's* mostly because it's the easiest thing to do for TV, especially before the CGI era. A forehead prosthesis, pointy ears, and body paint, and you're in business.

But go ahead with it, if you like... how your sapients look is only the least important thing about them anyway. Though could you perhaps avoid another of my pet peeves: breasts on non-mammals? Mammals at least have the excuse of needing something to nurse with, though no other mammals, not even our relatives among the apes, have human-like breasts. Reptiles and birds don't nurse.

There's another reason humanoids are popular: our visual systems, understandably, are designed to react strongly to other human beings. We immediately understand their body language and facial expressions; they trigger our social and erotic responses. If one of your characters is a gorgeous female, for instance, it's very hard to show this visually except by making her resemble a human girl.

For Almea, I enumerated a number of little differences from terrestrial humans— e.g. their lips don't have a philtrum, they have just four toes, they have some odd skin and hair colors, and they aren't as tolerant of dry and cold environments. These are really just nods to the idea that Almea is not Earth. I purposely kept their psychology and physical powers the same, figuring that special powers would feel like a cheat— in a fantasy, readers expect humans to act like humans.

If your characters are furries, consider giving some love to animals besides foxes, cats, and wolves.

Elves and dwarves

If you like the Standard Fantasy Elves and Dwarves, fine. After all, you're simply following the footsteps of Tolkien. *Or are you?*

In many modern conworlds, elves are a type of humanoid as I've described them above— humans with pointy ears and a Green Party membership. This isn't what Tolkien described at all.

Tolkien's elves are literary descendents of the *longaevi*, the near-immortal spirits of medieval literature. The *longaevi* or Fae are above all numinous creatures— they should awaken awe and a little fear. They are depicted as living in splendor and luxury, with immense vigor and lust for life (and sometimes just lust; they might take humans as lovers). Their theological status varies but seems to decline with the centuries; in the Renaissance attitudes darkened and they were classified as demonic.

For more on the character and history of the *longaevi* see their chapter in C.S. Lewis's *The Discarded Image*.

You needn't follow that tradition either, of course. But it's a reminder to aim high. If you have humanoid races at all, why make them nearly identical to humans? What's the point?

Orcs dark and dorky

The video game *Oblivion* has both goblins and orcs. Both are green and pig-faced, but the goblins are evil monsters and the orcs are citizens of the Empire— you can even play as an orc if you like.

Orcs are just a logical extension of the dubious fantasy trope that *ugly = evil*. The evil counselor is bent and lame; the future betrayer is sallow and eye-shadowed; the dark lord's minions are slavering subhumans.

How do orclings become evil anyway? Are they taught to be cruel and murderous by their parents, and if so doesn't that make their teenage years really rough? What happens if you take an orc kid and have it raised by hippies in Berkeley?

It's all pretty stupid and if you're contributing to it, you should stop. Following evil, or eeeevil, doesn't thicken your skin and make your teeth grow.

What can you do instead? Here's some ideas:

- Follow human history. There have been some pretty scary people: the Huns, the fascists, the Stalinists, the Assassins of Alamut, the medieval free companies of pillagers, the Thuggee cult, the Inquisition, the military juntas and warlords of contemporary Africa. Some of these were doing what they thought was right; others were pretty much villains taking advantage of the opportunities they saw.

- A variation of this is that orcs hate humans because humans hate orcs. Perhaps humans are the real villains here. The orcs may treat other orcs civilly... or try to; oppressed people can take out their grievances on each other. I know this is sounding like an After-School Special, but it'd sure beat another set of Butt-Ugly Badasses.

- Look at the animal kingdom. Dogs, for instance. In some ways their character is highly admirable— they're affectionate, loyal, and brave. But rats and squirrels sure wouldn't agree.

Would sapient species treat each other so badly? Well, look at how humans historically treated the apes. Till relatively recently, humans had no problem enslaving gorillas and chimpanzees, crowding them out of their forests, or even hunting them.

- You can have recourse to some sort of degenerative magic or science. The classic zombie, for instance, doesn't need much of a backstory. His brain is fried, so all he wants to do is attack others in order to spread the infection.

- Use symbolic or mythic associations rather than good/evil. For instance, species based on the medieval humors (sanguine, choleric, melancholic, phlegmatic) could be interesting. Or the five elements in Chinese thought: wood, fire, earth, metal, and water.

Is all this racist?

There may be a dark undercurrent to all the traditional fantasy races. The same genre which produced fantasy species, and some of the same authors, also talked about Africans and Asiatics in almost the same terms: the other races were ugly, primitive, perverse, and at best cunning rather than intelligent. There's an echo of this in Tolkien's description of Sauron's human allies.

You're probably insulated by time from doing the same, but please think twice about making your elves look like idealized Nordic fräuleins, and your dwarves look and talk like miniature Celts.

This doesn't mean I think that inventing humanoid species is forever tainted. For some reason, humans seem not to like to be alone in the universe. All cultures have told stories about other types of beings sharing the world with us; in the scientific era we fill the sky with aliens. It seems like an innocent and rather charming trait.

Would multiple sapients wipe each other out?

Some people have suggested that multiple sapient species are implausible, because one species would wipe out the others.

As with just about everything to do with sapience, we just don't know, because we only have one example. You can't reliably extrapolate from a sample size of one.

Our own history suggests contradictory answers. It's now believed that there were multiple humanoid species on Earth at once, for hundreds of thousands, perhaps millions of years. So coexistence is possible. Only maybe not, since in fact only *homo sapiens sapiens* survives today.

Species do tend to either crowd each other out, or separate or specialize such that they don't compete. This could work out several ways:

- Geographical separation. If a continent is isolated enough, it could develop its own sapient species. (Though it'd better be awfully isolated; there are unusual animal species in Australia or Hawaii, but the same old humans.)

- Habitat specialization. On Almea, there are separate sapient species that live in the seas and on land. On land, there are species adapted to the mountains, to the forest, and to the plains.

- Niche specialization. Species might be so different in size and eating habits that they largely don't compete. Perhaps one species lives as scavengers among another; or one is diurnal and vegetarian, the other nocturnal and carnivorous. Less benign forms of symbiosis are possible: predator/prey, master/slave, parasite/host.

Of course, once sapience evolved, mixing might develop. At this point you have to decide if your sapients are **separate species** or not. That is, can they have offspring together? If so one would expect widespread hybridization. (The D&D system where only half-breeds exist seems short-sighted. If interbreeding is possible, someone could easily be 3/8 human, 1/16 elf, 5/16 dwarf, and 1/4 orc.)

What makes a good sapient?

Here's a formula for you:

$$sapient\ species = culture + biological\ differences$$

So most of the work is the same as working out a particular culture (see p. 116).

But sapients get some physical differences as well— hopefully not just some tasks for the makeup department, but something more substantial:

- size
- lifespan
- number of limbs, digits, eyes, etc.
- senses: are there extra things they can perceive? are there human senses they lack? what senses do they use for communication? for art?
- food type: carnivore, omnivore, vegetarian, photosynthetic
- habitat: plains, mountains, forests, seas, outer space
- reproduction: number of sexes; does one sex dominate; how are offspring raised
- unusual physical abilities: flight, probing tentacles, claws or armor, infravision
- mental abilities, e.g. magic use, telepathy, healing, greater conscious control over their own emotions or memories

Whatever you pick, think out how it will affect their life and culture. A culture test or biography, for instance, should be very different than one for a human... if not, either you didn't pick a very exciting physical difference, or you didn't think it through.

- Thousand-year lifespans, for instance. How long does it take to raise a child? Even if it takes a hundred years, that leaves 800 years that an individual is neither a child nor raising one; what's the effect on family structure, on romance, on sex roles? How does the society keep from being so conservative it never changes? Since they're likely to live with the consequences of any major mess-ups (pollution, global warming, imperial decline), perhaps they deal with them more responsibly.

- Or take flight. It's not just a way of getting to point B faster; it's a way of *escape*. How could a dictator keep his subjects?

There wouldn't be chokepoints where merchants could be charged tolls or armies could be kept at bay. If flight is (say) five times faster than walking, then settlements might be five times less dense. When do the children learn to fly? This could greatly affect how families work and what houses look like.

Even for fantasy, my preference is for plausible biologies. The dark elves are said in some sources to live in caves. Uh huh. Even if the cave systems are far more extensive than ours, caves just don't contain much to live on, because there's no damn sun. I can buy them building their cities there, but then I expect them to possess the lands above for hunting or farming or whatever. Your goth spider-worshipping underground warriors are just not going to thrive on the occasional blind cave fish.

Aliens

Aliens are really just sapient species plus an ecosystem. That is, a fantasy species can just be tossed in the hominid bin— fantasy worlds are unapologetically earthlike. But s.f. worlds are supposed to be entirely different planets with their own evolutionary history. Instead of sapience developing in the great ape line, it occurred somewhere else.

What can I steal from humans?

Humanoid aliens are easier to identify with and less of a casting hassle, but they're not biologically plausible. Look at the range of vertebrates from whales to lions to kangaroos to snakes to velociraptors to owls to eagles. None of them look remotely humanoid. And animals that occupy similar ecological niches need not look particularly alike: compare kangaroos with cows.

It's true that some environments do produce convergent evolution. Plesiosaurs, sharks, and dolphins belong to entirely different classes of animals, but share a streamlined shape, heavy in the middle, due to the needs of swimming long distances in the ocean. Birds, bats, and pterosaurs have some similarities due to the nature of flight. But there's no reason to believe that sapience requires a body plan like ours.

Or more precisely, a case may be made that sapients could share *some* of our features:

- **Social structure**. Animals do need a certain intelligence to hunt, so predators are among the smarter animals... but they do just fine without sentience. It's fair to say that we use most of our own intelligence for dealing with the most complicated actors in our environment: each other.

  (A puzzling partial exception: the octopus is extremely smart while not being very social or even long-lived.)

- *K* rather than *r* strategy. These are terms from evolutionary biology; prototypically *r* species reproduce quickly and disperse offspring widely, while *K* species produce fewer offspring but invest heavily in their care. These terms are relative: compared to humans, rabbits are *r* strategists, but not compared to maple trees.

  As intelligence implies socialization and acculturation, it seems more compatible with the high parental investment of *K* strategists. (Larry Niven's Moties, who reproduce so fast that they're a threat to the whole galaxy, strike me as implausible, especially as the Moties are said to have a *K*-like refusal to tone down their reproduction to avoid problems with other species.)

- **Neoteny**, the retention of juvenile characteristics in adults. By great ape standards we're highly neotenous; or to put it another way, we look and act a lot more like baby than adult chimps. Young animals are exploratory and playful, characteristics that seem to feed into intelligence.

- **Omnivorism** might correlate with high intelligence, since it encourages quick adaptation, exploration, and extended local knowledge. **Carnivorism** seems to require more intelligence than herbivorism.

  A corollary might be **stereo vision**, which is associated with omnivores and carnivores. Hunting requires intense focus and perhaps a more sophisticated view of the world, while prey animals instead need wide vision to identify threats from all directions.

- **Mobility**. Though it's certainly possible to imagine a sedentary sapient— the Internet is full of them.

- **Manipulator** organs, such as hands. Dolphins may be smart, but they'll never get a technological civilization going with flippers.

- Since we live on **land**, we can accumulate goods, find shelter, grow crops, discover fire, metallurgy, and chemistry. A purely marine species might have trouble with basic technology. The sea also constrains body plans more.

- It's hard to imagine sapience without **language**, which allows us to organize our thoughts and speak about the past and future. We have (and the apes don't have) vocal tract adaptations that facilitate speech. Another species might not communicate with modulated sounds, but whatever medium it uses, its body will be adapted to modulate the hell out of it.

- We need enough **size** to support an elaborate, energy-munching brain. During our evolution from the other great apes, our brain size increased threefold. That suggests that we passed the minimum threshold for sapience somewhere in there, and that in turn casts doubt on sapients the size of dogs, sparrows, or beetles.

Other human characteristics are, at best, tangential to our sapience:

- Our **lanky frame**— our long arms and legs— is shared with other primates and developed for brachiation (moving quickly through the trees). There's no reason for canine or reptilian or insectoid sapients to have our basic body plan, unless they also went through a stage of brachiation.

- **Bipedalism** developed when we left the trees of the savanna, and hunted by running after game. (Fun fact: humans aren't the fastest of predators, but they have awesome endurance— their prey get away but can't sustain the pace.)

- Our reliance on **vision** is also due to our primate heritage, as is our fondness for vocalization. No reason another sapient species couldn't rely on different senses... though vision proved to be a fortuitous choice, compatible with easy, permanent recordkeeping (a.k.a. drawing and writing).

None of this is very limiting. I see no reason you couldn't have sapient creatures along the lines of large birds, velociraptors, tuataras, or most mammals.

Not really our planet

One justification for all those humanoids is that some human-like precursor race seeded the galaxy, somehow, with this shape. Larry Niven and *Star Trek* have both played with the idea.

Though it adds an epic grandeur to galactic history, it's poor biology; it's essentially creationism without God, a reflection of s.f. writers' greater interest in physics over biology. Our DNA confirms that we are very closely related to primates, and primates to all other mammals; we're clearly products of this planet. Nor is there room to add secret instructions in the mass of junk DNA in our chromosomes: anything not actually subject to evolutionary pressure is thoroughly messed up by mutations.

Entire ecosystems

Just as another planet shouldn't have hominids, it really shouldn't have our terrestrial classes of animals at all— even something as broad as mammals. Another planet's life forms should be *at least* as divergent as Australia's.

So ideally, you'll create an entirely new tree of life, and populate it with several thousand new species, working out all their interactions.

Yeah, I haven't done that either. (Though I know a biologist conworlder who's come close.) The usual expedient is to create a handful of species that are compatible with your sapient aliens.

Life is awfully variable on our planet. At the same time, to an anatomist, the similarities are striking. Limbs, for instance. As Neil Shubin puts it in *Your Inner Fish*, the limbs of everything above the fish level— dinosaurs, alligators, birds, bats, dogs, us— share a pattern: one bone, followed by two bones, then little blobs, then fingers or toes. Such structural similarities can be found all throughout the body.

And within those classes, the number of limbs maxes out at four. For all the variation among vertebrates, none has six legs; none has even developed four legs plus wings— wings have always developed from the front limbs. None of these classes developed a third eye, either. All have about the same digestive system, a linear track from mouth to butt. All have brains, spines, and blood.

So most of your non-dominant species should have the same body plan as the sapients. If you've got tentacled monstrosities in charge, their domestic and wild animals are probably similar, with variations in size, color, and proportion. Same story if your aliens have six limbs, or trilateral symmetry, or antlike segmented bodies.

Insects, arthropods, and worms are different, of course— not everything on the planet needs the same body plan.

An inspiring and informative sourcebook on inventing entire ecosystems is Dougal Dixon's *After Man: A Zoology of the Future.*

If you don't believe in evolution...

Don't sweat it; we're not going to argue about it here. We're talking about conworlds, after all; there's no reason your conworld couldn't be created by God, like Narnia.

Still, I'd suggest to you that God doesn't create randomly and neither should you. Cats are similar to lions, not just in appearance but in their DNA. It's a good idea to follow evolutionary principles anyway; just think of them as God's organizational system. Like an ideal programmer, God re-uses patterns in a systematic way.

The environment and the body

Body details aren't just arbitrary; they're exquisite responses to the creature's environment.

- The most striking physical fact about us, compared with our nearest relatives, is our lack of fur. This is a clue to our origin in the warm tropical savanna.

- Animals in cold climates tend to be large, with small ears, adaptations to conserve heat. Conversely, desert animals have large ears to help radiate heat away.

Heat exchange is a function of surface area, not volume, which is why the desert creatures need very large ears.

- I've referred half-jocularly to tentacles, but there's a reason these are largely limited to sea creatures— they're heavy. What is essentially a long, unsupported extra limb would be a liability on land (unless they're very light, like a monkey's tail, but these are not going to be lifting a lot of weight).

- Carnivores' teeth are designed for attacking and cutting— they're little knives. Herbivores' teeth are designed for grinding and chewing. Omnivores, like ourselves, get a little of both.

- As I've noted, predators often have eyes looking forward, to provide close focus and stereo vision; prey have eyes facing sideways, to provide near-360° vision to defend against threats.

- Thickness of limbs correlates quite rigidly with absolute size. This is because weight increases by powers of three, while limb strength depends on its cross-section, which varies by powers of two. As you get heavier, the limb has to get thicker.

Sadly, this means that the creepy thin legs of insects are due to their small size— you can't scale them up to elephant size and keep the thin legs.

All these guidelines must be adapted for **exotic planets**. For instance:

- A huge planet has higher gravity; animals are going to be bulkier, and very large ones may not be able to exist. A tiny planet conversely will have spindlier animals.

If you have sapients from such planets, they may be quite unable to visit Earth without special suits.

- A dense atmosphere could support larger flying creatures; a very thin atmosphere might support none.

Exotic biochemistries

If you're ambitious— and savvy about chemistry— you can consider changing the molecular basis of life.

On Earth carbon is key. **Silicon**, right below it in the periodic table, has some similar properties. For instance, silanes (hydrogen-silicon compounds) are analogous to hydrocarbons, and silicone (silicon-oxygen polymers) is similar to carbon-based plastics and proteins.

A carbon-based life form oxidizes carbon, forming carbon dioxide as a waste product— an easily dispersed gas. The counterpart is silicon dioxide, or silica— a solid at earthly temperatures, and indeed the major component of sand. Silica is a liquid above 1650° C, so perhaps silicon life is suited for conditions of extreme temperature or pressure.

Silicon is the principal ingredient in semiconductors... so AIs could be considered a form of silicon-based life.

Or life could be based on a solvent other than water. **Ammonia** (NH_3) is a possibility, though it's a liquid only at low temperatures or very high pressures. There are lakes of liquid **methane** (CH_4) on Titan, which has led to speculation about life that inhales hydrogen in place of oxygen.

The **extremophiles** are thought-provoking; these are organisms, mostly microbes, that thrive in conditions of high acidity or alkalinity, temperatures below the freezing or above the boiling point of water, etc. Hydrothermal vents in deep ocean are an example, featuring bacteria that rely on chemosynthesis rather than photosynthesis. These in turn support a chain of higher life forms.

Sexual display

All this sounds dreadfully utilitarian... isn't there a place for pure flights of whimsy? There is, in fact, approved by Darwin himself: sexual selection.

Basically, males and females just like certain species-specific body parts, and those develop into sexual displays: spectacular colors, crests, horns, long tails. If females like long crests, crests will get longer and longer. Human breasts, so unlike that of our relatives and quite useless to the baby, may have evolved in this way... in effect, because men liked them that way. (But there are other theories. One is that the protruding nipple is more convenient to the baby, especially as it has no fur to hold onto.)

There are theories that such displays advertise fitness— if a male can spend energy growing an impressive set of antlers, he must be healthy. But this doesn't change the essentially arbitrary nature of the signal.

Predators and parasites

If you're populating a D&D dungeon, or a horror level in a video game, you throw in monsters by the boatload. This maximizes the challenge for the player, but it's nonsense as biology.

Predators have a tiny fraction of the population of their prey, and require a larger territory. When humans were hunter-gatherers, population density might be as little as one human for 3 to 10 km^2. We have a population of billions because we largely support ourselves on grains. A civilization of pure predators would have a much smaller population.

We often project our own morality on predators— we picture them as cruel and murderous, or as badass hunters. But from their own point of view, they're just hungry for dinner. They're no more consumed by cruelty when hunting than a man ordering a hamburger. It's in a predator's interest to kill its prey cleanly and quickly... it can't afford prolonged fights and the inevitable injuries to itself. Likewise, most predators prefer prey comfortably smaller than themselves (e.g. cats vs. mice); if they go after large prey they do so in gangs. The biggest animals in an ecosystem will be herbivores.

Many writers assume that predator species would be particularly warlike and aggressive. And they might well dominate the galaxy— if interstellar wars were fought with claws and teeth. Technology equalizes individual differences; just as a peasant with a rifle can kill a highly trained samurai, a sapient herbivore with a phaser can blast a carnivore. The low numbers of carnivores would be a disadvantage, if it came to war.

Another model might be parasitism. One can imagine sapients living *inside* a huge beast or plant of some sort, but something big enough to be sapient isn't likely to be an internal parasite. More likely is something like the alien of *Aliens*, which uses other creatures to host its offspring. But note, such behaviors have to evolve in a pre-spaceflight context. Such parasitism again implies a much larger population of hosts; and parasites that entirely destroy their host species are foolish, since they will also wipe themselves out. Parasites and hosts co-evolve to make the infection less than completely devastating.

(Of course, the parasite might be in balance with its original host species, but out of balance when it's introduced into a new environment without those natural balances. So the *Aliens* species might well be horribly dangerous off its home planet. Our own history has many examples of diseases that devastated populations not adapted to them.)

The take-home lesson is that monsters, at least in s.f., should have a believable backstory. The classic bad example is the space slug in *Star Wars*... how the hell did these things get up there and how can they sustain their bulk merely on passing spaceships? Similarly silly are the D&D creatures invented to let game masters penalize the players for ordinary behavior: animated chests that eat people, worms that dive into the ears of those who dare to listen at doors.

A few neat ideas

Here's some ideas that (I think) haven't been done to death yet.

Multiple sexes

You might be surprised to learn that we have these on Earth. An example is certain slime molds, which have over 500 sexes. There's a type of mushroom that has over 20,000.

Don't expect the individuals to come in 500 varieties— slime molds all look pretty much the same. To biologists sex is determined by how many types of reproductive cells (zygotes) there are, and by which can mate with each other. (Zygotes of the same sex can't mate.) Most species get by with two sexes, but sometimes there are more.

Reproduction doesn't require an orgy of 500 zygotes— just as in humans, a new individual requires just two. One hypothesis about multiple sexes is that they offer an advantage in low-density species, as it's more likely that the first other individual a zygote meets is one it can mate with.

Different sexes

Another possibility suggested by biology: two sexes that aren't male and female.

What we consider male and female is really a constellation of traits that need not go together. Biologists use just one of them to decide the sex of a zygote: the really huge ones (eggs) are female, the tiny ones (sperm) are male. But some species have sex cells that are all the same size, so this rule can't apply. There's a type of green alga, for instance, that have two sexes labeled plus and minus.

There may be a reason we don't see such things at the macro level; but at the least we see that aspects of sex— zygote size, adult size, child-bearing, nursing, child-rearing, aggression, social dominance— need not be allocated between the sexes according to our own pattern.

We do see **hermaphroditism** among higher animals— a single sex, where each individual can mate with any other. (This too might be a key advantage for highly dispersed species, as you don't have to search for the right sex to mate with.) Sometimes it's a spur to creativity to subtract common features rather than invent exotic new ones.

One hermaphroditic species has a depraved, macho system: when two individuals mate, they "penis-fence"... attacking each other with dagger-like penises. The winner is whoever stabs the other first, injecting their sperm into the loser, who will then bear the young. Wouldn't that be great for a race of warriors? On Earth we're talking about flatworms, but you don't need to tell the warriors that.

A few species dispense with sex entirely, including some higher animals— the whiptail lizard, for instance, reproduces by **cloning**. (Curiously, the females mate with each other; this seems to stimulate egg production.) Reproduction without sex has evolved many times, but it's considered risky behavior— the exchange of genes during sex produces more genetic diversity, which is insurance against changes to the environment.

Colony organisms

The quintessential colony organisms are ants and bees, which in many ways act like a single organism. Our bodies are cooperative assemblages of cells which have almost entirely given up their struggle to reproduce— delegating this to the zygotes. Similarly an ant or bee colony delegates reproduction to only a few individuals, the queen and the drones.

But they're an interesting model for more than reproduction, because they suggest distributed intelligence: the colony as a whole is more intelligent than its members. We can imagine a species where one individual isn't sapient, but two, four, or a hundred are. (I included such a species, the Rifters, on Almea.)

Evolved humans

What would evolution come up with if allowed to work on humans for a few million years? Or what might demented genetic engineers come up with?

H.G. Wells was here first, projecting English class divisions far into the future with his Eloi and Morlocks; Olaf Stapledon's *Last and First Men* posits no less than seventeen further human species, while Dougal Dixon has been here too with *Man After Man*.

The ideas of brutes and enormous brains are easy satire. Subtler variations are more interesting: expanded memory, telepathy, greater adaptability to other planets, greater control over our own body. Those with weak stomachs will appreciate Iain Banks' suggestion of a conscious bypass of the digestive system.

Robots

By now robots are a hoary tradition in s.f., and every few months there's a new video showing some cute little robot mastering some new behavior. It's enough to paper over the fact that the s.f. stories are predictable— almost every one, starting with *R.U.R.*, explores the basic theme of robots rebelling against their inferior status— and the basic idea is kind of barmy.

What's the need for a general-purpose, man-sized robot? After all, anything a human-capable robot can do, a human can do, at minimum wage. Humans already *are* adaptable, self-reproducing, easily mistreatable, and rust-free.

What we need is more specific:

- Subintelligent robots— that is, **appliances**. You don't need a computer or an industrial robot that has full human functionality and argues metaphysics with you. You just want it to be reasonably clever.

  Many people want to talk to their appliances, but I'll put it to you that speech is a marginal UI, clunky and slow. I'm using a word processor right now... I don't want to have to say out loud "Move the cursor three lines down" or "Count the pages". I want to be able to do it in an instant using a UI gesture.

  You're never going to program your appliances by talking to them. Give emergency instructions, maybe. But determining day-to-day operations— i.e. programming— is an enormously complicated process requiring special skills and a particularly pedantic mindset. The basic problem is that our minds, and thus our needs, are situational. We can describe the general principles of accounting or painting or quantum teleportation, but there are always hundreds of details that we only remember when they come up. *Oh yeah, 501c corporations need a different form. I forgot, when the wormhole is full of T quarks you gotta use leftward denormalization.* Programming requires a mindset that systematically seeks out these situations and works them all out, and a formalization that makes it fast and easy to record them.

  A subset of useful appliances would be those that we incorporate into our brains and bodies, forming **cyborgs**. You can probably think of all sorts of useful applications, though based on past experience the major uses will be gamebots, music bots, and sexbots.

- **Specialist** robots. An example is the drones used in the Middle East: robots make sense here because they can go where US soldiers— expensive and a political liability— can't. It's easy to imagine other applications— deep-sea mining, exploration of Venus or Jupiter, radiation cleanup— though note that complete autonomy isn't always needed here; a remote human operator can supply the intelligence.

  What about child care or education? Perhaps everyone, as in Neal Stephenson's *The Diamond Age*, is supplied with an electronic super-tutor? I can see this as a niche product, based on a certain squeamishness about hiring help. Older societies had no such hang-up, and I doubt the economics. Automation is only cost-effective for high-wage jobs, and if you eliminate enough of those, humans become very cheap.

- **Massive minds**. If you need to run a government, a starship, or an interstellar megacorporation, you could use a mighty electronic brain. But you don't want human-scaled brains for that— you want minds with far *greater* memory, reliability, multi-tasking skills, and speed.

  That raises the question of who's in charge. In Iain M. Banks's Culture novels, the Minds are the masters— they essentially keep the humans around as pets, or because their eccentricities occasionally offer insights the ruthlessly logical Minds would never consider. Hans Moravec (in *Mind Children)* seems decidedly eager for AIs to replace us.

  But though it could be in *particular humans'* interest to get rid of most humans, it can never be in the interests of the species to eliminate itself. The CEO of that interstellar megacorporation isn't interested in losing his job, either. Those massive Minds will probably be designed as huge, amazing tools, with no more ability to supersede us than our other grandiose projects, from cathedrals to nuclear power plants.

Of course you can have robots and **robot societies** if you like. What would be their essential characteristics?

These will depend on their original purpose and subsequent history, as well as their mechanical capabilities. They'll be different, mentally and socially, if they developed from military drones, domestic automata, or sexbots. (Charles Stross's delightful *Saturn's Children* follows all of these in a world transformed by the loss of the robots' master, the human species.)

How are they **produced**? If they're made in factories, they're ultimately the thralls of the factory owners, and of course they'll have none of the biological concern with reproduction. If they're individually crafted, they'll have more autonomy, but will probably repair and upgrade themselves rather than reproduce.

It might be interesting to set up some form of sexual reproduction—not so much for the sex, though they might enjoy that, but to get the same advantages biological life forms: the fortuitous creation of new abilities by recombining existing progams and mechanisms.

It's often assumed that robots will easily master human speech, but will remain forever baffled by human **emotion**. This is quite backwards, so far as I can see. Human language is immensely complicated, and sixty years of intense effort hasn't gotten us much closer to general purpose text handling, much less speech handling. Emotion, by contrast, is simple and useful.

We're enamored of reason, because it seems to differentiate us from the animals— just see if you can create an industrial civilization, cat, without knowing multiplication! But you have to admit, reason doesn't prevent people from doing or believing absurd things. If our basic needs— eating, making a living, reproduction— could only be met by proper reasoning, most people would starve alone. Instinct, by contrast, is single-minded and reliable. Hunger makes you eat, lust makes you want to reproduce, fear makes you save your skin, no matter what damfool notions you have.

Many emotions, positive and negative, help us as social animals. Love and pity move us to help out others, especially the weak. Greed and envy help keep the alphas from taking too much. Embarrassment dissuades behavior too far from the norm. Gratitude reminds us to favor benefactors, resentment raises the price for unsocial behavior.

It makes sense that robots should be built with deep, hard-to-alter urges and failsafes that reinforce their purpose. If they're servants, that might be a slavish but envy-free devotion to human beings. If they're military androids, it might include a drive to seek out whatever meatbags— or enemy robots— they've been designed to kill. If they're corporation-running Minds, they may feel pleasure from maximizing the bottom line, irritation at governments and rivals, and benevolent concern for employees, graded by rank. Sexbots— well, you can figure that out.

Perhaps the neatest aspect of robots is also less explored: they can incorporate **any technological ability**. Here's an easy way to explore what it would be like to be a sentient being with computerlike memory, laser eyes, wheels, telescopes, infrared cameras, chainsaws, pepper grinders, whatever.

Robots might retain the mutability of computers or early automobiles: a few days in the shop and they've got a new ability. They would presumably retain the immortality of computer programs: their data and software, everything that composes their robotic personality, could be backed up and restored if the robot itself was destroyed. On the other hand, perhaps they are also plagued by the bugs and problems with interoperability that software is prone to. (To a programmer, the Hollywood trope causing the most eye-rolling is that any computer system, even an alien one, can connect to any other.)

Robots may not be a great practical idea, but they're a powerful expression of our age's **technophilia**. We love— and fear— our machines. Robots allow us to merge with our machines, to escape biological messiness, and at the same time to worry about who's in charge.

Animals and monsters

Creating alien animals and monsters is just like creating sapients, minus the sapience.

For fantasy, no one will think twice if you copy Earth creatures, though it's common to tweak them: change the size or make them talk.

(**Talking animals**, from Aesop to Chaunticleer to the Monkey King to Narnia to lolcats, are a perennial favorite. It's an attractive notion if you love animals, and also a great shortcut: if you see a talking dog or bear you can guess their personality. As conworlding, it's kind of incoherent... the animals either live exactly as humans do, which makes them little more than humans in costume, or they live exactly as non-talking animals, which doesn't take their new sentience into account.)

For s.f., I've already discussed the basic ideas: share body plans with the sapients; don't overdo the predators; bodies are adaptations to particular environments.

Think about how species **interact**. Predators and prey co-evolve. To use a silly example, if you give deer wings to get away from coyotes, then the coyotes probably need wings too.

Keep **sizes** in sync. If the main grazing animal is size X, predators will either be at least 2X in size, or they'll hunt in packs.

Fanasy/s.f. designers love huge animals, but size is also affected by the predominant vegetation: you're not going to get elephants or apatosaurs in thick forest. And the commonest animals will be small. Don't forget to create some vermin.

Sustenance

Peasants and nomads

Now that you have people, you need to feed them. Again, you may choose to just give them beer, wheat and pigs. You can live on ham sandwiches indefinitely.

Be aware that our crops are a mix of Old and New World. It bugs me that Tolkien's hobbits, in a mythical version of early Europe, are eating potatoes and smoking tobacco, both New World crops. (Hot peppers, maize, squash, and tomatoes are also New World and shouldn't exist in a medieval or classical European or Asian context.)

Agriculture developed in several areas, each with a distinctive **package** of local crops. The Middle East started with wheat, barley, and peas; China with rice, millet, and soybeans; Mesoamerica with corns, beans, and squash; the eastern Amerindians with sunflower, sumpweed, and goosefoot.

The individual crops are not always nutritionally complete, but the package is. Grains and beans each supply nutrients the other does not.

Often plants need some changes to be suitable for crops, and thus crop plants differ from their wild ancestors. These changes include:

- Increasing grain size: crop grains are larger— in the case of maize, spectacularly so

- Reducing bitterness— e.g. wild almonds are poisonous (which is often what bitter taste signals)

- Increasing oil production and the fruit-to-seed ratio
- Inhibition of seed dispersal (e.g. popping pods) to facilitate gathering
- Thinning seed coats
- Switching to self-fertilization, which allows plants to breed true

Plant genomes differ in how easily these adaptations are made. A single mutation, for instance, prevents peapods from shattering; another single mutation removes bitter amygdalin from wild almonds. The Middle Eastern grains are particularly easy to adapt to cultivation. By contrast it took thousands of years to produce large ears of maize, and oaks have never been cultivated to remove the bitterness of acorns, which depends on a number of genes.

For Almea, I created a package for each major climatic zone. For instance, here are the packages for the continent of Arcél and points east:

Region	Climate	Food crops	Textiles	Animals
Belesao / Ȟaibalai	Tropical	stripcorn, sorghum, teng bean	truca	nawr ox
Kereminth	Tropical	streff, hardroot, yam		pigs
Uytai	Temperate	millet, pell, ko bean, gram, potato	cotton, huar	sheep, notseh, sammule, piebird
Neinuoi / Western Sea	Temperate	rye, meigrass, bigbean, stoneroot, long yam	fluffleaf	

As you can see, these are all anglicized names, as I might use them in a history or a novel— they're the names English speakers might adopt if they reached Almea. Sometimes they're calques on the native terms (e.g. 'stripcorn' for Lé *desú*), otherwise loose phonetic adaptations (e.g. 'gram, pell' are *ħram* and *phel* in Uyseʔ). In other cases I just used an English term for a similar crop (e.g. 'sorghum' for Lé *né*).

Next I wrote a short description of each item and drew a picture, like this:

Pell (Uyse? *phel*). A tall branchy plant with large, rough seeds. The seeds are dried in the sun, which causes them to crack open; they are then soaked, which causes them to expand, shedding their shells, which float to the surface and are removed. The remaining porridge is cooked, or fermented into beer, or added to millet bread. It's higher-yielding than millet, but grows only in well-watered areas, such as river valleys.

None of this is necessary, but it allows at least as much realism as we'd expect in a story about China or the Inca Empire. You wouldn't buy a description of a Míng peasant sitting down in his toga to eat fish and chips. It should be just as jarring if your conworlders look, act, and eat like medieval Europeans.

For **textiles** see the section on clothing (p. 169).

Which **domestic animals** you allow can have a large impact on your culture. The Americas lacked horses or any large traction animals, which impeded plowing, long-distance communications and transport, and warfare. They lacked cattle and pigs as well, which reduced the opportunity to develop the nomadic lifestyle.

Not all animals are domesticable— Africans, for instance, didn't domesticate zebras, lions, hippos, rhinos, hyenas, or apes. (Some of these have been *tamed* but not domesticated: domestication requires breeding in captivity. Technically elephants have never been domesticated; working elephants are tamed from the wild.)

Jared Diamond notes the characteristics needed for successful domestication:

- **Diet**: carnivores have never been domesticated for meat; it's prodigiously inefficient. For one person fed on a carnivore's meat, you could feed ten on the animals the carnivore ate, or a hundred on the plants *they* ate.

- **Quick aging**. Elephants, for instance, take a dozen years to mature; no wonder it's faster to tame wild ones.

- **Easy breeding** in captivity. Tame cheetahs were prized by the Egyptians, but they refuse to breed in cages.

- **Docility**. This rules out obvious candidates such as the bear and rhino, but also the African buffalo, the onager, the hippo, and the zebra.

- **Herd structure**. Most large domesticated animals live in herds, with a dominance structure and overlapping ranges; these all make it easy to keep them together in close quarters. Deer and antelope, for instance, are fiercely territorial; males can't be kept together during the breeding season.

Types of agriculture

Though it's technically part of culture or technology, it's convenient to talk about agriculture while we're talking about crops, so you can tailor your conworld's crops to your sapients' needs.

There are three main types of agriculture, which have profound effects on culture.

- **Garden** or **shifting** agriculture. A patch of land is cleared, planted for a few seasons, and abandoned once the fertility goes down; the farmers move to a new plot and nature reclaims the old. This system is typical of tropical agriculture, partly because the rain forest tends to have poor soil. When population is very high this leads to desertification, but with medium populations it's a sustainable, effective use of resources.

- **Irrigation** agriculture depends on diversion of water from rivers. The classic examples are the rice paddies of southern China, and the intensive cultivation along the Nile and in Mesopotamia.

  Karl Wittfogel argued that such societies naturally led to **hydraulic empires** with a high level of state control, due to the needs of maintaining extensive water management systems. Leaving the system is difficult as the government controls the entire ecosphere, and overthrowing it will merely change who's at the top.

  Wittfogel's term "Oriental despotism" is unfortunate; Táng China (p. 238) was far less despotic than contemporary European states. And hydraulic states are certainly not eternal; China, for instance, hasn't had a dynasty that lasted more than 400 years. Ancient Egypt was despotic not because the Nile was irrigated but because it was compact and isolated, thus easy to unify and defend. As well, irrigation in such areas started out small and local.

- **Rainfall** agriculture depends mostly on rain rather than on irrigation; Wittfogel would argue that this encourages local autonomy if not individualism, as self-sufficient settlements can easily be created in new areas.

Agriculturalists are usually sedentary, but not always. The Apaches, for instance, would farm in the highlands in the summer, and gather wild foods in the lowlands in the winter.

Agriculture was preceded by the exploitation of wild grain, which also facilitated development of a number of ancillary inventions: sickles with flint blades, baskets, mortars and pestles, storage pits. This is typical of technological progress— an invention can't or won't be exploited till conditions are ripe.

Population

A major factor in the nature of society is **population density**. A land-rich society allows easy expansion. It's even argued that this correlates with polygamy, as fertility can be encouraged.

A high-density region is subject to much higher stress— the genocide in Rwanda was due not so much to ethnic tension as to desperation over land, with 10 million subsistence farmers in a nation the size of Vermont. When resources are limited, elites try to preserve their wealth by keeping their numbers down; fertility is discouraged, leading to restrictions on women's rights. High population also of course leads to environmental degradation— the majority of the population is likely to live barely above the starvation level, and to be highly vulnerable to drought and plague.

As Thomas Malthus pointed out, in premodern societies increases in productivity are soon eaten up by increased population. The average standard of living is nearly a flat line from the earliest Neolithic to about 1800.

For reference, here are Colin McEvedy's estimates of the population of Europe and the nearer Middle East over the centuries.

9000 BC	250,000
5500 BC	1 million
2250 BC	10 million
1275 BC	25 million
415 BC	40 million
AD 362	65 million
1483	88 million
1648	100 million
1715	118 million
1815	200 million
1910	425 million
2000	690 million

And here are some representative **city sizes** and populations:

Calah, Assyria	879 BC	358 ha	16,000
Athens	415 BC	225 ha	35,000
Classical Rome	1 AD	1380 ha	250,000
20C Rome	1931	6780 ha	1,000,000
Tokyo	2010	219,000 ha	13 million

(One hectare = 0.01 km^2 or 2.471 acre.)

Take care in comparing these to other sources, which are often inflated. Bigger numbers sound good, after all. Very few historical numbers are based on actual counts— Calah is one of the few that is.

Urbanism shouldn't be exaggerated in ancient times. McEvedy points out that a very misleading picture of Greece emerges if the name of a state, *polis*, is translated as 'city' or even 'city-state'. A typical *polis* was Megara, just west of Athens; it had a population of 24,000, of which just 3,000 lived in the little city (*asty*), also called Megara, that was its capital. That's an urbanization rate of just 12.5%.

(McEvedy's estimate for Rome is contested, but figures of a million or more make no sense; they require densities not seen anywhere on Earth, not even in places like Calcutta.)

Nomadism

Eurasian society is dominated by the clash between agriculturalists and nomads— going back to 2250 B.C., even before the horse was used in warfare, when the pastoralist Semitic Akkadians conquered Sumer.

The Eurasian steppe, which extends across the continent from Hungary to Inner Mongolia, has long been the power base for horse-riding nomads, and for one empire after another: Aryans, Scythians, Huns, Mongols, Turks. At various times nomads conquered the Middle East, Russia, India, and China; one group, the Mongols, created the largest empire ever. (See p. 248 on nomadic warfare.)

Nomadism supports a much lower population density than farming, but the nomads had a great military advantage: they were virtually nothing but army. The entire adult male population was mounted, and trained in the bow and arrow from an early age. Each man had several mounts, so fresh horses were always available. It didn't hurt that everyone was accustomed to butchering animals and to quickly dispatching predators.

Peasant societies, by contrast, didn't produce a natural cavalry, and peasant levies produced a barely competent infantry. The medieval European response was to turn its aristocracy into a professional cavalry; the Chinese and Roman response was to co-opt the nomads— intimidate the nearer tribes with raids, buy them off with tribute and titles, and if all else failed hire them to counter the tribes farther off. The Chinese preoccupation with the nomadic threat was a reason the capital ended up at Beijing, close to the steppe, and why China was much less interested in the sea.

To the civilized states the nomads were "barbarians", with implications of cruelty, alienness, and primitiveness. Their fear and anger were not misplaced; nomadic raids and conquests were enormously destructive. Central Asia, for instance, never really recovered from the savage conquest of Timur.

Civilized writers often fall into a pretentious disdain of their own society, so sometimes "barbarians" have been idealized as everything urban civilization is not— full of manly warrior virtues, free of urban luxury, corruption, and softness. Creations like Conan tell much more about their creator's values, or dreams, than about actual nomads.

In fact nomads were very appreciative of urban luxury... after all, that's what they swept in on their horses to loot. They were a good deal more open to agriculturalists' religion than vice versa— Kublai Khan sent to the Pope to invite scholars to explain Christianity to him; his descendants eventually settled upon another import, Buddhism. And as conquerors, they generally co-opted local elites and ran each country according to its customary laws.

As for *machismo*, it was urban and agriculturalist cultures that tended to show the greater sexism. Khitan women, for instance, were quite powerful, and even led armies; the Manchu ruling class of Qīng China didn't practice the foot-binding of the Chinese.

Nomads also co-opted the infantry and artillery of conquered agriculturalists— cavalry alone had no advantage in siege warfare, which was needed to conquer major nations. The Manchu had a good deal of help from Chinese warlords... there's always someone who prefers to be on the winning rather than the ethnically correct side.

What ended the nomadic threat? Partly this was due to stronger states, which however was merely a return to the efficiency of classical times. Gunpowder was also key— peasant levies could become effective with guns much faster than swords or spears.

The Arabs were not, as you might expect, nomadic horselords. Muhammad was an urban merchant. Arabia produces excellent horses, but not in Central Asian numbers. One of their great advantages was camels, which were used to travel great distances across lands their enemies considered impenetrable; but camels are unwieldly in battle. At Qadisiyya, the key battle in the defeat of the Persians, their army of 30,000 included a cavalry continent of about 7000. Once the caliphate was established, it did make extensive use of nomadic horsemen, but these were almost entirely Turks.

There is no steppe zone in the Americas or Africa comparable to that of Eurasia, so nomadism has been much less important there. In addition, of course, the Americas lacked the horse until European colonization. Subsequently the "horse Indians" developed a horse-based nomadic lifestyle.

Hunter-gatherers

Let's have some respect for the hunter-gatherers. They thrived for two million years, without ever destroying or overstressing the planet.

Moreover, they were taller, longer-lived, healthier and happier than almost any human society before our own. They were lean and fit, had a varied diet, and didn't work all that hard. Daniel Everett reports that the Pirahã, an Amazonian tribe, work 15 to 20 hours a week— the men hunting and fishing, the women gathering. Tool-making adds some time, but tools last for awhile. The rest of their time is generally spent hanging around. Add in Internet access and you've pretty much got the perfect lifestyle.

Living in tiny bands without animals, they avoid most of the diseases and parasites of settled populations, and their social structure is loose. There's simply no great reason to tolerate a tyrant— he can't provide greater resources than anyone else, nor does he have a security apparatus to harass dissidents. He can't even steal people's food, since it's gathered as it's needed.

There's one great drawback, but not one exclusive to hunter-gatherers: warfare. Humans can be brutal to each other— as can apes, for that matter. Marvin Harris suggests that warfare, by privileging the raising of fierce males, degrades the status and lifestyle of women. This seems to be true in some tribes, such as the Yanomamö, but not others, such as the Pirahã or Bushmen.

Hunter-gatherer women nurse their babies for years, which seems to inhibit conception; they bear babies about once every four years, while farmers may have children every other year. The burden of child-rearing is thus lower, too.

Hunter-gatherers know their environment in extraordinary detail— they know over a thousand plants and their uses, and of course all the animal life, and they notice things like where a stand of melons is growing, so they can go back to pick them when they're ripe. They understand that plants reproduce via seeds; why then don't they take up agriculture?

The better question might be, why should they? The species was doing fine, at least back when there were no agriculturalists to crowd hunter-gatherers off their lands. Look again at those work hours— far less than in any agricultural society. As one Bushman put it when asked why his people didn't grow crops, "Why should we, when there are so many mongongo nuts in the world?"

So why did agriculture eventually develop? There are many theories, none very satisfying. Climate change, for instance— agriculture started only a few thousand years into the current interglacial. Hominids have gone through at least five cycles of glacial periods and interglacials in the last half-million years; the previous interglacial, the Sangamon, is dated from 125,000 to 75,000 years ago— well within the period of anatomically modern humans.

On the other hand, about 50,000 years ago— during the last glacial period— we see a huge increase in tool complexity, and not long after that clear evidence of art: sculpted figurines, cave paintings. So perhaps human biology or culture reached some tipping point— we just wanted to tinker more.

Jared Diamond suggests that it was increasing population that led to agriculture. Perhaps because of the general good times as the glaciers retreated, populations started to rise. It may be significant that agriculture first developed in a relatively marginal area, the Middle East, where a scarcity of food might easily be felt.

Once the carrying capacity of the land was reached, people had to either limit growth or increase productivity. Perhaps both strategies were tried; but once agriculture started, it was unstoppable: the agriculturalists might be shorter, unhealthier, plagued by diseases and kings, but there were more and more of them. Fast forward 10,000 years, and the remaining hunter-gatherers have been crowded into lands useless for crops or herds.

Some environments are rich enough to support a high density of hunter-gatherers. The classic example is the Indian tribes of the American Northwest, supported by the region's highly fertile fishing.

Agribusiness

The Malthusian era, ironically, ended just in Malthus's own time. We live in an historically aberrant bubble of productivity growth, one that's led advanced nations to stabilize populations. Modern medicine nearly eliminates infant and child mortality, while in other ways child-rearing is much more expensive. (You can't make a profit off the little buggers, for one.) So the increased productivity translates into a higher standard of living.

Technically, American society is a mixture, with 70% of our protein coming from animal sources. But food production has become a minimal part of our economy. Less than 2% of Americans are farmers; most of us live in or near large cities. Contrast this with most premodern societies, where 90% or more of the people worked on the farm.

Ecological disaster

Some of the most malevolent actors in human history are not dictators but **diseases**.

The most spectacular example is the effect of European diseases— smallpox, typhus, cholera, and measles— on the New World. These spread quickly from first contact and facilitated conquest and colonization. When Hernán Cortés reached Tenochtitlán in 1519, half the population was already sick of smallpox; the same disease killed the Inca emperor Huayna Capac and his heir, leading to a civil war which Francisco Pizarro was able to take advantage of. When the Pilgrims arrived in Plymouth in 1620, they found the site depopulated by disease. It's been estimated that disease killed 90% of the inhabitants of the Americas.

Why did Eurasia abound in diseases it could pass to the New World? Jared Diamond posits that it's the continent's long association with domestic animals, whose diseases can spread to humans.

The Black Death, bubonic plague, exploded out of the steppe in 1346, and within ten years had killed 20 million people— in many areas, a third of the population. Worse yet, the plague returned intermittently till the end of the century. One effect was a labor shortage and a rise in wages. The general shakeup of institutions may also have facilitated the innovations of the Renaissance.

Epidemics tend to co-evolve to become less virulent over time— after all, if a microbe kills off all possible hosts, it's going to die out itself. The bubonic plague is a grim exception, since its primary host is rats— humans are merely an alternative when there aren't enough rats.

There are other forms of **ecological collapse** which humans bring on by themselves. One is salinization of the land caused by long-term agriculture. If this continues long enough, the soil becomes too salty to grow crops.

Another is deforestation, which not only limits wood (a very useful resource), but increases soil erosion; again, this leads to lack of fertility, as well as the silting up of rivers and deltas   The near total deforestation of northern China and subsequent soil loss resulted in the Yellow River frequently shifting its course, causing major and destructive floods.

It doesn't take long for salinization to become a problem. In 3500 BC the main crops in Sumer were wheat and barley; within 1500 years it was almost all barley, which is more resistant to salt. By 1800 BC crop yields were a third of what they had once been; the city-states of Sumer became marginal and political power shifted to the north. The area had recovered by the time of the Islamic conquest— only to collapse again centuries later, about the time of the Mongols. In the 20C archeologists digging in the Iraqi desert marveled at the lush world depicted in the tablets they were reading.

The picturesque landscape of the Mediterranean lands, dominated by olive trees, vines, low bushes and herbs, is the result of deforestation— there used to be plenty of forest. (The "cedars of Lebanon" referred to in the Bible are nearly gone.) As early as 590 BC the Athenian legislator Solon proposed a ban on the cultivation of steep slopes in order to prevent soil loss.

The Maya, originally garden agriculturalists, built an extensive urban and agricultural civilization, clearing the forest to build permanent fields. But as the population increased, crop yields dropped, silt damaged the raised fields in the lowlands, and social unrest grew. The civilization collapsed, and its cities were reclaimed by the jungle.

Salinization can be put off by leaving fields fallow, and by manuring (this was unavailable to the Maya who had no large domestic animals). Terracing helps reduce soil loss (but doesn't eliminate it; the Greeks and Maya were both great terracers). When problems start to occur, moreover, it becomes harder and harder to do the right thing; the perceived need is *more land*, and people start to cultivate more and more marginal soils, and reduce rather than increase fallow periods, bringing the disaster closer.

In a sense dark ages are nature's way of recovering after a too-intensive period of human development.

Most of these ills are due to agriculture, but hunter-gatherers can cause devastation too, by **overhunting**. The large animals of the Americas died out at the same time as initial human settlement.

Fantasy/s.f. food sources

Anthropology stops here, but we don't have to. Food could come from other sources:

- hunting alone (for a carnivorous species)

- photosynthesis (for a plant-derived species)

- magic

- vats of algae formed into food-like shapes, injected with flavors and nutrients— yummy!

- anything you want, constructed molecule by molecule using nanobots

- the less successful members of society. Cannibalism can't be the primary food source, however. Carnivores require several times their biomass to support their population— if a species only ate conspecifics, it would quickly die out.

Whatever exotic system you choose, decide **how much work** it involves. Does it take the whole population most of their work week, as traditional agriculture did? Is it a trivial economic sector, as in our society? Or something in between?

What sort of population **density** is supported? One person in a square mile, like some hunter-gatherer lifestyles? Huge megacities?

What **resources** are needed, and who controls those? Are they evenly distributed through the land or concentrated in easily defended clumps? Are they sustainable? How easy is it to create a new settlement, especially for a dissident group?

What are the **environmental effects**, especially as the population density grows? How high a population could the planet support this way?

History

History and culture determine each other, so which do you do first? I'll suggest history, since you can write an outline history without a detailed understanding of your culture.

Filling in an outline

Earlier (p. 10) I suggested a narrative, two-line summary of the course of your culture, the sort of thing you could pitch to a bored movie exec.

Let's examine one of these and fill it out more:

It used to be...	and now it's...
two separate nations	united, with cultural remnants of the former independent countries

Create a table comparing our own history with your conworld's. This is going to be fast and breezy— just a dozen lines long, on a more or less logarithmic scale. Put in the two events we have somewhere.

BC/AD	Earth	Mil.	New world
-9000	Agriculture	0	
-4000	Urbanization	5	
-3000	Writing; kingdoms	6	
-2000	law codes; chariots	7	
-1000	cavalry; alphabet; coins	8	
-500	Greeks; rise of Rome	8.5	
1	height and fall of Rome	9	
500	Dark Ages; Táng; Islam	9.5	
1000	Medieval era	10	two separate nations
1500	colonialism, science	10.5	
1750	Europe conquers world	10.75	
2000	Modern times	11	united, with cultural remnants of the former independent countries

There are two reasons to include the précis of Earth history: to remind you to outline the whole of your history, and to serve as rough defaults. A blank line can be assumed to be similar to Earth's development at that period.

So the current time in this world is comparable to our present? Meh. Let's say we want a Renaissance-like world. So let's move the events back, and also create some provisional names.

BC/AD	Earth	Mil.	Novazema
-9000	Agriculture	0	
-4000	Urbanization	5	
-3000	Writing; kingdoms	6	
-2000	law codes; chariots	7	
-1000	cavalry; alphabet; coins	8	
-500	Greeks; rise of Rome	8.5	
1	height and fall of Rome	9	two nations, Joausi and Mounia
500	Dark Ages; Táng; Islam	9.5	
1000	Medieval era	10	
1500	colonialism, science	10.5	united, er, Joausimounia
1750	Europe conquers world	10.75	—
2000	Modern times	11	—

I moved the component nations 1500 years back— the exact date can be adjusted. So there's a technological as well as a political difference between the two periods.

Trying to name the united land brings us to the first of many questions about making this history more specific: which nation won? Or is the union something so new it got a new name?

But a single change of state is boring. Why not let both nations win, each in turn? And only then, perhaps, a new nation emerges.

9	two nations, Joausi and Mounia
9.5	Joausi conquers Mounia; many rebellions
10	Mounia re-emerges, takes over Joausi
10.5	formation of united Naeja Republic
10.75	—
11	—

How did we get from a revanchist Mounia to a new republic, though? Maybe another civil war, but we more or less did that. Perhaps another nation, Ombuto, invaded, and it was in pushing out the invaders that a new national identity was formed.

That's a good start, but where did Joausi and Mounia come from? Let's give them very different histories:

	Joausi	Mounia
6	first city-states along great rivers	
7	empire of Kinyr	
8	nomad invasions: proto-Joausians conquer Kinyr	cities form
8.5	a dark age— some foreign or Kinyrian rule	diverse littoral people create mercantile republics in a former barbarian area
9	Joausi nation	unified Mounia
9.5	Joausi empire	Conquered by Joausi; many rebellions
10	ruled by Mounia	Mounia re-emerges, takes over Joausi
10.5	Ombuto invasion; formation of united Naeja Republic	

One nation derives from nomadic conquerors; the other from maritime city-states. We begin to get a picture of how their values differ, and even what they might fight about.

Map time

It's hard to get much further without a map. Note that some bits of the map are already determined: Joausi must adjoin a region suitable for nomads; Mounia is littoral; there must be a fair amount of room for Ombuto, a nation that can threaten them both.

You'll probably have a lot more world than you have countries at this point. In the example we have three nations. Presumably Mounia and Joausi adjoin; but what's to the north, south, east, and west? Ombuto is one of those directions, but what's beyond it?

So add some names to the map— you can always change them later. While you're at it, name some of the major regions within the two main nations— these will be useful as you add further history, as they may have been nations themselves at certain periods.

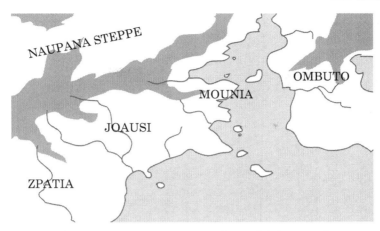

The dark shading indicates mountains, which partly protect the southern nations from the steppe.

A historical chart

Now that we have multiple nations, let's expand the chart, one column per region:

	Zpatia	Joausi	Mounia	Ombuto
6		city states along great rivers		
7	early kingdoms	empire of Kinyr		first kingdoms
8		conquest by Jouausi nomads	cities form on coast	three-way war
8.5	Vlapuyn unites Zpatia, forms empire	dark age— rule by Zpatians; rebellion by Kinyrians	littoral people create mercantile republics	early Ombuto empire
9	collapse; dark age	Joausi kingdom	Mounia united	nomad conquest
9.5		Joausi empire	ruled by Joausi	warring states

| 10 | divided into small states | conquered by Mounia | Mounia re-emerges, becomes empire | rise of united empire |
| 10.5 | eastern states occupied by Naeja | Ombuto invasion; Naeja republic | Ombuto invasion; Naeja republic | invades Mounia |

This sort of chart is easily converted into a graphic. Keep the basic idea: regions across the top, time down the sides. But present the information graphically. Color in each of the nations; make the size proportionate to how much of the region they control. Here's the above table turned into a chart:

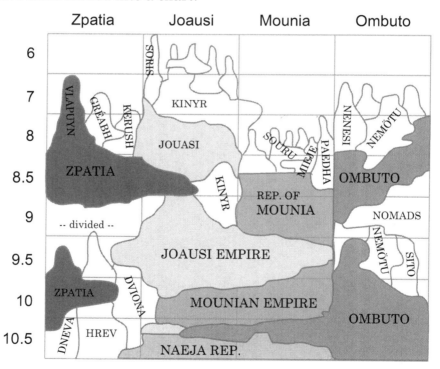

The graphics allow a lot more detail in the same space. E.g. I was able to suggest the back-and-forth of the struggle to form Ombuto, rather than just label this spot "three-way war"; it's also possible to see stages in the conquest of Mounia and the emergence of Naeja.

Avoid the pattern of "state emerges, stays the same till it's conquered". E.g. look at Souru and Mieje, two of the city-states that formed the Republic of Mounia: the scalloped border between them indicates that they alternated periods of dominance.

Also avoid kingdoms or city-states that are all the same size. Some should be much larger, some much smaller.

When you develop historical details, be bold. A sort of psychological block can develop— you've labeled a portion of the map "Mounia" and you think of it as always being one country. But few nations have a simple history. Apply the principle we started with at smaller levels: this region is now X, but it used to be Y.

Historical atlas

The historical chart can now be turned into historical maps. As a boy I discovered Colin McEvedy's *Penguin Historical Atlases*; in four slim volumes he covers the whole of European and Middle Eastern history, with several maps per century, plus a brisk, wry, and informative commentary. Companion volumes treat North America, Africa, and the Pacific. These books are invaluable for giving a wide perspective on history, but McEvedy is also a master at lapidary character portraits that bring history to life:

> Fortune smiled on Spanish arms but Ferdinand deserves his traditional share of the credit. Ever willing to compromise, always offering to take the smaller half, he usually ended up with the whole bag.

You can draw horizontal lines across your chart at key points and use these as guides for making the map. The main idea is that you are translating diagrammatic conventions to geographical facts— e.g. "half of Mounia controlled by Joausi" must be translated into an exact division of the territory.

Formats

My historical atlas of Erelâe includes maps for 43 dates, from the remote paleolithic (-25,000) to Almea's present, Z.E. 3480, plus 13 supplementary maps covering things like terrain, cities, and languages. And this is still only about 1/4 as large as McEvedy's coverage of the West.

You can do far less than this, of course— a couple of maps of "ancient times" may be all you need. But the more maps you have, the more *story* you have in your history. You accumulate a rich cultural lore and a set of past heroes and villains.

Movements and borders are constrained by **geography**. I recommend including the major mountain ranges on your base map. These make natural boundaries— e.g. the Pyrenees separate Spain from France, the Alps protect Italy, the Carpathians form a minor barrier around Hungary. (Mountains paralleling the coast, such as the Atlas range in the Maghreb, are less important for history).

Be aware of **ecological boundaries** too. The most important are those between climate zones, such as tropical, temperate, and arctic. People are unlikely to expand into areas where their crops don't grow— or where the local diseases kill them off.

Just as important is the distinction between areas suitable for cultivation, and those best suited for nomadism— the steppe. These boundaries are somewhat permeable: a strong nomadic nation can force the agriculturalists off grassland, though not forest.

Know where your major rivers are; these are natural transportation arteries and sites for cities, and their basins make a natural ecological zone. The area separating river basins will be higher ground and form a natural boundary.

Another natural ecological zone is the littoral, areas in close contact with the sea. A very convoluted coastline, as in Greece and western Anatolia, extends the littoral zone. A littoral zone makes a natural maritime nation, distinct from the nations of the interior. The ancient Greeks by preference colonized nearby regions that also belonged to the littoral zone: the Crimea, the Mediterranean islands, the boot of Italy. A relatively straight coastline produces only a small littoral, less likely to form a distinct nation.

A lesson from terrestrial history: few regions belong to the same people forever. Think in terms of population movements. As a corollary, the majority population of almost any nation originally came from somewhere else. (This is sometimes reflected in the people's mythology— though a more prestigious place of origin may be substituted, as the Romans claimed to descend from Troy.)

Movements trigger counter-movements. E.g. the movement of the Huns into Europe impelled a number of Germanic peoples to try their luck in the Roman Empire. Or the movement may be a counter-invasion: the ancient Persians' attempt to conquer Greece ultimately led to the Greek conquest of Persia.

Methods

The first version of my historical atlas was done on paper. I created a base map with only oceans, rivers, and mountains, and took it to a printer to get a hundred pages printed in a light blue color. That was enough to do the atlas, then redo it better.

Now that color printers and photocopiers are available, you can easily make your own blank maps, and with far better colors.

These days, though, you can get better results entirely on the computer. You can proceed in several ways, most but not all of which involve handing money to Adobe.

See the Maps chapter (p. 285) for how to create the actual maps. Some programs you can use for the atlas:

- A good paint program, or to use the technical term, anything but Microsoft Paint. Create the base map— just the geographical features, no lettering. Start from this every time you need to make a historical or other kind of map.

- **Photoshop**, or **GIMP**— any paint program which supports layers. Now you can place the oceans, rivers, and terrain on separate layers, and each historical map on its own layer above those. Each bit of text gets its own layer— this can quickly get out of hand, so this is perhaps the best solution only if you need a handful of maps, rather than 50.

- **Illustrator**, or **Inkscape**. Put the base map as a bitmap on one layer. Everything you need for one map— borders, towns, text, transparent regions to color in the countries— can live in a separate layer. You can easily switch between maps by setting their layers' visibility.

- **Flash**. I used this method for the atlases of Arcél and Skouras. Flash is two-dimensional: it has *layers* and *frames*. The layers will work like Photoshop: one for oceans, one for rivers, one for boundaries, one for names, etc. The frames correspond to each of your maps.

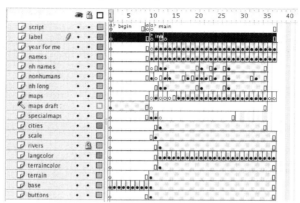

Flash makes it easy to share elements between maps. In the example, the base map, terrain colors, and rivers are shared between all maps. The "nonhumans" layer contains only a few different frames, as the boundaries of the nonhuman states change much less often than those of the humans.

Best of all, the atlas can be played as a movie, and you can see your nations wax and wane over time. You can also add controls to hide or show the layers; my Flash atlases allow the viewer to step through the maps with or without layers for the terrain, cities, language colors, or political colors.

Example: Novazema

Here are three rough maps of Novazema, at three points within the last row of the graph.

First, here's the beginning of the Ombutese invasion: Ombuto has occupied the coast nearest its own territory.

You can add new details at any point— I've added some tribe names to the steppe area. Adding names is a good first step, but get into the habit of thinking about the stories behind them: what makes this place different from that place over there? Terrain, language, religion, what? If the difference is cultural, when did it arise?

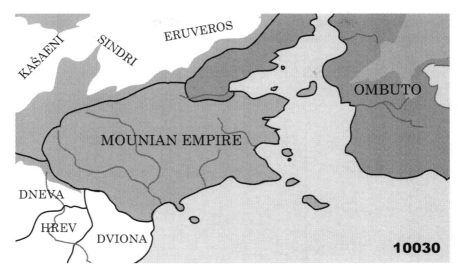

10030

The map below shows Ombuto in control of both countries, but rebellions have occurred in each. Perhaps these almost fail before they overcome old antagonisms and decide to work together to expel the invaders.

Now that we're looking at individual maps, quirks of geography— or just whim— can suggest additional stories. The island of Akaerti is either another rebellion, or was never conquered by Ombuto.

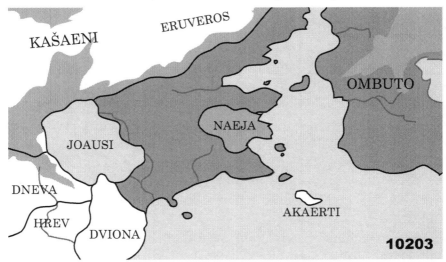

10203

Marginal areas should have changes too. Here the Kašaeni have absorbed their neighbors, the Sindri.

Here's the present state of affairs, after the Naeja Republic has not only kicked the Ombutese out, but taken some Ombutese territory, and conquered Dviona to the west as well. Ombuto's weakness has allowed a buffer state, Ndato, to form.

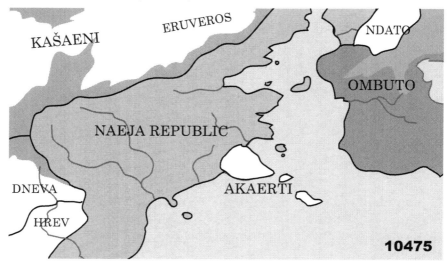

It looks like Akaerti did its bit in fighting the Ombutese, but refused to join the Naeja Republic.

Iterative development

Don't try to rush through a project as large as a historical atlas. The Atlas of Almea I posted on my website is about the fourth version I did, and by the time you're reading this I may have revised it again. If you're in a hurry, do the historical table and just a few maps.

Your first map is likely to be breezy and characterless... a bunch of similar-sized kingdoms that bubble up into empires and divide for no apparent reason. That's fine— inspiration can flag. This is one reason to create rough draft maps at first, so they're easy to go back and revise later, as you think of new and better things to happen.

It's also a good idea to stop after the rough draft stage, and work on the culture, religion, and technology, using the following chapters. A rough history is enough to inform your cultural creation— if you want to say "Religion X was invented in Y", you have some names for possible Y's and your map suggests propagation routes. You'll know what your main culture's neighbors are and something of what makes them tick.

But for the polished version, especially the commentary, the more you know about the culture the better. You want to know not just what happened, but why. The meaningless unions and divisions of the rough draft can take significance as dynastic quarrels, religious splits, the result of mercantile success or military advances, the consequences of corrupt emperors or ecological crises.

If you're working out **languages** at the same time, think about what happens to entire language families. An empire normally imposes a standard language, which then splits into daughter languages over the course of a millennium or two.

You'll need a naming language for each region of your map; some of them should be related and look somewhat alike. Working out the full culture, religion, and history of your main conculture is difficult without working out its language, or at the least a lexicon of a few hundred roots.

Example: What's next for Novazema?

For the maps of Novazema, the maps suggest a story, but it needs to be fleshed out. Why did the Mounian empire fall so quickly to the Ombutese— was it decadent, unpopular, or simply technologically backward? What allowed the rebellion to begin? Was it merely an ethnic rebellion, or a new ideology, as suggested by the new name Naeja and the change from empire to republic? Why wouldn't Akaerti join? Why did the republic, founded to counter a foreign invasion, turn around and occupy one of its neighbors?

Think about *who* did these things— who were the Ombutese kings; whose idea was the republic?

Look at the more static areas of the map— it's not very realistic that pretty much nothing has happened in Dneva and Hrev for the last five centuries. And perhaps because I didn't put the steppe into the historical chart, there's no interaction here between its inhabitants and the lands to the south.

The reason why

Why did Ombuto invade?

- Arashne the Great, the favored prince of Ombuto, after consolidating his power, sought eternal glory, setting himself against the canny and brave empress Kiraeku of Mounia (the Great Man theory)

- Trade, even Ombuto's internal commerce, was dominated by Mounians; if they were conquered this engine of wealth would be Ombuto's (the economic explanation)

- Arashne's line and upbringing was Sito, disdained by the Ombutese proper. He thus had a burning urge to prove himself and quash dissent (the psychological explanation)

- The Ombutese nobility was feudal and war was their *raison d'être*; the best way to keep them from rebellion or frivolity, and to strengthen the state, was an external war (the cultural explanation)

- Sithiswe, the god of Peace, entered on his long cyclical sleep, leaving Harana the goddess of War as his regent. Men had no choice but to fall into war (the mythological explanation)

It could be all of these, of course. Your history becomes more interesting, in fact, the more reasons you add. You can start, as we did above, with mere statements of fact like "Ombuto invades", but the world starts to seem real once you can explain *why*, on several levels.

Who's talking?

The commentary for my atlases takes a pseudo-scholarly tone, but that's only one alternative.

Historians aren't omniscient; for Almean studies I allow my point of view to be limited by native sources— e.g. little archeological information is available, and I describe conflicting sources and historical mysteries. If you prefer, of course, you can know everything about your world.

Or you can take a native point of view: e.g. the history of Novazema might be relayed by a Mounian, with appropriate biases and gaps in knowledge— this can be a lot of fun to write. I've mentioned the *Count of Years*, a native Almean history. *Oblivion* and *Skyrim* , are filled with stories, poems, and bits of history or ethnography all written by natives.

Native writers might simply wish to relate the facts as they know them; or they might have an agenda. Perhaps our Mounian wishes to glorify the old empire, or justify the new republic, or advance a religious revival. The narrator might even be unreliable— events can be narrated in a way that suggests a different story or interpretation to the reader.

Here's the same event narrated in three different styles:

Academic: Arashne spent two years mustering his army, ferrying troops to Paedha, the Mounian port his father had captured. There were endless delays due to the scale of the operation; the force was not ready till early fall. Eager to make use of the remaining campaign season, he ordered the attack to begin. But the delay had allowed Kiraeku to move a hastily raised army into position, and as winter fell the invasion petered out at the gates of Mieje, just 100 km into Mounian territory.

Partisan: The alien despot launched a sneak attack at harvest time, with over 200,000 death-pale Ombutese and thousands of traitorous Paedhans. Forewarned in time, our brave Empress Kiraeku personally led the loyallest of her troops, a bare 50,000 stalwalt fighters, to meet the invaders with their cruel curved swords. The horde was halted at the desperate battle of Mieje, but the invaders remained outside the city and were rumored to be fetching cannons. Reinforcements were few; fear led many to desert Mounia at the hour of her greatest need.

Religious: These were the dark times of Harana into whose hands the world of mortals was delivered; Lord Arashne made sacrifice and drank blood in Her worship. Possessed by the goddess, the Lord and his warriors burned with wrath and they advanced into the heathen lands causing great devastation with sword and lance and musket. They halted before Mieje as even Harana must not act in the night of the year, the season of the Nameless God.

Cities

These maps— to say nothing of modern politics and economics— give the impression that history is all about countries. This is highly misleading; it's all about the cities.

Why are cities important?

- They're key **military** strongholds. A rural area can't resist an invading army; a city can, and in fact conquering a country, as opposed to ruling it, can't be done without taking the cities— a formidable task before cannons were invented.

- Because of this they're the safest place for rulers to hang out, and thus they become centers of **administration**.

- They're **economic** powerhouses, before modern times the site of all manufacturing and banking, the endpoints of trade routes. They generate wealth that rulers can tap in its most convenient form, money.

  In Europe town culture— the literal meaning of *bourgeois*— was the origin of the middle class, and thus of republicanism and capitalism.

- For all these reasons they become **cultural** hubs, the home of artists, writers, theaters, and universities. Cities also become the focus of **language** varieties; a standard language is almost always the speech of a prestigious town.

- Most important, perhaps, they're the center of **innovation**— even advances in agriculture such as mechanical reapers and electricity begin in or near cities. The Renaissance began in the most urbanized parts of Europe, northern Italy and Flanders.

For many reasons (including high-speed transportation and the fad for nation-states) the 20C was a rough time for cities; Americans may still feel that cities are swamps of poverty and crime. Historically it was quite the opposite: the cities were rich and far safer than the countryside. (Unhealthier, though. Dense populations breed disease, attract vermin, and create loads of waste.)

For more on this I recommend the books of Jane Jacobs, cited in the reading list; also see the essay on cities on my website.

What do you do with this in your conworld? Well, create cities, for one. That's why I have a cities layer in my atlases, so I can see where they are.

- In earliest times, kingdoms are likely to be city-states. When one gets strong enough to conquer the rest, the empire stage begins.

- If a nation is conquered in stages, this corresponds to taking one city after another.

- Some regions, such as ancient Greece and medieval Italy, never really coalesce as nations, but remain patchworks of city-states.

Cities aren't interchangeable; cities and whole regions develop specialties— e.g. the wool trade in medieval Flanders, or the auto industry in 20C Detroit. A specialty may develop by accident, but once it exists it's self-reinforcing: support industries grow up, skilled workers abound. It's not easy to bite into such an area's market share (but when it happens, it's likely to be a major economic event).

Cities can last thousands of years, but they can be abandoned in a dark age or a conquest, and not all are reestablished. So don't have the same cities in every epoch.

See also p. 91 on city sizes, and p. 297 on city plans.

Cycles

Are there cycles to history? Nations certainly have their ups and downs; so do economies. The Chinese have long noted a pattern of vigorous rulers at the beginning of a dynasty and weak ones later on. In the last few centuries Western nations seem to alternate between periods of revolution or reform and reactionary cooldowns.

Attempts to set fixed years on apparent cycles require a bit too much special pleading. For conworlding, cycles are a reminder to *have stuff happen*. Throw in a major war, a revolution, a great intellectual discovery, a plague, an ecological disaster, a new religion, an orc invasion.

Alternative histories

Instead of creating a world from scratch, you can take ours and tweak it. The usual method is to take a single event and have it come out the other way: e.g. Hitler won (Philip K. Dick, *The Man in the High Castle*), or the Reformation never happened (Kingsley Amis, *The Alteration*), or a Jewish homeland was set up in Alaska rather than Palestine (Michael Chabon, *The Yiddish Policemen's Union*).

Or there may be an ongoing difference. In Alan Moore's *Watchmen*, the difference is that superheroes are real in the Watchmen world. Or your goal may simply be to insert a fictional country into the map of Europe.

The advantage is that you already have your planet, with a full history and set of cultures up to the point of divergence. You'll need good research on the period of divergence, however, to make your alternative history plausible. Reversing the last battle of a war is usually not convincing: you have to address the *reasons* for the victory. If Napoléon had won Waterloo he would likely have lost the next battle, perhaps when the Austrians or Russians arrived. (As Ken Hite and Mike Schiffer point out, the *real* divergence in many an alternate history is "so-and-so wasn't as much of an idiot as in our timeline".)

If the divergence is quite early, you'll be doing quite a bit of conworlding. E.g. if Persia had beat the Greeks, the world would look very different 2000 years later. And even if you just make the winning side *last longer*, as in the ever-popular ongoing Roman Empire, clothes and language and religions won't be the same as in the 1C.

The process is most impressive if you think out second-order effects. For instance, Amis has Martin Luther becoming Pope; one result is that his puritan ideals prevent Michelangelo from designing St. Peter's.

Four centuries later, Amis has Jean-Paul Sartre becoming a Monsignor. This sort of thing is hard to resist, and of course it supplies you with ready-made personalities, but I find it hard to swallow. If the big picture is radically different from our timeline, there's no reason the little details are the same long after the point of divergence.

Don't forget demographics. By Hannibal's time Rome had a 4-to-1 population advantage and was unlikely to be conquered by Carthage. There are similar problems with attempts to make a successful Confederate States a real rival to the USA.

Lost cause histories are the bread and butter of alt history, but be careful if you sympathize with the lost cause: you may be tempted to write a utopia, and utopias kill storytelling.

Culture

What's a culture? Everything that's not biology nor individual choice. To be specific, this chapter will cover things at the level of the whole society: culture tests, government, law, and the economy. The next chapter will look at things at the individual level: family life, clothing, architecture, and other aspects of daily life. Religion, magic, technology, and war get their own chapters.

Many things we imagine are universal– how men and women relate, rules on invitations and gifts, how negotiations proceed, how much you can get from your family, attitudes toward nudity or fidelity— are really cultural.

You can also work backwards: take what seems to be a commonplace of human experience (e.g. "people prefer girls to old women") and imagine a society where the opposite holds. It'll make your culture at least distinctive, and at best fascinating.

Culture tests

A good way to begin describing a country is to write a culture test. The best way to explain these is to show you one. There are a couple dozen more available from my website, for both real and imagined countries.

Skourene culture test

Skouras is a region on my conworld Almea; it's a maritime culture, comparable to ancient Greece or Phoenicia. The culture test is intended to apply only to urban residents, as these are the dominant and most interesting class.

If you're Skourene...

- You think the gods are important— everyone should have one. But you can't imagine telling someone outside your *bsepa* (your extended family) who to worship. In some foreign countries the rulers tell you who your gods are. Crazy!

118

- You're reverent to all gods— who needs supernatural enemies?— but you reserve your sacrifices and requests for the two gods of your *bsepa*, one male and one female.

- You can ask the gods for things because that's their job: they're helpers and guardians. Things can become gods— some gods even used to be human beings— and they can cease to be gods. The world, including its gods and people, was originally created by Ksaragetor (who is responsible for all good things) and Gamagetor (who was not so good at his job and created all the messed-up things); but no one worships them or knows much about them.

- You can read— how would you do business without it? You enjoy reading stories, the convoluted history of the Skourene states, sermons, poems, satires, philosophy, treatises about your trade, and much else.

- Games are simply training for war: running, swimming, archery, rowing, wrestling, spear-throwing, sword-fighting. If you're male, you like to participate in these and watch exhibitions by masters— or even better, fights with captured prisoners. If you're female, you grew up playing at these things too, and can pursue the first three as an adult, if you care to.

Would you eat that? I'll have a slice

- We're here to work; if you get tired of doing one thing, do another; if your feet hurt, do the accounting; if you're sick of the city, take to the sea. This isn't to say you can't enjoy yourself with food and drink and amusements, but don't tell me you want to do that *all day long*.

- You like to eat a big meal in the evening, at home with your family; but you usually buy your lunch in the market, or take some business associates to an eatery (*tnasali*).

- There's very little that you wouldn't eat. If you travel to faraway places and see exotic animals, your mouth waters.

- You don't like to live far from the water, and you take a morning bath every day if possible— if you're poor, right in the ocean or the river; if you're better off, in the heated city baths.

Do I get paid for taking this test?

- If you need a letter or package sent to someone in the city, there are messengers who will take it— you just flag one down in the street.

Barefoot, shaggy fellows, but reliable. There are services between cities, considerably more well-heeled.

- You have no objection to walking, but who has the time to walk all the way across town? There's carriages for that; or you take a skiff along the waterfront. To get to other cities, of course, you take a ship.

- You're proud to be part of a free people, which is ruled by its own *bsepas*, meeting in a Senate, and not by "kings", as the foreigners are.

- People can have lighter or darker skin, or hair that ranges from black to brown to straw color. It doesn't mean anything. You don't entirely trust someone from out of town, though.

- You think that most problems can be solved if they're thought about long enough— and if you can be the first to think of it, there's probably money in it.

- Disputes that can't be solved any other way can be taken to the courts— a scary prospect, as the judges are empowered to probe into every aspect of your life. The better way is to talk to the higher-ups in the *bsepa*, and they'll work it out for you. You'll owe them a favor; but that's better than the courts getting their hands on you.

People and other people

- Humans aren't the only people on Almea. There's the *ṭailuadnir*, who live in the sea; you don't want one as an enemy, and you're not sure if you want one as your friend, either. Not that they'll *harm* you, no.

- Then there's the *atingetoro*— little, fierce, mostly friendly guys from the mountains, who come round to sell gems and minerals and metals they've dug up, and beautiful things they've made out of them. You've learned the hard way not to play drinking games with them.

- Then there's the *geŋŋialgirigi*— mischievous little devils who are an excellent reason not to go into the forest, where they live. Farms near the forest will leave out food for them, to appease them. There are other monsters up in the mountains or the steppe.

- You're not the sort of hick who only knows one language. You know your own city's language and that of a few other Skourene cities. Possibly Axunašin, Jeori, Mei, or Tžuro as well.

One of them said Almea is round, if you can believe it

- Each of the *bsepas* has a tax levied on it, which goes to pay for defense, the courts, roads, public entertainments, and the dole. You grumble over it, but you pay your share.

- You learned to read and write and calculate at home, and you learned morality and worship from the *bsepa*'s priest. Some of the philosophers offer lectures; it's often worth paying a few coins to hear what they have to say. Sometimes you learn something; sometimes you just laugh at the crazy old greybeard's ravings.

- Years are reckoned by the *groparam*, the triennial Trucial Councils between the three delta cities. The three Senates meet together, and there's competitions and feasts and performances. Complicating the chronology, they're not held if the cities are at war with each other.

- You grow your own vegetables in a plot by your house, and perhaps raise chickens as well. Everything else you buy at the market.

- There used to be a proverb that "Skourenes don't fight Skourenes"... would that it were still true. Some city will get too big for its breeches and need taking down.

- Your own city has come out on the wrong side of a war or two, and perhaps lost a good deal of its colonial empire. Skouras has never been conquered by foreigners, however, and it's hard to see that it ever could be.

Why you'd better get along with your mother-in-law

- Marriage, like any business of importance, is arranged between the *bsepas*. It takes time to get used to being married, but you end up loving the person almost as much as your own relatives.

- In the old days, a man joined his wife's *bsepa*. These days a firstborn son may bring his wife into his own *bsepa* instead— at least, if his is richer.

- A man can only have one wife; but some men— lucky bastards— can support a mistress or two. In colonies, where the supply of women is low, a woman is sometimes married to two men.

- It's not really right for men to sleep with other men, outside of special circumstances like a long campaign or a trading expedition. But it's an impure world, and what happens behind closed doors is the least of our worries.

- You call a person by his name. Foreigners make this complicated by having multiple names and making you guess which one to use.

- Nudity is best indulged at home— except when bathing, of course. Some women like to dress in the shameless Axunemi fashion, showing their breasts.

- There are houses (*rubnakalir*) that will rent a room to a stranger. It's better to stay with a friend or relative, though; through the *bsepa* you'll have these anywhere in your city's empire and sometimes elsewhere in Skouras.

- Whatever sort of business you have, gifts and meals will help it along. But it's going a little too far when people expect to have their vices satiated, or get rich at official posts.

Give me that old five-tone music

- The only money you entirely trust is gold, but it's more for saving than for buying things. For that, you use silver coins, or promissory notes from a bank.

- The simplest way to run a business is within your own family or *bsepa*— there's a tradition for it, trustworthy workers, and financial help. But you can have a family firm with nonfamily employees, or work for a large concern that has lost any family character (though in many ways it acts like a *bsepa*).

- If there's no wine available, you'll consent to swig down some of the westerners' foul rye beer.

- Music is decaphonic and polyrhythmic, based mostly on drums, horns, wooden flutes, and sitars. But there's an undeniable charm to country music, with its pentatonic scale, simple rhythms, and reliance on reeds and bagpipes.

- If you're sick, there are people who will do disagreeable things to you and charge you for it and leave you just as sick. Better to go to a hermitage for rest, steam and cold water baths, and massage.

- As a citizen, you have the right and obligation to serve in the army, when your city is attacked or when arrogant outside cities need to be punished. Only a crazy person actually likes it, but it's got to be done.

Barbarians and where to find them

- You may trade, you may farm or fish, you may make things— it's all business. If you're not in charge, you think you should be.

- Proper streets are paved, and the major roads into the hinterland too.

- The people upriver— from Miligenḍi and Papliopagimi and such places— are not much better than rustics or barbarians; they only feel comfortable with despotic governments and too much religion.

- The colonists— a term which you apply to anyone who lives south of the delta, even if their cities were founded half a millennium ago — are rough around the edges and a little too excitable and full of themselves. The Guṭleliki are the worst— proud and vulgar.

- The Axunemi and Jeori are warlike, priest-ridden, and oppressed by their 'kings' and 'lords'— a fat, idle class who are treated like gods.

- The only safe, civilized places in the world are Skourene cities. There are some places in them you wouldn't advise a stranger to go alone, of course. Rural areas are unsafe and depressing. Forests, mountains, and deserts are nasty, dangerous places. If you can't smell the sea, it's no place for you.

"Can I take this road to the city?"
"Reckon not. They already got one"

- The ideal girl is a little pale, a little thin, a little naive, and a little fiery. Once married she loses the first three qualities but makes up for it in the last.

- The best jokes are told about the *guṣourianda*— the people of the hinterland. Most are dimwits, but there are also stories of clever *guṣourianda* teaching a lesson to a foolish city slicker.

- Everyone knows that Skouras is the richest land under the sun. Why are things so expensive, then?

- The most important thing to know about someone is what *bsepa* they belong to.

- If you run a firm, you choose who will run it after you; it doesn't have to be one of your children, but if it's not, you'll adopt them. They'll get the bulk of your personal wealth as well. Land belongs to the families and so it doesn't change hands when someone dies.

Mess with me and I'll call Grand-Uncle

- The biggest holiday of the year is the celebration of the harvest (*Raḍḍoug*); the most important is the blessing of the spring planting (*Raḍḍinoum*). At those times, and no others, you feel great solidarity with your rural brethren and your farmer ancestors.

- You can name most of the *bsepas* in the delta cities and their relation to your own, and you're pretty well informed about the other major cities, too.

- If you run into trouble you would turn first to your *bsepa*. If they can't help or you have no family, you have to rely on the dole. The city will give you food and a place to sleep, but you have to wear special clothes and do menial work, like street-cleaning. You hope you never have to use it, or if you do, that it won't be long.

- There are some professions, such as medicine, magic, architecture, and the martial arts, that you can only learn by apprenticing yourself to a master. Others, like writing or the law, are just talents which some people can do and others can't.

Space and time

- It's very rude to make an appointment and not keep it. On the other hand, you don't expect to get someone all to yourself— you join the people hanging around with him, and the amount of attention you get is finely calibrated to your relative importance.

- If you're talking to someone, you're uncomfortable if you're not close enough to make a point by grabbing their arm or tapping their chest.

- You don't haggle for cheap things, but if it's expensive, you make a production out of it.

- You can show up at a friend or relative's place uninvited. If they're really busy, though, you'll only get a glass of wine and some honey cakes, not a meal.

- It's extremely impolite to refuse someone outright; also to boast about your own abilities or wealth. On the other hand, there's no need to hide your feelings just because of someone's rank.

How do you write one?

What are you doing as you write a culture test for your culture? Making decisions, mostly, and inventing details that help show what it's like to belong to that culture. The points above are selected to tackle a wide variety of issues— marriage and sex, economic life, attitudes toward the past and foreign countries, values, religion, government.

The idea is to make statements that are true of 90% of the described population. E.g. the American culture test has "You are not a farmer", since farmers are a tiny percentage of the population. "You're a Christian" wouldn't quite make it, since under 80% of the population identifies as Christian.

If you're baffled, go point by point through this culture test (or look at the ones online at http://www.zompist.com/amercult.html) and say to yourself, "Self, how would this go in my country?" If you're not sure, go on to the next point. Or write something tentative and go back to it later.

You don't have to make every point a major difference from your own culture, or the Standard Fantasy Culture— but think of every point as an opportunity to do so, or at least to look at things from different eyes.

Reading the tests can help you realize just how variable cultures are— attitudes we've always taken as universal turn out to be much more parochial. And writing them is a good first step in bringing a world alive, and learning to speak for the natives.

Monoculture

It takes work to devise a culture, so it's understandable that many creators stop at one. This is especially evident in s.f., where most alien races and human colonies have precisely one civilization per planet... sometimes just one climate per planet, too.

On our own planet, culture is fractal— there's variation at every level. There are major civilizations: European, Islamic, Indian, Chinese, African, Andean, Mesoamerican. Each of these is divided into ethnic groups and religions. The ethnic groups are divided into provinces, the religions into sects. Your province or state is far from uniform; your city is divided into neighborhoods each with its own character; even a small school is divided into factions and cliques. Graham Robb's *The Discovery of France* is an eye-opening exploration of just how diverse a premodern nation is.

How do you simulate this without working out a thousand cultures in full detail? By **incorporating diversity** as you design any culture.

- When considering aspects of culture— or biology— you should sometimes answer "**all of the above**". Whether it's hairstyle or form of government or number of gods worshipped, this produces areas where variation is to be expected.

- Ask yourself where **disagreements** occur. What are the controversies in your society? What do people fight about? (This is valuable for storytelling too: people talk about their disagreements far more than their common values.)

When creating culture tests, we look for things 90% of the population would agree on. Creating controversies, look for things 40-60% of the population believes. If just 10% believe something, they're likely to be persecuted dissidents.

- Outline some **subcultures**. Even within one nation, there will be groups isolated or organized enough to have their own distinctive mores and values. E.g.:

   ° Immigrants. Make sure you have a story on why they got there... are they conquerors, traders, refugees, job-seekers, former slaves, or mercenaries?

   ° Remnants of an earlier population— like the Celts in Roman Gaul, the Indians in the US, the Ainu in Japan.

   ° Religious minorities, like the Jews in Europe, the Muslims (*Huî*) in China, the Zoroastrians in India.

   ° Certain professions, especially despised ones like grave-diggers and thieves, might band together, providing the support system they are denied by larger society.

It's worth considering why these groups don't assimilate. This is less of an issue in premodern societies, where communities could easily keep to their own neighborhoods under their own laws, using their own language. But reasons will vary: a despised minority may be kept at bay by the larger society; a conquering minority wishes to maintain its monopoly on power; a community of traders needs to foster its relationship to the outside world; a religious sect has divine orders not to mix with the world.

- Diversity may be **chronological**. If there's been a major change— e.g. a foreign conquest, the overthrow of a king, evidence against the prevailing religion— there will be factions that liked the old situation and are threatened by the new. Almost any change can be opposed by somebody... electric lights were surely despised by the gaslight industry.

Try to get beyond **single-adjective cultures**: e.g. "warlike", "commercial", "spiritual". It's a good place to start, but no culture is uniform. The medieval aristocracy, for instance, was as "warlike" as any Klingon, but knights and lords were also obsessed with courtly love, beautiful art and clothes, and often religion. Some liked fighting for its own sake, some undertook war out of duty, some avoided it. And a civilization needs more than one skill to survive; the most successful empires also have a genius for administration, urban life, agriculture, and engineering.

Rulers

It's all about power. Who's on top, and what can they do to whoever's on the bottom? Any establishment will have a self-myth where the people on top *deserve* to be there— but, well, they would, wouldn't they? Things may look very different from the bottom. Take Jeff Alexander and Tom Bissell's hilarious piece from *McSweeney's*, imagining Howard Zinn and Noam Chomsky watching *The Lord of the Rings*:

> ZINN: Well, you know, it would be manifestly difficult to believe in magic rings unless everyone was high on pipe-weed. So it is in Gandalf's interest to keep Middle Earth hooked.

> CHOMSKY: How do you think these wizards build gigantic towers and mighty fortresses? Where do they get the money? Keep in mind that I do not especially regard anyone, Saruman included, as an agent for progressivism. But obviously the pipe-weed operation that exists is the dominant influence in Middle Earth. It's not some ludicrous magic ring.

There's an underlying optimism to most s.f. and fantasy. We like the occasional horror story, but we rarely read an entire novel where the Evil Overlord wins, or where technology ends up destroying us all.

In history, however, the overlords do often win. And after they do, they're the ones who hire the scholars or troubadors and control the theologians, so their version of events is what comes down to us as history and even as the judgment of the gods. (We never hear the Carthaginian side of the Rome-Carthage wars.)

That's not to say that negative opinions are suppressed. When the overlords die, historians can be more honest— especially if it's convenient to their successors. As well, what we consider damning evidence was often no big deal, and thus appears in the historical record because no one bothered to censor it.

There are limits to power, as well. There are always ambitious men who see a better ruler whenever they pass a mirror. The peasants can always rebel. And though the cruelty of ancient rulers is striking, if rulers went too far they made too many enemies, and usually met a bad end.

So let's take a look at rulers and what they do.

Choosing rulers

One way of classifying governments is by whether authority ultimately rests with an individual, a small group, or a wide base of society. The key word here is "ultimately": obviously power can be shared, and monarchies can be weakened or watered down to share aspects of the other systems.

Autarchies

These are realms principally ruled by one person, though they vary in how absolute the ruler's power is, and in how the ruler is chosen.

- The ruler may be selected by the leading clans, or nobles, or even a wider collection of stakeholders (e.g. the College of Cardinals). The advantage is that you get the best guy; the disadvantage is that the losing candidates may beg to differ.

  Arguably the golden age of the Roman Empire was the 2C, when emperors hand-picked a competent successor. Marcus Aurelius blew it by choosing his idiot son.

- Rule may be hereditary, which avoids contention, at the cost of having a large number of incompetents in charge.

  Primogeniture isn't always the rule; sometimes the previous monarch chooses; sometimes the royal family makes the choice. In royal Uganda the chiefs chose a new king from the old one's sons.

- A general or warlord may take over. From the 200s on, this was essentially the Roman system: a general would be acclaimed by his troops as emperor. Legions closer to the capital had an advantage; on the other hand troops on the frontiers were more experienced. Rome's history is not a good advertisement for this system, which led to inflated soldier salaries, near-constant civil war, devastated civilian populations, and declining military preparedness. Post-colonial Africa has suffered from more than its fair share of these bully boys as well.

- Rulers may emerge from a ideological movement: John Calvin's theocracy in Geneva; the Supreme Leaders of the Islamic Republic of Iran; the General Secretaries of communist regimes.

- The term *dictator* comes from an earlier stage of Roman history, in which rather than the two consuls normally appointed by the senate, a single ruler was named to deal with an emergency.

- Democracy was once distrusted by political scientists because it had a tendency to produce tyrants— much of the *Federalist Papers* is an argument on why it wouldn't happen this time. Hitler received a plurality of votes in an election, then used all the power of the government to stack a new election which he 'won' and used as a mandate for seizing absolute power. Napoléon became emperor out of the chaos of the French Republic.

- Some writers (e.g. G.K. Chesterton in *The Napoleon of Notting Hill*) have suggested that choosing a ruler randomly would produce as good or better results than any of the above methods.

Oligarchies

These are ruled by a group— wider than an individual, pointedly much smaller than the general population. The group may be defined in various ways:

- the leaders of clans or tribes
- the nobles as a group
- the top merchants in a town; this is the natural government for city-states
- a military class, such as the Janissaries
- pirates, bandits, or mafiosi
- a separate species

The ruling group may or may not be defined as a formal council or legislature. In some of the above cases there may be a monarch, but one with severely limited power.

Democracies

By this I mean states that are ruled by a relatively large subpopulation— thousands or even millions rather than dozens or hundreds. (No state is run by "the people" as a whole; children, at least, are always excluded, and often other large groups.)

There may be a property requirement, as in ancient Athens. In England before the 1832 Reform Bill, just one in eight Englishmen could vote. This made the British elitist and conservative in our view, frightening populists by continental standards.

Hunter-gatherers require little government, often resisting anyone who tries to set themselves up as an autarch; they may thus be classified here.

The standard class

Another way of grasping the values and power roles of a society is to identify the standard class— the group whose interests are assumed to be those of the nation as a whole. This is usually broader than the ruling class; we might say that these are the people the ruling class had better not offend. Examples:

- In Ancient Greece, the citizens— that is those who held property, voted in the assembly, and had the right and duty to serve in the army.
- In the Roman Republic, the knightly and senatorial class; in the Empire, the army.

- In medieval Europe, the noble class, including knights and churchmen. (The urban burghers were important because their money was needed to finance wars, but they were unable to translate this into more than transitory political power.)

- In imperial China, the scholars, those who had passed the civil service examinations.

- In Tibet from the 1600s, the monks— up to one third of the male population; the country was ruled by their leader, the Dalai Lama.

- In modern America, the businessman. "What's good for GM is good for America," as the president of General Motors said in the 1950s.

- In Xurno, one of the nations of Almea, it's the artists, who took control during a revolution.

- In communist countries, in theory the "workers", in practice the Party.

The standard class may be evident from a glance at a typical city: what are the largest buildings? In the medieval city it'd be the local lord's castle and the cathedral; in an American city, the headquarters of corporations.

What do governments do?

This may seem obvious— just look at existing governments. But the activities of government were often much more restricted in premodern states— even as their pretensions were higher. Adam Smith considered the idea of a general sales tax completely impossible.

Absolute power

In some cases the answer is *Whatever the sovereign wants*. The early Roman Emperors are an example; when a nutter like Nero or Elagabalus donned the purple, there was no institutional bound on their power; they could only be removed by coup d'état.

Some extracts from A.A. Goldenweiser's description of the Baganda monarchy give the flavor of absolute rule:

[The King] ate alone, served by one of his wives, who, however, was not permitted to see him while he was engaged in eating. "The Lion eats alone," said the people. If any one happened to come in and overtake the King in the process of eating, he was promptly speared to death by the latter, and the people said: "The Lion when eating killed so and so.."...

All the land belonged to the King, excepting only the freehold estates of the gentes, over which the King had no direct control. Contributions to the state in taxes and labor were, however, expected from these estates. The king had the right to depose a chief at will....

The king was expected to visit the temple of his predecessor, which was in charge of the dowager queen. When about to leave, the king would suddenly give an order that all persons who had not passed a certain spot arbitrarily named by him, should be seized. This order was at once carried out by his bodyguard, and the persons seized were bound and gagged. Then they were sacrificed to the ghost of the dead king.

As society becomes more complex, and as rulers show their fallibility, such systems become hard to sustain. Tyrants become targets; weak or very young rulers tempt regents or generals to take power. A council of nobles, the bureaucracy, or even the palace eunuchs may become important counterweights.

Custom may make it harder for the sovereign to do as he likes. The officials of imperial China would remonstrate with decrees they disagreed with; though he might take action against them, he couldn't do without them. The officials were all trained in the ancient classics, which had much to say about the character of the ideal monarch.

Not infrequently an important official becomes the real ruler, keeping the monarch only as a puppet. The Frankish Mayors of the Palace were examples, till Pépin took the throne for himself. Another is the shoguns of Japan, who didn't even bother to rule from the city the emperor lived in.

Death

Perhaps the basic governmental power is to wage war. Sometimes a monarch only has significant power in wartime.

It takes a good deal of organization to maintain a large standing army, at least for a non-nomadic states. Huge empires such as Rome and China might have several hundred thousand soldiers on hand, but only during periods of strength; yet both had to hire barbarian auxiliaries to meet foreign threats.

Civil war and barbarian invasions sapped the strength of the western empire; perhaps more importantly, *foederatii,* barbarians settled within the boundaries of the empire, removed those regions from the tax base. A mark of the decline in military readiness is given by the size of the army Justinian of the Eastern Empire sent to reconquer Carthage and Italy: less than 15,000 men. More than a thousand years later, Europe had not much advanced: in the 1630s Gustavus Adolphus of Sweden was able to cut a large swath through Germany with an expeditionary force of just 20,000 men.

The benefits of keeping the peace over a large area are great. Or to put it another way, the alternative is that economic life is sapped by the local warlords or bandits, or by fear of the next city-state over.

Taxes

The other universal power of government is to maintain the elite in sumptuous style. To modern eyes this may look like nothing but stealing resources from the producers, but in older times taxation was considered the obvious prerogative of those who owned the land. As late as the 19C, a rich man who had earned his wealth was considered something of an upstart; gentlemen collected rent.

Taxation in kind can be used to stockpile against famine, a practice noted in the Old Testament.

To regulate taxation, the state may undertake censuses, draw maps, and maintain archives of land ownership and boundaries. (As a corollary, one of the first priorities of a peasant rebellion was to burn the local tax records.)

It's hard to cite typical levels of taxation, because taxes were constantly changing. The ruler's boundless needs drove him to devise new taxes; but this was offset by the fact that one of his most effective rewards was exemption from taxation. Poor recordkeeping and corruption made state revenues unpredictable.

As a data point, in Táng China, free peasants owed 3% of the harvest for each adult male in the family, plus a length of linen or silk for each woman; men also owed three months a year of labor.

Public works

Often only the state has the resources for large-scale works: irrigation or transport canals, aqueducts, paved roads, sewers, forts, city walls, mines. Some governments provided temples, arenas, theaters, schools, libraries and scriptoria, observatories, public baths, fountains and parks, mills, shipyards. Of course, they also constructed palaces for the comfort of the rulers and for official business.

The economy

In some early kingdoms, such as Egypt, any economic activity above the level of a single farm or workshop was organized by the state—everything from mining to metallurgy to issuing money to lumber extraction to armaments to shipbuilding to salt panning.

The Anatolians of about 600 B.C., followed quickly by the Greeks, are considered the pioneers of market economies, and the inventors of coinage. In these states many economic functions were taken over by private parties, though the state was likely to keep a hand in. Much of Adam Smith's *The Wealth of Nations* (1776) is spent arguing against the idea that the state should closely regulate trade so as to benefit its own producers and manufacturers.

States may organize transportation and communications networks. The Romans are famous for their roads, the Chinese for their canals (the empire preferred these to trade by the open ocean, which was much harder to protect and regulate). The original couriers unfazed by "rain, nor sleet, nor gloom of night" were messengers of the Persian empire. The Incas, lacking pack animals, maintained a corps of fast runners.

People have long recognized that some industries are noxious or destructive; these might be limited by the state, or restricted to certain areas. As mentioned, the Athenian Solon proposed to prohibit farming practices that fostered deforestation.

Religion

Few premodern states were entirely untangled with religion. On the other hand, not all belief systems are centered around temples and priesthoods, and some have no organization above the level of a local cleric. We'll get back to this in the chapter on religion.

Culture

The state may or may not intrude in personal morality or marriage. Marriage might be regulated instead by families, ethnic communities, or clerics.

Public education is a relatively new development, though Hàn China had schools to prepare students for the civil service exams. Schools were mostly private affairs, or run by religious groups.

A relatively modern concern is the codification of an official language, such as the Accademia della Crusca for Italian, founded in 1582.

In a fantasy culture, an area to explore is the relationship between government and magic, which would surely be as complicated as that between rulers and religion.

Future functions

Future societies will vary greatly in the specifics, but some general principles may be useful. Governments are likely to be necessary, or impose themselves, in certain areas:

- Projects too big for individuals or groups— terraforming, building ringworlds, establishing hyperspace waypoints.

- Managing externalities, i.e. effects of private activity with no direct price, thus not addressed by the feedback mechanism provided by the market. Almost any s.f. technology could generate social or environmental headaches. The mother of all externalities is life support on a space habitat; "do as thou wilt" doesn't work when malice or accident can destroy the whole ship.

- Arbitration between competing actors, a function that becomes more important as society becomes more complex.

Imagine the legal system of a state consisting of predators from a gas giant and herbivores from a terrestrial one.

It's easy to imagine governments becoming more intrusive: spybots could monitor everyone; songs might monitor who listens to them, weapons who fires them and who they're fired at, cars what damage they cause. Or perhaps corporations assume this power— or parents, or schools, or religions.

On the other hand, the same power could be used to increase citizen involvement (crowdsource the legislature!) or to reduce externalities (e.g. if individual pallets can be tracked, perhaps pollutants can be too).

Law

The idea of law has many sources: monarchical decrees; morals preached by the priests; custom; bureaucratic precedent; rights granted to favored nobles or demanded by obstreperous ones; rules proclaimed by the founder of a dynasty. Law need not be universal— often it applies very differently to different classes, and it may never be fully applied to the king.

There isn't always a court system— laws may be enforced directly by the monarch or by the bureaucracy. If there are courts, private advocates may or may not be tolerated.

The sovereign generally enforces a level— perhaps a low one— of public order. This is easiest to do in the cities, which are the safest regions in premodern societies: rural areas are easily terrorized by gangs, and only a strong state can prevent this. Bandits on the road didn't come in ones or twos, but in swarms a few dozen strong; when they were strong, traders or pilgrims had to travel in caravans.

Custom and non-state law

This vague term covers "how we always do things", and it can be an obstacle even to absolute rulers. The Ugandan kings described above (p. 131) were given enormous power by custom, but were also bound by traditional rules.

Laws aren't always enforced by the state; guilds, clans, or temples may take this role instead. In areas run by gangs, gang leaders enjoy taking a judicial role— everyone likes to consider themselves as benefactors.

Babylonian law

The Code of Hammurabi, dated to 1790 B.C., shows a fairly sophisticated legal system. Cases were decided in courts by judges, who would interrogate the parties to the case and witnesses; there are no mentions of lawyers. There are punishments for false accusations, and an insistence on proof and evidence (e.g. adultery could only be proved by catching the participants in the act). One law refers to a trial by ordeal:

> 2. If any one bring an accusation against a man, and the accused go to the river and leap into the river, if he sink in the river his accuser shall take possession of his house. But if the river prove that the accused is not guilty, and he escape unhurt, then he who had brought the accusation shall be put to death, while he who leaped into the river shall take possession of the house that had belonged to his accuser.

It seems that the canny criminal would make sure he learns how to swim. But this is the only such law; everything else relies on evidence, witnesses, and oaths. Medieval European law was a lot worse.

The law is often remembered for its "eye for an eye" severity; but quite a few severe infractions are simply payable by fine, especially if committed against the lower classes. Women have substantial rights, and freedmen and slaves have certain protections. Some laws precisely quantify the worth of the various classes; e.g. if a man strikes a pregnant woman and causes a miscarriage, the fine varies by her class: 10 shekels for a free-born woman, 5 for a freedwoman, and 2 for a maidservant. Intent was taken into account; some penalties could be reduced if the accused swore that the damage was unintentional.

Topics include theft, the treatment of slaves (including penalties for runaways and those harboring them), merchants and their agents, the maintenance of irrigation works, required military service, sexual crimes (adultery, rape, incest), divorce, dowries, inheritance, adoptions, and violence between citizens. Certain prices are set (e.g. hiring a ferryboat costs 3 *gerahs* a day), and penalties are set out for malfeasance by physicians, wet-nurses, veterinaries, builders, shipbuilders, tenant farmers and herdsmen.

Roman law

Roman law was codified around 450 BC in the Twelve Tables; it mostly addressed private or civil law: marriage, succession, wills, property, the power of the *paterfamilias*. It was supplemented by creative interpretation as well as by new laws issued by the Senate or the plebeian assemblies.

A lawsuit was brought to a magistrate, one of the higher republican officials, who would conduct a preliminary investigation. If he found the case had merit, it would be assigned to a judge, a private citizen agreeable to both parties. The magistrate could issue instructions to the judge, in effect another source of law. In the provinces, however, cases were heard by imperial judges.

From the -3C a new profession emerged, the jurisconsult— one who gave advice on matters of law. These were men of high rank, acting out of civic duty— their services were free. Their opinions were highly authoritative, not least because magistrates were politicians, not jurists. They did not plead cases themselves, and looked down on the *advocati* who did— essentially professional orators.

There were oddities by modern standards. As Paul Veyne recounts, a large landowner might invade a smaller estate with an army of slaves. The wronged estate owner could sue— but it was his obligation, not the state's, to seize the defendant and bring him to court, generally impossible unless one had powerful friends.

The emperors gradually acquired a monopoly on legislation, and also had the right to dictate how a court should rule— though they generally followed precedent.

Justinian codified the entirety of Roman law, incorporating Greek and Christian ideas. His *Corpus Iuris* (534) consists of four books forming a general survey, 12 books of law proper, and 50 books of excerpts from the classical juriconsults— intended to entirely supersede them. These 66 books suggest the elaboration of Roman law in the millennium since the Twelve Tables.

Chinese law

Different Chinese traditions have very different attitudes toward the law.

- The Legalists believed that humans were inherently evil and must be controlled with explicit laws (*fǎ*) and harsh punishments. They underlined state power and disdained tradition. They were strongly favored by the first emperor, Shi Huangdi— but he was widely regarded as a despot, discrediting Legalism.

- The Daoists valued individual liberty and minimal government— the *Dào Dé Jīng* advises non-action: "When the Master governs, the people are hardly aware that he exists." It's a spiritual treasure but not much of a legal system.

- The Confucians didn't trust law so much as ritual (*lǐ*), not just ceremony but the whole ordering of society— inferiors being deferential, superiors being compassionate. The good example of the Emperor was key.

Law was not transcendent; it was purely a tool of government. Its only source was the emperor's command; imperial China never developed any tradition of consultative assemblies. The emperor relied on the scholar-officials to draft laws and correspondence, though he was always free to change them.

The local magistrates, also products of the civil service exams, tried and decided cases; there was no profession of jurists. They had no time for small disputes, and civil disputes could only be heard if framed as criminal complaints. Under these conditions the peasants resorted to the arbitration of community and clan leaders instead.

Cities did not have any separate legal status— unlike in Europe, where the *bourgeois*, literally the town dwellers, gained freedom from feudal lords and were granted self-government.

Under the Táng, punishments for grievous crimes might apply to the extended family as well. On the other hand emperors were given to issuing blanket pardons, so if you weren't actually killed your sentence might be lifted after a few years.

Economy

The **economy** is, basically, *work*— what we do to support ourselves.

In primitive societies, everyone does the same work— hunting, fishing, gathering, herding, farming— though there may be sex or age specializations. Even the chief or king lives pretty much like everyone else. Though it accounts for most of the species' history, we hardly think of this as an economy; it's merely a lifestyle. Economies kick in once you have **specialization** and **scarcity**. No longer is everyone doing the same thing; there must therefore be mechanisms to share the wealth... probably unequally.

Fantasy writers generally either copy the modern American or medieval English system... doesn't every town have a market and use coins? But these things were once innovations.

It's all too easy to introduce a major distortion into the picture and not take account of its economic effects. The standard D&D world has an astonishing amount of currency tied down in dungeons, mined only by adventurers... why don't the kings, a class habitually short on cash, send in the army? For that matter how can the mountains of Middle Earth support an army of orcs far greater than that wielded by human agricultural societies?

Types of economies

The first level of intensification of production is **redistribution**. We might say that these are proto-states so primitive that they haven't learned how to oppress. A "big man" or a chief encourages the people to produce more than they usually would; the excess is then consumed or given away in enormous feasts, leaving the Big Man with nothing but prestige and the need to do it all again.

These feasts serve to increase production without central control, creating a buffer for hard times and redistributing goods from fortunate to less fortunate areas. If you've had a good year, you share; if not, you benefit from the success of those who did.

Once a ruling class has developed, we find **command economies**, where large-scale production is organized by the state. In its most extreme form, all production is centrally organized; luxury goods are a perk of state; key resources are state monopolies, perhaps collected by state-run expeditions; trade is negotiated with other rulers. The prototypical example is ancient Egypt. In our time communism reverted to a command economy as a radical reaction against capitalism.

The Mesopotamians had a class of merchants, and their trading expeditions might be financed by private investors as well as by the temples and the state. Without coins, it was necessary to come up with a package of goods that could be bartered; e.g. a -19C Akkadian expedition invested 2 minas of silver to purchase 5 gur of oil and 30 garments, traded in Bahrain for 4 minas of copper.

The **market economy** was pioneered by the Lydians of Anatolia and the Greeks starting in the -7C, when markets and coins first appear in the archeological record. Markets allow goods to be distributed efficiently, without armies of bureaucrats, and allow a looser social system. They also adapt quickly to change, from new technologies to natural disasters, without anyone having to make explicit decisions.

Nonetheless the state was always a major economic actor. Romans might grow rich and gift their towns with a public building; but only the Roman state could build those enormous aqueducts, roads, and mill complexes. States often maintained a monopoly on important goods— e.g. half the Táng state's income derived from its monopoly on salt.

Imperial China constructed networks of canals, including the Grand Canal which allowed the south's agricultural surplus to be shipped to Beijing... this despite the fact that the country bordered an ocean. The empire preferred to focus trade on the canal, which was safer and easier to control.

Anglo-American culture is mercantile; we admire the man who buys low and sells high. This attitude was generally not shared in early societies. Warriors, priests, and scholars were likely to have higher prestige than merchants, and there was often distrust or disdain for people who merely carted merchandise around for a profit, seemingly adding no value. A medieval mystic, Gerard Groote, declared that "Labor is holy, but business is dangerous."

As late as 1776, Adam Smith declared that only the landowners could be trusted to increase the nation's prosperity; merchants and manufacturers were too apt to create cartels and artificial restraints on trade.

Trading may be closely tied to raiding— the Vikings, for instance, would seize goods by force if they could, and trade only if the locals seemed able to defend themselves. A mercantile nation may handle trade between third parties, and form a neighborhood in every port, sometimes resented by the less commercially gifted locals.

Trading posts easily become colonies and then imperial enclaves, whether Philistines in North Africa, Greeks all over the Mediterranean, Arabs in East Africa, the British in India, the Portuguese and then the Dutch in Indonesia.

Travel

A key characteristic of premodern societies is **slow transportation**.

- Human **walking** speed is about 5 km/h or 3 mph. The winner of the 40 km marathon at the 1896 Olympics took just under 3 hours, probably a good approximation of the maximum long-distance speed before modern training; this amounts to 13.3 km/h or 8.3 mph.

  Neither pace can be sustained all day, of course. A large army, marching 8 to 10 hours a day, might count on making 30 km or 20 miles a day— but a half or a quarter of that if they were foraging (i.e. plundering the areas passed through to support themselves).

  The Incas organized runners (*chaskikuna*) in a relay system, allowing messages to travel at 250 km / 160 miles per day. Quite impressive, but a message from one end of the empire to the center would still take 12 days.

- **Horses** can gallop at 40-48 km/h (25 to 30 mph), but not for more than a couple miles. But again a relay system helps. The Pony Express averaged just 9 mph. In 1808 a noble rode across Scotland at an average rate of 15 mph. The ancient Persian messengers, the ones undeterred by rain and sleet and dark of night, could get a message across the empire at 300 km (190 miles) per day.

This heady clip of course doesn't apply to cargo transport. Merchants plied the same Persian route at about 30 km (18 miles) a day.

- **Camels** walk at 3 mph, though they can briefly gallop at 12 mph. A camel caravan traveled 25 miles a day. **Oxen** travel at 2 mph.

- **Tanks** can travel at 70 km/h (43 mph) on good roads. The speed of a blitzkrieg was 30 to 50 miles per day.

- **Sailing ships** can't travel as fast as a horse, but can go all day and night. But more importantly, they're compact and *safe*. A small sailing ship can carry 60 tons of cargo, which would take at least 20 horses to haul; even this comparison is misleading as such an expedition would need a beefy security force and food for them and the horses. In a premodern state, most long-distance trading was thus done by water— the waterways were its transportation system.

Steamships can travel faster than sailing ships, but require a network of coaling stations. The worldwide British Empire had plenty of these but the U.S. did not, so U.S. oceangoing ships depended on sail throughout the 19C.

Some average speeds and cargo capacity for ships, given in knots (1.8 km/h; 1.1 mph):

	tons	*kn*	*km/day*	*mi/day*
Trireme not under sail (-5C)	36	6	250	150
Caravel (15C explorer)	60	4	175	100
Carrack (16C cargo)	300	4	175	100
East Indiaman (17C cargo)	600+	4-5	200	120
Clipper (19C)	800	16	700	400
First steamship (19C)	3000	11	450	300
Steamship c. 1900		22	900	600
Steamship c. 1950		35	1500	900
Aircraft carrier (WWII)	21,000	14	600	400
Modern oil tanker	500,000	15	600	400
Nuclear submarine	350	20	850	500

One economic consequence of all this is simply hassle— the logistics of communications and travel made long-distance trade difficult. In well-organized states that maintained good roads and kept bandits in check, staples like grain and farm animals could be exchanged; in troubled times these could only be traded locally, and only compact, high-value items were traded long-distance.

Another is that prices and economic conditions could vary wildly by region. The price of wheat, or the ratio of gold to silver, was quite different in different countries.

Enterprises

How are large enterprises financed and run? And who can you really trust to do them?

The state has been a major economic actor since the Sumerians: securing resources, running factories, trading with other nations. Many of the things it does for its own use—building roads, protecting against bandits and invasions, running a postal service and a court system— may be extended to private actors as well. It's a relatively late development for the state to do things for the benefit of private enterprise, such as granting patents.

The state has already solved the problem of getting people to do what it wants. For everyone else, the problem is trust: are you going to hand your money or projects over to complete strangers in a city three months' travel away?

Local resources can be combined in interesting ways:

- A group of people can contribute a certain sum each month, distributed as a sum to one member, who uses the capital to start a business. This method is used today within immigrant communities who aren't likely to get a traditional loan.

- You can simply hang out in a central location with people in your line of work. The insurance giant Lloyd's of London started out in 1688 in Edward Lloyd's coffeehouse, where sailors, merchants, and ship owners met.

There are other ways to facilitate long-distance projects:

- A family can operate as a business; the early German and Italian banks ran this way. You can trust even remote family members better than strangers.

- Temples or religious orders may directly engage in trade, facilitate money transfers, or help travelers. Medieval monasteries were often industrial operations, as well as careful landlords with an interest in long-term development of their property.

- An ethnic or religious minority may trust one another more than strangers. In many areas of the world some displaced minority took on most local commerce— e.g. Indians in East Africa, Chinese in Southeast Asia.

The corporation per se, which brings together unrelated strangers and treats them as a legal entity, depends on many tools and conveniences: insurance, banks, a strong court system, an educated work force, a culture that discourages corruption. But above all it requires fast communications; it's no coincidence that the golden age of the corporation came soon after the invention of the telegraph.

Once you have a banking system, banks can create money. E.g. if Roger deposits $1000 in the bank, he probably doesn't need the money right away; the bank can lend it out to Ann. Ann spends half of it but deposits $500 in her own bank account. The bank happily lends that out to Múr. The money has more than doubled: Roger still has $1000 in the bank, Ann has $500 in the bank and $500 in goods, and Múr has $500 in hand.

The bank is in trouble if everyone wants their cash all at once (a bank run); but this can be avoided by setting a reserve requirement. The process is rather disturbing to those who want to think of money as a commodity, but it's the foundation of the immense investment power of modern economies.

Advances in finance as as important as those in technology. Britain's rise as a naval power, for instance, was financed by the Bank of England, and the railroad boom in the US was largely financed by British investors.

Scarcity

Without scarcity, there's no trade and really no economy. It worked for a couple million years for our hunter-gatherer ancestors, but since then, there's been goods that not everyone can have.

This is hard to miss in a premodern society, as many goods are produced only in particular areas: fish in the sea; horses in the steppe; furs in the forest; gems and metals in the mountains. Each crop has its best growing area— e.g. rice needs waterlogged paddies, olives and oranges need a warm climate.

A new invention may suddenly change the fortunes of its supply region— when bronze was first used, for instance, tin became a key resource. The growing use of gunpowder made the saltpeter deposits of the Atacama desert valuable.

Manufactured goods depend on expertise and a network of suppliers, which may at first exist only in particular areas. Silk was once restricted to East Asia; wootz iron to India; fine woolens to England.

Certain jobs, such as trading, software, and moviemaking, are **scaleable**: sales can be multiplied independently of the work itself. It takes the same effort to trade a hundred shares as a million; it's no harder to write a bestseller than a niche book. Compare jobs like farming, barbering, or dentistry, where more customers means more work.

As Nassim Taleb points out in *The Black Swan*, technology moves jobs into the scaleable category. No matter how fabulous he was, a premodern musician could only satisfy a few hundred people in one town. Today he can sell millions of CDs, putting many local musicians out of work. The rewards in scaleable jobs are lopsided.

I emphasize this mostly for s.f. writers, who sometimes like to create utopian communities where everyone has access to everything. Iain Banks creates something like the ultimate consumer paradise in his Culture novels, largely by inventing an infinite energy source, 'gridfire'. But this doesn't address the inequalities produced by scaleable jobs. E.g. one of his characters designs space habitats for a living— as each one can house millions of people, few people can aspire to such a job.

If you're not so utopian, make sure you think about what goods are scarce, who controls them, and what happens when people can't get at them. We can live without silk clothes; it'd be more dire if someone got a monopoly on a space habitat's oxygen supply.

Money and prices

There may be a bewildering variety of **coins** in use; in Shakespeare's time, for instance, there was the pound, the angel, the noble, the crown, the shilling, the sixpence, the groat, the half-groat, and the penny. We might have a similar list, of course, if we had no paper money.

Note that the relative value of gold, silver, and other metals is not fixed, but varies according to their supply; and that coins may circulate outside their country of origin. (The American currency is called the dollar because of the prevalence of the Spanish dollar at the time of independence.)

Here's a table of prices in Shakespeare's time (from an edition of the *Major Plays* edited by G.B. Harrison, 1948, as well as *Daily life in Elizabethan England* by Jeffrey L. Singman, 1995). As few readers are likely adept at handling pounds/shillings/pence in their heads, I've stated all prices in terms of pence only.

The vertiginous scale of class differences should be apparent; also the relative expensiveness of food and drink for urban laborers.

Wages

nobleman, income	per day	1600
skilled worker, without food and drink	per day	10 - 14
skilled worker, food and drink supplied	per day	6 - 9
boy	per day	5
captain (of 200 men)	per day	96
sergeant	per day	12
common soldier	per day	8
payment for a play		1920

Food and drink

beer, good quality	quart	1
butter	pound	4
cheese	pound	1.5 - 2
eggs	dozen	4
beef, good quality	pound	3
chicken	whole	10
tallow candles	pound	4
pepper	pound	48
wine	quart	12

tobacco	ounce	36

Travel

meal at an inn		4-6
bed at an inn		1
horse, hiring	per day	12
coach, hiring	per day	120

Clothing

tailored suit	216
satin doublet (fitted jacket)	480
canvas doublet, officer's	173
woman's gown	2400
woman's working dress	240
shoes	12
white silk hose	300
satin cloth per yard	144

Goods

soldier's sword and dagger	96
soldier's helmet	96
sackbut (a musical instrument)	480
knife	4
spectacles	3
Bible	480
horse	240 - 480
bed	48
theater admission	1 - 3

More data points, courtesy of Adam Smith: in 1776, the wages for a common laborer in London were 18 pence a day; in Edinburgh, 10 p, and in rural areas, just 8. Rising productivity, centering in the cities, was beginning to raise the standard of living— even more so than the wage figures indicate, as the price of food and clothing was lower than in Shakespeare's time.

Future economies

I'll happily make predictions about war or religion, but predictions about future economies are the one thing likely to make me look ridiculous in five hundred years. The nature of the modern economy would be incomprehensible to a man of the year 1500; Adam Smith with his long disquisitions on wheat prices, agricultural rents, and tariffs looks quaintly out of date.

Capitalism keeps inventing new goods and new markets. This is how it defeats Malthus— we live in a bubble where new ideas increase productivity faster than we can reproduce. It's also why you can never just extrapolate current trends— e.g. predict that the economy will simply collapse when the oil runs out. Not to make light of the adjustment needed, but when it does run out, the economy will look different. A late 19C observer might have predicted that cities would soon be covered in horse manure to their rooftops.

The previous revolution occupies a smaller and smaller slice of the economy. Agriculture is now less than ½% of the US economy; and manufacturing is about 12%. The service sector now predominates, at 80%. Whatever replaces it will start as a fringe activity, grow to encompass a huge fraction of GDP, and then shrink in turn as it's outmoded.

The products of capitalism get more and more complicated: reinsurance, derivatives, iPod covers, bagel slicers, virtual world memberships, virus checkers, low-sodium organic soy sauce. I imagine half the economic transactions from the year 2500 would require a lengthy explanation before we even understand what they are.

Over the last three centuries, the overall trend has been toward **automation**. Old sectors of the economy don't just shrink because they're old, but because ways were found to do the work of hundreds with one worker and a machine. When this process isn't balanced by the creation of new products and services, it results in mass unemployment rather than prosperity.

For this reason I couldn't quite buy the society depicted in *Ghost in the Shell*. Robots seem to do everything in society... what do the people do? If the answer is 'not much', doesn't the price of labor drop to near zero and thus become competitive with the robots?

Taking a bird's eye historical view, current arguments over the **size of government** are hair-splitting, like controversies over the human and divine nature of Christ. The main battle is over: all precapitalist systems, as well as totalitarian control over the economy, were outperformed. Robber baron capitalism didn't work so great either; government is needed to set the basic framework for economic competition and even out its rough edges. Not that new systems can't emerge; it's just unlikely that they'll be repeats of the old systems, especially the absolutes (total or zero government).

One area which might be transformed in the future is **management**. Smith thought that the corporation had little future; a firm needed the strong hand of an owner at the top. He was wrong, but capitalism hasn't been able to decide if the best managers are entrepreneurs, hired managers, or major stockholders, nor whether the best workers are mindless drones, hands-on tinkerers, or empowered decisionmakers. Personally I think that the hierarchical top-down structure will one day seem as inefficient and antiquated as absolute monarchy.

Western culture has increasingly emphasized **individualism** over community; the American ideal seems to be citizens without strong ties to extended family, ethnic group, location, or religion. Not coincidentally, this sort of citizen makes the best employee for corporations. This could easily change, especially as the US won't be the top nation forever. A swing of the pendulum back toward stronger communities seems likely. Charlie Stross points out that robber baron capitalism would be a recipe for disaster on a small space habitat.

I also expect that our current heuristics on government, management, and economics will slowly be replaced by science. Most political arguments are a clash of morals and values, conducted that way because we don't have enough solid data. I can't imagine the world of AD 3000 working that way. When you don't know how to cure a disease, it can be blamed on bad air, or iniquity, or the Jews; when you know how to cure it you just do so.

Future society might also develop different attitudes toward change and toward technology itself. We're still half enraptured, half frightened at our own headlong progress— both tendencies being well manifested in s.f. The google-eyed fascination should damp down in the next thousand years. On Almea, I have a sentient species, the iliu, with 40,000 years of civilization. They have very high technology, but they're no more captivated by it than we are by fire. Indeed, miniaturization and specialization have developed to the point where their technological footprint is small, and they've purposely moved to a lifestyle reminiscent of their own ancestral environment.

Apocalypse now!

Of course, maybe in your imagined future everything collapses. I'm a sucker for a good post-apocalypse myself. One cheap error is to assume that civilization will just revert to some particular earlier period. Some survivalists seem to assume that after the collapse the world will look pretty much like 1840 again.

But history doesn't neatly repeat. A collapsed society may simply disappear, as the Norse Greenlanders did. The fall of Rome didn't make people revert to Celtic and German paganism or chieftancies. And for that matter the mindset of 1840s America— relatively unpolluted, thinking itself with some reason to be the most advanced nation on the planet— would be very different from a 2140s America devastated by social and economic collapse, surrounded by enemies, out of resources, and full of environmental disaster areas. I'm afraid *Fallout 3* would be a better model.

There can also be local declines. Jane Jacobs describes a settlement where her aunt was sent as a missionary. The aunt wanted to build a church from the large stones found in the riverbed; but the locals patiently explained that this was impossible. As everyone knew, mortar could only hold small stones; and even those could only be used for small structures like chimneys, certainly not a whole wall. This was not the Third World; this was 1930s North Carolina, and the people were descendants of people with a long tradition of stonemasonry. Such stories are hard to imagine in today's highly interconnected world— but an interstellar society might have such isolated pockets.

Daily life

This is really a continuation of the Culture chapter, but with the focus on everyday life rather than entire societies.

Sex and sexism

Humans are pervs... their laws, culture, and religions are obsessed with sex.

Is sexism avoidable?

Let's hop right into the maelstrom, or (joke imminent) the femaelstrom: sexism. For the most part our ancestors' views on sex are unpalatable, even ludicrous. A realistic portrayal of medieval sex roles would be too.

One possible response: just ignore it. In *Oblivion*, for instance, players, bandits, fighters and magicians, pirates, and orcs can all be male or female. Beginning stats may be affected, but they all balance out (e.g. Dunmer females lose in Endurance what they gain in Personality).

I'm not bothered by this— games and even fantasy novels don't have to be realistic. There's another approach, though: try to understand the biological and cultural bases for sexism, and address those directly rather than simply erase the problem.

Not all historical cultures were equally sexist; it's worthwhile to consider the variation that existed. And there's even more variation found in other species, which can be adopted for your conworlds or aliens.

Historical sex roles

Here's one mitigating factor, though it's a bit of a downer: life sucked for everyone! Or more generally: for the vast majority, life in agricultural and early industrial society involved hard work and plenty of it, for both sexes.

As a pioneer woman succintly put it: "Everything on this farm is either heavy or hungry."

The upside of this is that class trumps sex. In an egalitarian but sexist society all men may feel that they outrank all women— except for their mother— but in a stratified society, upper class women outrank lower class men. Chaucer's depiction of the Wife of Bath shows how formidable a medieval woman might be. In cultures from ancient Rome to imperial China, women might be regents for young heirs and rule the country. Some kingdoms could be ruled by queens in their own right. In medieval times there were monastic orders which were entirely female-run; a large noble household was often run by the noblewoman.

Dorothy L. Sayers in *Are Women Human?* points out that women's work was economically significant. In hunter-gatherer societies women often do the gathering, which produces half or more of the tribe's food. Hammurabi's law code describes tavernkeeping as a female occupation. Clothing is often a female industry— stolen from women by the industrial revolution. Women helped their craftsmen husbands in medieval times and could inherit the business upon their death. Among California Indians, artistic creation was a female monopoly, as it consisted of basketry (a category that included most household goods).

The notion that women should only be occupied with bearing children was a conceit of the Victorian upper classes.

The position of women improved or degraded over space and time, sometimes in surprising ways. The Spartans, those military juggernauts, were noted for their proud, independent women— this scandalized the Athenians, who thought women should stay at home. The Neo-Confucian thinker Zhū Xī, writing in the 1100s, pushed Chinese society in the direction of rigid respect for authorities, resulting in much greater restrictions on women.

Women had more independence among the nomads of the Eurasian steppe than in China. They had property rights, they could initiate divorce and remarry, and elite women could hold high office, even military office. They cared for the herds along with the men, rode horses, and defended their settlements when the men were away.

Yingtian, wife of the Khitan emperor Abaoji, accompanied her husband on military campaigns and received ambassadors with him. Abaoji died in 926. There was a tradition of wives being sacrificed upon the king's death, but she stated that her sons were young (they were in their twenties) and the country needed her. However, she insisted— over the Khitan nobles' protests— on having her right hand cut off to be buried with Abaoji. This did nothing to lessen her power: she was able to overrule her husband's choice of heir and impose what she considered a better choice. And it ended forever the custom of sacrificing the widows of Khitan kings.

What factors are most important in maintaining sexism?

- The male monopoly on **war**. Marvin Harris argues that this is the primary factor— that the premium on raising warrior boys makes girls less valuable.

  Read enough history, and it's striking how every society seems to have a few exceptional warrior women: China's Fù Hǎo, Vietnam's Trưng sisters, France's Joan of Arc, Arabia's Mavia, Artemisia of Helicarnassus, India's Lakshmibai, the Hausas' Amina, the Apache Lozen, the Soviet Lyudmila Pavličenko, and on and on. For the curious I've provided a fuller list on the web resources page.

  Though many of these women were royalty, some organized female armies as well, and there are other peoples where women routinely fought alongside men. Weapons are found buried with women in Scythian graves; the Romans found women fighting among the Teutonic tribes. In modern times there are many stories of women disguising as men in order to fight— e.g. the first US woman to receive a military pension, Revolutionary War fighter Deborah Sampson.

- Lack of **birth control**. Hunter-gatherers have children at intervals of about four years; for agriculturalists it's about two years. Women are obviously not restricted to only child-rearing, but if there's always young children around, their options are limited. As a corollary, women are freer when they can control conception and birth.

- Authoritarian **religions**. The Abrahamic religions were harder on women than paganism; the Confucians more so than Daoists or Buddhists.

  An obsession with virginity is especially destructive for women; it can cause men to sequester women, to make their lives miserable if they stray, and in extreme cases even to mutilate their bodies to prevent sexual arousal.

- **Limited land** held by an elite— such as the medieval European aristocracy. Such an elite does not value fertility, which in a primarily agricultural society can only dilute its wealth. You want to raise a son to inherit the estate; daughters are something of a liability, and you actually pay someone to take them off your hands.

  In land-rich societies, by contrast, fertility is welcome— as is polygamy. Women are valuable and a husband has to pay a price to marry one.

Biological sex roles

Biology offers some generalizations on male and female appearance and behavior:

- Males tend to be **larger**; the size discrepancy (*sexual dimorphism*) correlates, we may say, with the nastiness of the males— e.g. male gorillas are 1.5 times the size of the females, and a single male maintains a harem; gibbon females are almost the same size as males, have a considerable degree of choice over their mate, and live in long-term monogamy.

  Humans are on the low end of the sexual dimorphism scale— the male/female size ratio is 1.1. If you think this means that males do all the heavy work, think again. An anecdote from Jared Diamond:

  > Once [in New Guinea] I offered to pay some villagers to carry supplies from an airstrip to my mountain camp. The heaviest item was a 110-pound bag of rice, which I lashed to a pole and assigned a team of four men to shoulder together. When I eventually caught up with the villagers, the men were carrying light loads, while one small woman

weighing less than the bag of rice was bent under it, supporting its weight by a cord across her temples.

- Males expend little **energy** in producing and distributing sperm; females invest much more in producing eggs and bearing young. Their mate selection strategy accordingly varies: for males there is no cost and much to gain by inseminating as many females as possible; females are more picky as they're making more of an investment, and prefer monogamy.

But it's much more complicated than that. Within the same species, males may try different strategies: e.g. some male chimps bluster and cow the females into submission; others form friendships with females and mate behind the alphas' backs. Male parental involvement is a good evolutionary strategy: being a strong caretaker and protector makes it more likely the small fry will thrive and reproduce. And females even in pair-bonding species play around— getting the best of both worlds: viable genes from the strongest males, nurturing from the gentler ones.

Some females are well defended against male violence— the porcupine, for instance, isn't going to have sex unless she feels like it. (Though this isn't without its kinky side... foreplay consists of drenching the female with urine.)

- There's something of an **arms race** between the sexes, waged with changes to the genitals. The very promiscuous chimpanzees have evolved enormous testicles, so as to produce a huge amount of sperm— the better to fertilize you with, my dear. (Male gorillas, who keep their harem sequestered, have small testicles.)

When a drone mates with a queen bee, his penis detaches, acting as a genital plug to prevent other drones from mating with her. Male squirrels insert a gluey "copulatory plug" with the same purpose— though the female may later remove or eat it.

The bedbug, perhaps in response to such obstacles, developed "traumatic insemination"— the penis skips the genitals entirely and pierces the female's carapace, inserting the sperm close to the ovaries. In some species the females have evolved a swelling that guides the penetration and is filled with hemocytes that combat infection.

Or a male may kill a female's offspring, to make sure the next ones are his— a behavior observed among lions and chimpanzees among others.

Humans are unusual among the great apes in that estrus (the female's most fertile period) is hidden. Most likely this increases pair-bonding by divorcing sex from reproduction. The males can't be sure of reproducing by focusing on the short period of fertility, so they have to be around all the time.

All that said, there's immense variety in the animal kingdom, and there's all sorts of wacky sexual behavior.

- Close to home, bonobo females are nobody's patsy. Females don't let themselves be dominated by the males— in captivity, they are even dominant. The alpha male more or less decides where the troop moves... unless vetoed by the alpha female.

  Bonobos also use sex as a form of social bonding and conflict resolution; they don't pair-bond, and female-female sexual contact is very common— male-male contact also occurs, though less frequently.

- It's not always the female that raises the young. After laying an egg, the female emperor penguin (star of *March of the Penguins*) skedaddles off, leaving the male to brood the egg— all the more of a sacrifice as the penguins mate in a remote area and the male has no food for two months.

- Some species reverse the amount of effort put into the genetic package. Many species (including species of firefly and salamander) create and deposit a huge sperm packet, which not only provides a huge number of sperm but a significant gift of protein. I borrowed this idea for one of the sapients of Almea, the ktuvoks.

- In some species, nature seems to have decided that males are just vehicles for sperm. Beehives are almost entirely all-female affairs; drones are raised in small numbers for reproduction only, and die after mating. At least they're not eaten, as in many spiders and mantises. (To be fair, among bristle worms, it's the female that dies after laying her eggs, and she is sometimes eaten.)

The male green spoon worm is 200,000 times smaller than the female; after finding his mate he enters her body and takes up residence in a little sac in her reproductive system.

- The spotted hyena has a real matriarchy, and these dames are tough. Their clitoris has expanded into a pseudo-phallus, and it's not only used for mating but for giving birth. Packs have a dominant female, and all males (except her cubs) rank under all females. Normally cubs are born in pairs— and one immediately kills the other. A single spotted hyena can kill a wildebeest three times its size. They're also able to eat and digest bones.

For much more on unusual animal sex, see Olivia Judson's *Dr. Tatiana's Sex Advice to All Creation*.

Matriarchies

Part of the fun of fantasy and s.f. is that you can explore neat ideas that human history hasn't bothered to try out. One of these is matriarchy.

If you'd like to build your own:

- If you can play with the biology, consider using some of the ideas above, such as small or reversed sexual dimorphism, biological protection against rape, and male care for the young.

- At the cultural level, you can supply reliable birth control, plenty of land, and of course an ideology of feminine superiority.

- If you're working with humans, don't just reverse everything in premodern societies. There are biological differences after all: women are still the ones to get pregnant and nurse, which take far more of an investment than insemination. At least some of male violence and female bonding is hormonal.

For Almea I created a female-dominated civilization, the Bé. Here's a partial description of Beic mores; see also the biography of Múr on p. 30.

The following description applies to the poor— the majority of the people. Their life is not that different from peasants, fisherfolk, and craftsmen in any pre-modern society. Both sexes work hard; marriages are arranged by the family rather than by the participants; women marry in their late teens and have many more babies than survive to adulthood. The major differences from most other societies:

- Women are the acknowledged **leaders**. They are usually older than their husbands; they control the family's wealth; inheritance and naming are matrilineal; husbands join the wife's family and take her name. Women are considered smarter, tougher, more even-tempered, more virtuous (yet, when they are bad, more evil). Men are recognized for their strength, but the comparison is inevitably made to the even stronger nawr ox. Men are considered the more emotional sex, and the sexual tempters.

- Society is organized into extended family groups called **bands** (*jɔ*), led by an elder woman (*hɑ́ɔ*) and consisting of her descendants, plus males who have married into the family. When the elder dies, the two oldest daughters become the nucleus of their own bands, unless the family is too small. The optimum size for a band is one to three dozen people.

  Bands rather than marriages are the basic economic unit: members work for the band as a whole, and wealth is pooled. Raising children is a task of the entire band.

  At this level of society a band's wealth mostly means land, so splitting the band means **dividing up land**. However, bands don't legally *own* land— noble families do; poor bands simply have the right to work somewhere on the estate, and the nobles don't care how many bands there are.

  More importantly, the Bé are relatively land-rich. The majority of land at any one time is uncultivated. When a band splits, it will abandon its old fields and begin two new plots. This practice helps maintain the ecological health of the jungle.

- Since women are not the property of men, there is no cult of virginity, nor any concern that women be faithful to their men. Nonetheless a woman is not supposed to have sex till a few years after menarche. They're expected to devote themselves to learning their band's work and ways.

- Men technically do not **marry** a woman; they marry into a band. (Indeed, the word for marriage, *jɔhù*, means 'band entry'.) As marriage is not the basic economic unit, marriages are not accorded the importance they have in our society— both parties are free to terminate it. Men will not lightly do this, however: since wealth stays with the females of the band, leaving the band will almost always be a severe economic loss. Moreover, bands are reluctant to accept older males.

  Moralists spend much more effort exhorting women to keep their men— a clue that, often enough, they do not. On the other hand, if a woman has tired of a man, she can stop sleeping with him without kicking him out of her band (which is the elder's prerogative anyway). The band won't lightly give up an extra pair of hands.

  A marriage is sought for a particular girl in the family, when she's old enough. It's not inappropriate, then, to use the terms 'husband' and 'wife'. Nonetheless, sex between any band members of the same generation is licit. To put it bluntly, a man can and probably will sleep with his wife's sisters, and with her cousins if they are part of the band. His primary pair-bond may even shift to one of them. The Bé like to say that their morality allows the male (considered the randier, more animalistic gender) to stray, but within bounds.

  Marriages are sought with allied bands; these are often ultimately related, but the rule is that one cannot marry into bands which have split off from one's own within living memory. (In our terms, you can't marry your cousins, because they're probably in your own band, nor your second cousins, because their band split off only a generation back; but your third cousins are fair game.)

- Young women bear and nurse **babies**, but that's the extent of their formal responsibility. Past infancy, the primary caregivers are younger girls, middle-aged women, and older men. (This wide range is considered healthy for the child.)

  To put it another way, a young girl is learning the skills needed for her band's lifestyle; that includes raising children, so she helps out. A healthy young woman, however, is best used working at the band's primary economic activity. As she ages, she has more time for leisure pursuits— including caring for children. When she becomes an elder her primary responsibility is governing the band.

  Boys will help take care of younger siblings, but it's not so important for boys to learn the band's ways— they'll be leaving it when they marry. Thereafter, their primary task is working to help support their new family. Their working life is longer mostly because of sexism. As old men, however, they're not expected to work hard, and they have little role in running the band, so they're most useful in taking care of the children.

This probably raises many questions; you can read the Almeopedia for more. You may think it would go a different way— fine, on your planet it will.

The *jɔ* structure is partly based on the largely female-dominant Moso culture of East Asia. It's also an attempt to provide an extended family structure that would free women from being bound to child-rearing for most of their lives.

Another interesting approach is Sheri Tepper's *The Gate to Women's Country*, in which women run the towns. Men are allowed to live with them, but most live in barracks just outside the towns and engage in frequent war. I can't explain much more without spoilers.

Marriage

There are several decisions to make about marriage.

- Are marriages **arranged**? In premodern agricultural societies, arranged marriage was generally the norm. Among the well-off, marriage cemented ties between families or even nations, and were far too important to leave to the individuals involved. For other classes, as among Indians today, it was felt that mature older people could make a much better decision than rash youngsters.

    Among the medieval European nobility, people still fell in love, but this had little to do with who they were married to. Courtly literature offered a complex standard of behavior for such adulterous affairs.

- Who is **out of bounds**? In our culture this is largely a matter of avoiding incest. But many cultures divide people into groups and specify complex rules on which groups can and can't intermarry.

    The simplest such system is two **moieties** or halves. E.g. the Tlingit are divided into Raven (*yéil*) and Eagle (*ch'aak'*) moieties (in some areas the latter were Wolves instead). A Raven could only marry an Eagle and vice versa.

- Whose family does the couple live with? In **matrilocal** societies, the bride stays with or near her parents; her husband may or may not live with her. Among the Moso, for instance, a man visits a woman at night, and helps little with child-rearing.

Matrilocality does not mean matriarchy. Among the Iroquois, a man was absent for half the year raiding, trading, or hunting; the rest of the year he lived with his wife's family. Under these circumstances a man's wealth would pass to his sister's son or to his brother— that is, to the nearest male relative within his own clan; his own children belonged to his wife's clan. (Given the social mores, this also made genetic sense: his heirs were certainly genetically related to him; his wife's children might not really be.)

In **patrilocal** societies the bride goes to live with her husband's family; this has historically been the pattern for about 70% of societies. Most modern societies are **neolocal**, meaning that the couple sets up a new household separate from both sets of families— a consequence of highly mobile societies where people routinely move long distances to study or work.

- Is the family line **matrilineal** (inherited from the mother) or **patrilineal**? Western European culture is patrilineal, in that names and titles are inherited from the father.

Inheritance of ethnicity may be more complicated. In Arabic culture an Arab man's children are all Arab; this is why (say) Egyptians consider themselves Arabs. The Spanish in the New World, however, didn't consider a man's child Spanish if the mother was Amerindian or black. Traditionally one can only be a Jew if one's mother is Jewish.

In the premodern world wealth was not easily acquired, and it would quickly be subdivided into nothing if all children inherited equally. In Europe, the traditional rule for the elite was primogeniture: the eldest son inherited the estate. Some cultures, including parts of medieval Japan and England, practiced ultimogeniture, where the last son inherits the estate, or a larger share, perhaps on the theory that older sons already had an estate, or to reward the youngest son for taking care of his elderly parents.

Cultures differ in whether women inherit at all, and if so whether they get a full or a half share.

- Is a payment required, and who gets it? Does the man pay a **bride-price?** This seems to be associated with regions where population density is relatively low, land is cheap, and there is no great social stratification, such as traditional sub-Saharan Africa.

  If the woman's family must pay a **dowry**, the implication is that female fertility is something of a negative; this suits areas where population increase threatens to reduce the standard of living, and where elites don't want property to spread to lower strata.

- How many wives? Having multiple wives is **polygyny**; according to the *Ethnographic Atlas Codebook*, 85% of the 1231 societies surveyed allowed polygyny. Thus it's monogamy that seems to demand an explanation.

  Nonetheless, polygynous societies can hardly supply multiple wives to every man; polygyny is a privilege of the wealthy and powerful.

- How many husbands? **Polyandry** is quite rare, but it's practiced among some Tibetans; this is a difficult environment where limiting population growth is highly desirable.

Many of these choices are more male- or female-centric, and it's safe to say that the more of the male-centric choices are made, the more male-dominant the society.

The family

In most premodern societies the **extended family** is more important than the nuclear family. You may live with them, or next door to them. They're your social network, your judges, your protectors and avengers, your investors, your safety net in bad times.

In ancient Roman society, for instance, the *paterfamilias*, the head of the family, not only retained authority over his adult sons, they could not sign contracts, free slaves, or make wills without his consent, nor did their money belong to them. (This was an extreme, however; the Greeks were surprised by such strictures.)

As a corollary, the modern idea of teenage culture is a novelty. In most cultures, a male adolescent simply begins living and working as an adult, though at a junior level, and is often forbidden to marry till he is well established.

In Rome, however, young elite males were expected to be rowdy and sexually indulgent— breaking into shops, visiting prostitutes, getting into fights.

Birth control

It's no coincidence that sexual liberation came on the heels of effective birth control, nor that moralists of all religions preach fidelity. In premodern conditions, chastity is the only sure way to avoid disease, and since a woman could hardly avoid pregnancy, it was best to be married before having sex. Anna Magdalena, second wife of Johann Sebastian Bach, bore thirteen children between 1723 and 1742, meaning that she spent half her time pregnant.

!Kung hunter-gatherer women have babies only about every four years. They nurse their children till the next child is born, which seems to inhibit ovulation. On the other hand they live in a desert and have a low fat intake, so it's not clear that this is truly representative of the ancestral environment.

There's always been a strong demand for birth control, and where any demand exists it will generate a supply: acidic vaginal suppositories, oiled paper used as a cervical cap, herbal concoctions. But these methods seem to have been no more effective than most of the premodern physician's toolbox— that is to say, variable at best, fatal at worst. The condom, originally made of animal intestine, appeared only in the 17C.

In Roman times the herb silphium apparently inhibited conception; it only grew in Cyrenaica, was highly expensive, and seems to have been overharvested to extinction.

Abortifacients can be more effective— but mostly because they're poisons, with a high risk of harming or killing the woman.

The simplest premodern birth control is infanticide— usually done soon after birth before any bond can develop, but there may also be a pattern of preferential neglect. This is so effective among the Yanomamö that the sex ratio at puberty is 154 males to 100 females. But it's by no means limited to primitive societies; in the 18C poor women in England regularly dropped unwanted babies in the river, left them in trash barrels, or rolled over them in a drunken slumber.

More benignly, you can try abstinence, or non-reproductive sex. However, many of these activities were considerably less attractive with premodern hygiene. Oral sex was once considered highly perverted— the premodern nose was accustomed to a workout, but there were limits.

I go over all this grim history not to encourage you to reproduce it, but to suggest that you think about how to avoid it. It's not realistic to depict a premodern society with modern promiscuity and sexual equality with no explanation; it's like outfitting your windy and stinky old castles with jacuzzis.

The simplest though the least original method is to posit a herbal mixture that really works. It could be interesting to place limits on this: where do the herbs grow? are they rare or common? do the religious authorities approve?

You can also tweak your biology. Queen bees can determine whether an egg is male or female, and it's easy to imagine a species with greater control over ovulation or conception. (Though the genes may have reason to distrust the brain, as discussed above, p. 84. They'll be screwed if the brain decides not to reproduce at all.)

Cultural norms may help— e.g. many societies practice sexual abstinence during nursing, perhaps accompanied by rationalizations such as that semen would poison the milk.

Homosexuality

So, there are two types of people, people who love the opposite sex and those that love the same sex, right?

Nah. It's much more complicated than that. Let's look at a few examples.

- In ancient Greece and Rome, men routinely took male lovers as well as wives.

- In Latin America, only bottoming is a sure token of being gay— a man who penetrates another man may consider himself straight.

- Among the Azande of central Africa, male warriors would take on a younger male lover, even paying his parents a bride-price. The relationship would end when the younger boy reached maturity. Marriages were polygamous, and lesbianism was common among wives. The Atanda of Australia and the Keraki of New Guinea had similar customs.

- Male homosexuality is required among the Etoro and the Sambia of New Guinea— it's believed that young men must ingest the semen of older men in order to attain maturity and impregnate women; there are also severe time and place restrictions on heterosexual sex.

These examples suggest that sexual orientation is a continuum, not a binary opposition, and can bend very far depending on cultural mores. It can also vary over an individual's lifetime; there may be a good deal of adolescent exploration, and occasionally a dramatic change in orientation in later life.

I don't mean that homosexuality is a choice. As it's found among animals, it's a part of biology. But it's more complex than a single binary parameter.

For reference, I'd love to give you a percentage for homosexuality, but the numbers are all over the place. For the U.S., on the low end, a Census study found 0.5% of the population living in a same-sex relationship; on the high end, Alfred Kinsey found 37% of men reporting at least one homosexual experience.

So, how is homosexuality expressed in your society?

- It's considered wrong. This is a minority view: an anthropological database, the Human Relations Area File, reported that of 76 societies where homosexuality had been studied to some extent, only 36% considered it unacceptable.

"Wrong" covers a lot of ground, however. It could mean:

° Evil, and punishable by death or imprisonment, as in Leviticus or Victorian England. This should be put into perspective: Leviticus also dictates the death penalty for adultery, incest, spiritism, and cursing one's parents.

° Disreputable but not criminal, like being a Jew or an actor in Elizabethan England.

° A character failing, like drunkenness.

Lesbianism may be treated differently— or ignored; Leviticus doesn't even mention it.

- It might be tolerated if kept discreet. Note that societies differ in how much *any* sexuality can be expressed in the open, and which sorts of things were considered sexual. In the 19C Japanese men and women bathed together, but the Japanese were scandalized by Westerners kissing in public.

- It may be regarded as a private matter, so long as it didn't interfere with one's duty to beget children, as in premodern China.

- It might be fully indulged, as in Greek and Roman society. The ceramics of the Moche, in Peru, depict both gay and lesbian acts.

- It might be allowed to a certain subclass of people (see the next section), or within sex-segregated institutions such as monasteries and the military (as in feudal Japan).

- It might be obligatory, as for the Azande, Etoro, and Sambia.

Though we might pride ourselves on our openness to sex, many cultures would complain that we inappropriately sexualize everything. Men holding hands or kissing may have no sexual meaning; two people setting up a house together (like Holmes and Watson) doesn't imply a sexual relationship.

All this can make it hard to know for sure what's going on in history. Michelangelo, for instance, wrote love poems to boys and created beautiful images of male bodies, but a contemporary biographer, Condivi, describes him as "chaste". Interpreting Chinese sources is complicated by the lack of gender-specific pronouns and the use of highly allusive language (e.g. "countenances of linked jade"). (Of course there are plenty of clear references too; what's difficult is getting an overall perspective.)

Cultural sexes

Biology says there are two sexes, but cultures don't have to agree.

Many North American Indian tribes had a category, called "two-spirits" (*niizh manidoowag* in Ojibwe), for those with a mixed masculine and feminine nature. These often took on special roles within the tribe, e.g. shamans, prophets, storytellers, matchmakers. They might have either heterosexual or homosexual relationships.

In northern India, the *hijra* community includes eunuchs, transvestites, homosexuals, and hermaphrodites, considered an alternate gender. They too have a cultural role, though an uncomfortable one: they sing and dance at weddings and births— often uninvited; they'll offer their blessing for a fee and a curse if none is given.

One of my Almean cultures, the Ezičimi, considered that there were three sexes: male, female, and *ewemi* (literally, 'middlers'):

> The *ewemi* were those that didn't fit the fairly rigid sex roles of the Ezičimi bands. It was said (usually by outsiders; Ezičimi explanations tended to the tautological) that these were the unmanly men and the mannish women, and when we learn that many of them were homosexual, we may think we have their number. But the Ezičimi were using their own categories, not ours.
>
> The prototypical Ezičimi man was a warrior, strong and hard; the prototypical woman was a mother and wife, hard-working and nurturing. Men who were not good with weapons, who messed around with herbs or (later) books, were likely to be classified as *ewemi*. Same story with women who resisted marriage, or preferred books or bows to babies. A fifth or more of the population was considered *ewemi*. Only a fraction of these were actually gay or lesbian; we could equally call the *ewemi* 'geeks' or, more nicely, 'intellectuals'.
>
> *Ewemi* did not dress like women or like men; rather, there were separate dress styles for each sex. *Ewemi* dressed in long robes and followed an aesthetic that hid their biological sex; they were expected to marry only other *ewemi* (male or female).

Clothing

If you see a foreigner, the first thing to strike you may be what they're wearing. In a visual medium, you hardly need those place subtitles ("Venice, 1690")— the clothes on the first person we see will do the job.

Alison Lurie wrote a book called *The Language of Clothes*, and indeed, our clothes have a lot to say about us: our sex, our age, our wealth, often our profession or our passing mood.

Ironically, it may be the last thing a conworlder thinks about. And it's not as easy as devising a coinage system or a list of gods; it requires us to think visually, and know something about how clothes are made.

Cloth and how to make it

Clothing starts with cloth, which in turn goes back to the fauna and flora of your world. Here's a whirlwind tour of types of cloth:

- Animal **skins** make good clothing, once the animal is removed. If you scrape off the fur you get **rawhide**. Skins didn't become really useful till the invention of the needle, some 40,000 years ago.

  The minimum equipment for preparing rawhide is a scraper; later cultures used a dull knife. The process can be facilitated by soaking in a solution of lye or lime.

- Skins are made into **leather** by the process of tanning (named for tannin, an acid derived from oak bark). Tanning makes the skin softer and allows it to last indefinitely— rawhide decomposes.

  Tanning is a somewhat unattractive process: the fur might be limed with urine or lye; then dung or animal brains were pounded into the material. Even in a society used to strong odors, you didn't want to live next to a tannery.

- **Textiles** are cloth made from fibers of various types:
  - **Plant** fibers, which range from the extremely coarse (grasses and rushes, mostly suitable for making rope,

mats, sacks, hammocks, and very rough clothing) to the very fine (such as the near-transparent Egyptian linen).

○ **Wool**, made from hair (goats, sheep, camels, llamas, rabbits). I've always thought of wool as scratchy, but fine wools such as cashmere and vicuña are very soft.

○ **Silk**, made from the cocoons of the silkworm; silk produces the finest and softest natural fiber.

○ Various **synthetic** fibers, such as polyester and nylon (polymers, a type of plastic), or fiberglass.

Textiles start out as short loose fibers. These can be mashed and rubbed together, which is how you get **felt**; this was the favorite fabric of the Central Asian nomads.

You get a more durable fabric by spinning and weaving. **Spinning** aggregates fibers with a strong twist. The easiest and earliest method was to use a spindle, a simple device like a top; it acts as a weight and spins the thread, and the newly formed thread can be wrapped around it. Hand-spinning takes much more time than weaving; women often kept their spindle with them to do some spinning at idle moments.

The spinning wheel greatly sped up the process, though quality was low till the foot treadle was invented to power the wheel, allowing the spinner to use both hands to control the fiber as it was spun.

Weaving is the process of making cloth on a **loom**. The simplest loom is a framework to hold an array of parallel threads, the **warp**; these could be stretched tight with a backstrap. The weaver then interweaves a thread at right angles to them, forming the **weft**. (Warp and weft may be of different fabrics or colors, and for fancy effects one can alternate colors, forming a pattern.) Hand-threading is very slow; an early improvement was the **heddle**, a rod which lifted every other thread of the warp.

A slightly more elaborate version is the vertical loom, with the warp threads attached to the framework at the top and held taut by weights, or tied to a bottom frame; this also had the advantage of allowing a wider cloth to be woven.

Even before steam power was applied to clothmaking in the 1700s, the use of spinning wheels and large frame looms transformed clothmaking from a home craft to an industry: cloth became something you bought rather than made.

Types of clothing

There's a wide range of clothing that doesn't require much fitting or sewing:

- **Loincloth**: Put a short thin cloth between your legs; tie it tightly round your waist with a cord. A variant is to use a long enough cloth that the material itself can be wrapped around the waist, though a belt may still be a good idea.

- **Toga**: Take a very long, wide cloth; wrap it around the waist, then throw the excess over one shoulder. The weight of the toga would hold it in place, but it wasn't suitable for hard labor, and thus was an indicator of elite status.

- **Poncho**: Take two pieces of cloth about six feet long; sew them together except in the middle; put it over your head. If you sew the sides together (leaving armholes) you're on your way to a tunic or shirt. Make it longer and you've got the long simple robe worn by both sexes in early medieval times.

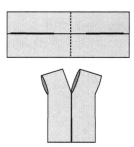

– 12.5 ft –				Collar
Sleeves	Body	Body		Overlap

– 14 in. –

- **Kimono**: The kimono is made from a single bolt of cloth with no waste. Follow the recipe for the poncho, but use a longer cloth so it comes down to the feet. Add two more pieces of cloth that drape over the shoulders, forming sleeves. Kimono are properly sewn together only very lightly, at cleaning time, which makes them easy to wash and to adapt to changing figures.

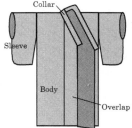

- **Skirt**: Cut a length of cloth so it wraps once around your waist, sew together. It can be made longer and held up by straps to form a basic dress.

- **Cape**: Take a large squarish piece of cloth. Drape over the shoulders; bring the corners together and fasten with a clasp, pin, or even a loop of cloth.

Our clothes (pants, shirts, dresses) are of course **fitted**, which involves measuring, cutting complex shapes out of bolts of cloth, and sewing together. These can be made to fit the body much better, but they are more specialized work and do not use the cloth as efficiently.

Infinite variation is possible: color; type of fabric (coarse or fine, stiff or soft); length and thus amount of coverage; thickness of belts; amount of decoration; accessories (hats, headbands, collars, cravats, shawls, veils). Sometimes hats, belts, sleeves, or shoes grow long extensions, such as the long pointed shoes and pointy hats popular in the 15C, often mistaken as typical medieval wear.

The basic templates can be combined or **layered**, of course. A medieval peasant might wear a light tunic, a thicker cloak, and leggings. The properly attired noblewoman of Heian Japan wore no less than twelve layers of kimono. Often you want to show off the fine underlayers, so undergarments peek out at the edges, or are glimpsed through slashes or slits in the outer layer.

The type of clothing interacts with other aspects of lifestyle, such as furniture. Liza Dalby points out that kimono are impractical with chairs— you have to perch on the edge; the obi (stiff tied sash) doesn't allow you to lean back. The kimono was designed for kneeling on the floor. In this position Western clothing is highly uncomfortable, but the kimono flatters the figure and the obi offers back support.

The language of clothing

A culture has not only a style of clothing, but a set of variations that tell much about the individual.

Unsurprisingly, the main signifier is quality. The well-off wear better, softer fabrics, more layers, and more decoration. Dyes have been sought after for millennia, and the strongest colors are often expensive and thus markers of high status. Tyrian purple, for instance, is harvested from a type of snail; as 12,000 snails are needed to extract enough dye for a single garment, it was restricted to royalty. Cochineal, made from a scale insect, was the most important export of colonial Mexico after silver.

Sumptuary laws, which restrict certain clothing to certain classes, are common. In Táng China, for instance, commoners were supposed to restrict themselves to undyed hemp. Such laws are repeated often enough that it's clear they were frequently violated.

It may be equally important to be sophisticated. Geisha, for instance, wear kimono in slightly more subdued hues and a subtly more voluptuous line than middle class women, and pride themselves on matching kimono to the season according to complicated cultural conventions.

A perennial approach to sophistication is to dress like prestigious foreigners— elegant Romans dressed like Greeks, Japanese like Chinese; today male leaders around the world use Western suits— essentially a version of 19C British formalwear. Exotic dress can be worn as a novelty (Mandarin collars, harem dresses) or as a political statement (Nehru jackets, Palestinian keffiyehs).

It's an oddity of recent Western culture that men dress drably, while women have a wide array of styles and colors. Historically men were just as apt to compete in the richness and color of their clothes. Male and female outfits may or may not be sharply distinguished.

Clothes become associated with professions, and these may become markers of values or even intent. In ancient Rome the toga was the dress of the senatorial class, very different from the armor and skirts of the soldier. Emperors were often military men, and whether they wore the toga or a military outfit was a signal of which class they intended to favor. Blue jeans, originally a marker of the sturdy working classes, became the uniform of the young. The hip-hop style of sagging pants originated in prison, where belts were banned, and neatly shows the reverse prestige operating in a marginalized community.

Authority figures in the Middle Ages wore long robes— as opposed to the peasants' short tunics— and this has persisted in the robes worn by priests, judges, and academics.

Children often wear simpler garments than their elders. Roman children, for instance, wore a simple tunic. In Europe young boys wore dresses similar to those of their sisters well into the 20th century.

As Lurie points out, changes in fashion reflect larger social trends. With the French Revolution, the elaborate and colorful dresses and coiffures of noblewomen went out of style; the new style was simple white gowns, appropriate for the bourgeois democratic era, and based on lingerie, or the simpler outfits worn by children. Male attire became far more restrained, distinguished by fine tailoring rather than striking color. (Styles don't stay simple for long; by the end of the century women were wearing corsets and long skirts with a ballooned-out shape built out of whalebone.)

When to be nude

Another clothing option is to wear none, or not much. Looking through a history of clothing, it seems there's been a general tendency to wear more over time. Some of it was climate, of course— you don't need to wear anything at all near the Equator, and not much in Egypt or Cambodia. But you can also find bare breasts in early Anatolia, Germany, and North America.

Perhaps nudity goes out of style because it's associated with poverty or low status. Slaves might go naked in ancient Egypt; till relatively late poor children went naked in many cultures, saving the expense of clothing them.

Ascetics may wear simple clothing, like Mahatma Gandhi's loincloth; as a further step the holy man may wear nothing at all. Isaiah preached naked for a time (Isaiah 20:2-4), and in a religious ecstasy King Saul took off his clothes and prophesied (1 Samuel 19:23-24). Traditionally Indian sages often went naked.

In special circumstances nudity may be a signal of elite status. Athletes competed nude in ancient Greece, and a marker of high status in modern Europe is the freedom to fly to a warm beach somewhere and wear as little as possible.

The unfashionable human body

That's the title of a fascinating book by Bernard Rudofsky, chronicling the ways humans disfigure their bodies for the sake of fashion.

Foot binding is the most infamous example: for nearly a millennium, Chinese girls had their feet broken— all but the big toe crammed under the foot. Then the arch was broken and the heel and big toe pressed close together. This caused enormous lifelong pain, difficulty in walking, and malodorous infections, but a tiny foot that looked fetching in tiny shoes (though less so when the shoes were removed), and a cautious, swaying gait that men considered highly erotic. Curiously the Manchu rulers of the Qīng dynasty forbade their own women from binding their feet.

The Victorian corset was not quite as cruel, but still painfully constricted the waist and forced the internal organs downward; no wonder women were depicted as frail, fainting creatures.

We don't do any of that anymore though, do we? Look at your feet. The big toe curves inward a bit; the little toe may curve back the other way, especially for women. This isn't natural; this is what shoes do to us. For contrast, Rudofsky shows the foot of a Roman sandal-clad foot with completely straight toes. He also mocks the designers of women's shoes for apparently believing that the big toe is in the middle of the foot.

Architecture

Houses are almost as distinctive as clothing. What does the architecture of your people look like, what is it made of, and how is it decorated?

How to make a hut

The dwellings of primitive peoples are not arbitrary, but adapted to the climate, rainfall, local materials, and degree of nomadism.

- In the rain forest, there's no need to protect against the temperature, so walls may disappear. Instead there's a parasol-like thatched roof to provide shade and protection against the rain, and sometimes a raised floor to protect against vermin. Houses are made of the most prevalent materials: trees and leaves.

• The hot deserts feature blistering daytime heat and cold nights; clay and stone absorb heat during the day and radiate it at night, mitigating these extremes. Walls are massive; roofs in low-rainfall areas can be flat.

• Nomads favor tents, with a light framework covered by skins, felt, cloth, or bark. The diagonal willow framework of Central Asian yurts folds up to a compact bundle.

• The dome shape of the igloo deflects winters storms and efficiently encloses space. Snow is a good insulator, and body heat and an oil lamp create an inner glazing of ice that seals the surface and reflects heat. When outside temperatures are -25 to -35° C, the inside temperature remains just above freezing.

Another factor is the **number of people** per house. The Yanomamö build a single house for an entire village— really a large ring enclosing a circular inner courtyard. The Plains Indians built earth lodges 12 to 18 meters wide, large enough for an extended family.

The problem of roofs

Architecture, as opposed to a dude making himself a house, happens when you're building something big, and facing the fundamental problem of how to roof it over.

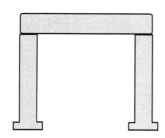

The simplest construction is **trabeated**: a flat lintel rests on vertical posts. The force on the posts is vertical and entirely compressive. That on the lintel is more complex: compressive on the top, tensile on the bottom. Stone and wood are strong only under compression, thus aren't suitable for long trabeated spans.

In the third dimension, the pillars can become walls; or you can stick with pillars or columns for an airier building.

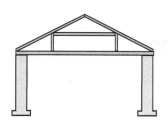

Longer spans are possible by using a **truss**, a structure composed of narrow beams, strengthened with diagonals. (Triangles add stability because they can't buckle.) A truss is stronger and much lighter than a solid beam of the same length.

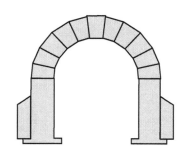

Arcuated construction relies on the arch; the Romans were the first to fully exploit arches. The wedge-shaped stones (voussoirs) are easier to handle than lintels, and an arch can cover longer spans.

The voussoirs eliminate tensile forces and thus nicely fit stone and wood, but the arch generates outward force, requiring buttresses on the sides.

The arch need not be a half-circle; variations add a particular character to the building. Gothic arches have the advantage that the two arcs need not be the same height, while the parabolic arch eliminates the need for side buttresses.

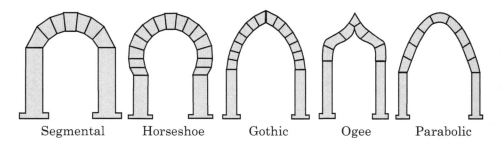

Segmental   Horseshoe   Gothic   Ogee   Parabolic

A circular arch can be extruded into the third dimension, forming a barrel vault, or rotated to form a dome.

Walls don't need to be solid; a set of columns as in a Greek temple, or a row of arches as in a Roman aqueduct, are equivalent to a wall.

Materials

Architecture was transformed in the 19C by mass-produced **iron**, which is not only stronger than wood and stone but much better at resisting tensile force. Iron frameworks, or steel-reinforced concrete, can be much lighter and taller than traditional buildings.

Since iron rusts, it generally has to be covered. This bothers some architects, as the structure of the building is hidden— indeed, a building can now deceive the world, looking like it's made of brick or pure concrete when it relies on a steel skeleton.

Steel beams support two structural innovations:

- A lintel can be balanced on just one pillar if a counterweight is added on the other side, forming a **cantilever**. As the weight can be hidden, the visual effect is of a large rectangle extending into space without visible support.

- A block can be **suspended**: supported by cables, themselves hung from larger cables attached to huge pillars. The suspension bridge is the most familiar example, but roofs can be suspended as well.

Shapes

Primitive houses are often circular; the **circle** encloses the most space per length of wall, but it's harder to combine into larger structures. Large buildings usually end up rectilinear.

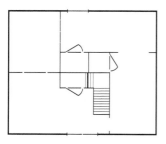

Most architects start with a big geometric shape and subdivide it.

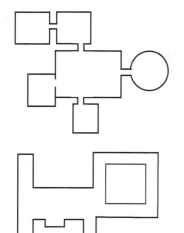

An alternative is to add rooms as discrete units, with an irregular perimeter, a plan which may appeal to more romantic tastes.

Somewhere in between, the building can incorporate wings and courtyards, inside and outside. Negative space is as much a part of the design as positive space.

Civilizations, epochs, and architects differ in their appreciation for **symmetry**, uniformity, and large-scale order. An organic or haphazard plan may have a retro charm, or a modernistic edginess.

Similarly, some people like Zen **simplicity**, some like extravagant ornamentation. But things that look arbitrary or decorative often are not. The flying buttresses of a medieval cathedral are functional, supporting the outward pressure of the arcuated walls; the beams of a truss or the columns of a temple are similarly structural.

Function

How a house is built tells us much about the values of the residents. Which are the biggest, grandest rooms, for instance— those intended to receive guests, or those for the private life of the family? Are there rooms for servants? Is the kitchen a small mean room or a luxurious status symbol? Is the house decorated according to male or female taste?

Do children get their own rooms? Do the servants? Go back far enough and a large household lived and slept in one big room— if nothing else, because that was the room with a fireplace. Most premoderns would be amazed not at the size of American McMansions but at the fact that they house only three to five people.

As a civilization becomes more complex, both buildings and rooms become more specialized. Before the modern era no one needed a train station, a missile silo, a computer room, or a garage. On the other hand, few houses today need a granary, a stable, a music room (that is, for making music), or a sickroom.

Architects also face new logistic problems: they not only have to fit in the rooms, corridors, and stairs, but elevators, ventilation shafts, wiring, plumbing, heating and a/c. An s.f. house might need life support, robot storage, teleport pods, and the central A.I. core...

A Verdurian house

Here's a house I designed for a middle-class family in Verduria:

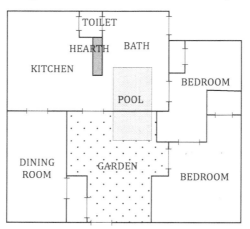

I used a number of features inspired by Christopher Alexander's *A Pattern Language*:

- An **intimacy gradient** from public (the dining room at lower left), to the kitchen/bath area, to the private bedrooms.

- The use of **negative space** to define areas such as the garden.

- **Light** can enter all of the rooms from two or three sides.

- Offset walls in the bedroom area create semi-private **niches**.

The focus of the house is the kitchen and bath, where the family spends most of its time. The latter includes a pool that extends into the garden. For a poor family, this would be the whole house— beds would be fitted along the side walls.

And more...

This section is a frank miscellany of things that didn't fit in anywhere else.

Politeness

I've covered the linguistic aspects of politeness in the *Language Construction Kit* (p. 145). Here I'll cover various nonverbal aspects.

Personal space

As noted in the culture test (p. 124), cultures vary in how much personal space people expect, with comical effects when cultures mix. My high school psychology class did a neat exercise: the class was divided in pairs; one half the students (unbeknownst to the rest) were told to try to move just a foot away from their conversational partner. The others, quite unconsciously, moved back. You could see each pair constantly moving around the room.

Americans expect to have their own space— the nuclear family can come in, but they'd be decidedly uncomfortable with the lack of privacy in a Yanomamö village, a Roman senator's house, or a Bedouin chieftain's tent.

Some s.f. writers, taking this attitude to the extreme, have imagined worlds with a positive horror of any direct physical contact.

Loose and strict time

Many cultures are notoriously lax about time: if you're asked to come at seven, you're expected to show up a couple hours later; if you have an appointment with an official, you might wait all day, then be told to return tomorrow.

We're used to clocks accurate to the minute, and the strict schedules they allow, as well as transportation that matches this accuracy. Laxity over time may be a holdover from the era when time was measured in hours at best, and a visit anywhere could be expected to last days or weeks.

Requests and orders

Richard Feynman told a story about going to a seminar in Japan; he wanted to stay in a Japanese-style inn rather than the Western-style hotel his fellow physicists were staying in. But somehow this proved to be an enormous problem. The Japanese organizer was polite but kept bringing up one objection after another. It took half an hour to get down to the real objection: if Feynman was in another hotel, the bus would have to make another stop in the morning.

"No, no! In the morning, I'll come to this hotel, and get on the bus here," Feynman said.

And so it was settled. Only it wasn't; some new obstacle had come up. This time it took fifteen minutes before it was out in the open: the mail was delivered to the other hotel. Feynman promised to pick his mail up when he walked to the other hotel, and the problem was solved.

This sort of thing is insanely frustrating to Americans less patient than Feynman. Why don't these people say what they mean?

The key here is that in many cultures, indirection is polite. Directly stating a price, or a refusal, is disturbing, so these are obscured. Japan is what's been called a Guess culture, rather than an Ask culture. In an Ask culture, you can ask directly for things— you accept that the answer may be no. In a Guess culture, you don't ask directly unless you're sure the answer is yes. You put out subtle feelers, in hopes that the hints will be taken and you'll get an offer.

A Japanese person would have either intuited the reason for the organizer's reticence (rather than, in effect, forcing it out of him), or backed off when the request ran into obstacles; one can also be more direct once a personal relationship is established. People within a Guess culture get along fine; it's the conflict of cultures that causes frustration.

Meals and drinks

We've already talked about the chief crops (p. 86) and domestic animals. But there are other questions to answer:

- What do you add for flavor? The Romans, for instance, were fond of fish sauce (*garum*). The Chinese favored pickled vegetables.

- When is the chief meal? Laborers prefer to eat at noon; urban sophisticates like to dine at night.

- What's a typical meal? The Verdurians of Almea, for instance, like to wrap meat or vegetables in a thin bread, much like a tortilla.

Before modern sanitation alcoholic drinks, apart from their amusement value, were *safer* than water. Also note that distillation wasn't available in ancient times.

Schooling

Mass education is a modern phenomenon— literacy was traditionally restricted to a minority, sometimes a very small minority... though since they're the ones who write the books, their point of view is overemphasized.

Schools are ancient— there were schools for scribes in Sumer— but they were at first restricted to an elite. Plato's Academy was founded in 387 BC, though it was more of a scholars' circle than a university. The Imperial Academy was established by the Hàn dynasty in China in the -2C, and eventually had 30,000 students. Some disciplines established their own schools; medical schools existed in the Islamic world by the 7C.

An Egyptian text used as a writing exercise reminds the students of their favored status:

> Do you not consider how things are with the farmer, when the harvest is taxed? Grubs have taken half the grain, the hippopotamus has eaten from what is left. There are mice in the field and the locust swarm has come... [The tax collectors] say "Hand over grain!"... He is stretched out and beaten... his wife is bound in his presence....

> Let me tell you how the soldier fares... how he goes to Syria, and how he marches over the mountains, his bread and his water carried on his shoulder like the load of an ass... His

drink is foul water... If he gets back to Egypt, he is like worm-eaten wood, sick and bedridden.

Religions may take on educational functions, whether it's adolescents being taught the ways of the world in primitive tribes, or education in the scriptures. Most of the European universities started as religious institutions.

Craftsmen took on apprentices to learn the craft, a practice at least as old as Babylon, as they are mentioned in Hammurabi's code— an apprentice was considered an adopted son, and could sue his master if he failed to teach him his craft.

Medieval misery

I don't think the medieval stink has been expressed more memorably than by Patrick Süskind, in *Perfume*, speaking of 18C France:

> The streets stank of manure, the courtyards of urine, the stairwells stank of moldering wood and rat droppings, the kitchens of spoiled cabbage and mutton fat; the unaired parlors stank of stale dust, the bedrooms of greasy sheets, damp featherbeds, and the pungently sweet aroma of chamber pots. The stench of sulfur rose from the chimneys, the stench of caustic lyes from the tanneries, and from the slaughterhouses came the stench of congealed blood. People stank of sweat and unwashed clothes; from their mouths came the stench of rotting teeth... even the king himself stank, stank like a rank lion, and the queen like an old goat, summer and winter.

This is on Süskind's first page, and it masterfully tells us that the world he's describing is different from ours, in some very unappealing ways.

The past is a foreign country. On the other hand, it's only the narrowest and rudest sort of tourist who visits a foreign country and complains incessantly that things aren't as good as they are back home. These things would all immediately assault our nostrils, but the people of the time certainly didn't feel the same way about them. (Or more precisely, they made distinctions. Everyday sweat was one thing, but please keep the tannery on the outskirts of town.)

Rather than washing, people might rely on hiding the stink with perfumes. A Táng prince chewed on a mixture of aloeswood and musk when with guests, so that whenever he spoke they would sense a pleasing fragrance.

Attitudes toward bathing have widely varied. Bathing every five days was good enough for the Táng; the Cambodians and Koreans were considered a little strange for bathing daily. On the other hand Western traders stank; but then this would be hard to avoid after a six-month journey.

Stench was only part of the general misery. Barbara Tuchman's *A Distant Mirror* is a vivid evocation of the horrors of the 14C: in addition to the general corruption of the clergy, the oppression of the peasants, and the irresponsibility of the nobles, there was the Black Death that killed a third of the population, vicious pogroms against Jews, the Great Schism, and the Hundred Years' War. One of the worst scourges was the free companies, groups of mercenaries who simply prolonged wartime pillaging into a full-time occupation. Lacking a standing army, the kings could not suppress them, and indeed had reason not to, as they could be hired for the next war.

This isn't to say that life was uniformly awful, even for the poor. There were islands of prosperity and beauty, and the seeds of future progress. Nor were all lands as disordered as medieval Europe.

Again, you don't need to dwell on this— unless you want to; perhaps you like grim conworlds. But some idealization is fine; art need not be didactic.

Lords and slaves

A time traveler from a land where you call the CEO by his first name— or a hunter-gatherer— would be equally nonplussed at the staggering hierarchy of premodern states. Lords were prickly and arrogant; only relatively recently were the powerful expected to treat their lessers with friendly courtesy. Tuchman records some blood-curdling diatribes against the lower classes; one Duke not only called the peasants dogs but liked to force them to bark.

At the same time, their inferiors need not be abject. As C.S. Lewis points out, slaves in Greek and Roman comedy are cheeky, knowing, full of tricks, and highly self-interested— more like Figaro than like

Uriah Heep. St. Augustine's mother was berated by her slave-girl for her drinking; Odysseus in a play is insulted as never having a "freeman's thought"— meaning he is always calculating, never acts freely and generously.

Didn't the lower orders ever rebel? Of course they did; they could easily storm the local keep and massacre the inhabitants. Rebellions were usually beaten down, but it took time to organize a counter-force. Cities rebelled too, and having more money, plus walls, they were trickier to subdue. Sometimes it was easier to grant them certain liberties rather than sack them.

Xenophobia

I've always been fascinated by the foreign. I like learning languages, reading about foreign and historical cultures, meeting people from distant lands. I'd love to have access to the galactic Internet.

This has probably always been a minority taste; most people don't cotton to strangers. Every group has disparaging terms for non-members. And many things create groups of insiders and outsiders: race, religion, class, customs, and above all language. If you can talk at all, there's some chance of coming to terms.

But groups differ in their openness:

- A primitive tribe may have a very narrow world, without much interest in or sympathy for the tribe down the next jungle trail. Jared Diamond describes New Guineans from different tribes meeting and exchanging long lists of relatives. They were trying to find a common relative so they'd have reason not to kill each other.

- Large empires, amalgamating many peoples, end up cosmopolitan in spirit: Persia, Rome, the Islamic caliphate, India, China, and the US were all used to multiple religions, ideas, and ethnic groups. But their tolerance and interest may end at the border.

- A nation isolated by natural barriers, like Japan or Britain, may be open to foreign ideas but decidedly uncomfortable with foreign people.

- A small unprotected nation has a complicated relationship to the outside world. It may have a strong pride and sense of identity— the ancient Jews, for instance, refused to fall into the melting pot of the Roman Empire. It may also feel a sense of precariousness and peripherality alien to the citizens of empires: they've been invaded many times, and too much happens outside their borders to be ignored.

Xenophobia may be tempered by the hunger for novelty. A stranger can tell you stories you've never heard before, perhaps one reason why many cultures preach courteous treatment of outsiders.

Both fantasy and s.f. introduce separate species into the equation. I would expect these would generate a greater sense of difference than any human division. The happy melting pot depicted in many works strikes me as implausible, at least outside artificial environments such as a university or diplomatic compound. I like C.S. Lewis's description of Ransom's first meetings with the *hrossa* of Mars: it was both like speaking to a human and like being with an animal— sometimes an uncanny and disagreeable sensation.

Amusements

What do your people do for fun? Here's some ideas and examples.

- Hang around and **talk**— this seems to be the favorite activity of the Pirahã. Storytelling is surely almost as ancient.

- **Feasts**; as we've seen (p. 140), this is the origin of economic activity, as Big Men organized redistributive bonanzas. Even when the flow of goods became a steady stream from peasant to king, canny rulers still knew the power of giving away food. The Roman emperors issued a wheat ration to almost the whole population of Rome.

- **Music**, including song and dance. You could make a living doing this in medieval Provence or the shogun's Japan— *geisha* originally meant 'artist'.

- **Vice**: gambling, intoxication (by drink or other substances), and whoring are as old as civilization.

- **Theater**, as for instance among the ancient Greeks. The medieval guilds put on mystery plays, based on Biblical stories but including a heavy helping of verse and comedy. Acting was a fairly disreputable profession in Renaissance England— thus the use of boys to play women's roles in Shakespeare's time.

- **Illusions** have always been popular; all the better if the marks thought the trick was real. If magic exists in your world, maybe some magicians earn a living as street performers. Illusionists would likely still exist... or even magician/illusionists whose act is a mixture of real and fake.

- **Athletics**, an obsession of Brits, Americans and ancient Greeks.

- **Baths**, popular in ancient Rome and in the Ottoman Empire; still highly popular in Japan.

- **Board games**: the ancestor of go was played in China 2500 years ago; chess originated in India 1500 years ago. The earliest known board game is the Egyptian *senet*; boards have been found in burials of 3500 BC.

Religion

You want a religion for your conculture. You can come up with half a dozen god names and call it a day. But let's say you want to get beyond that.

Religion is a misleading term, because to many people it just means Christianity. I prefer *belief system*, since it covers things that act like religions but don't seem to fall under the term, like Confucianism or communism.

Everyone has a belief system, just like everyone has a skeleton. It's not a bad thing, really. You don't want to go through life believing nothing, or believing everything, any more than you want to toss out your skeleton.

The best practice for creating a religion is to have one of your own. It's hard to imagine what people get out of worshipping and praying if you've never done it— though I'll do my best to explain below.

For Christians: Is it OK to create a religion?

It's just as OK a creating a fictional villain. A Christian writer like G.K. Chesterton wrote a lot about murderers and thieves; he didn't in the least approve of murder or theft, nor did he worry that his stories would tempt his readers to these sins. No one's going to join your fictional religion.

I hope you'll approach your fictional religions, like your villains, with Christian compassion. We're all fallen, but likewise there are glimpses of the Light everywhere. A fictional religion that simply worships evil is as cheap and unconvincing as a fictional villain that cackles and curls his moustache.

The more interesting question may be, how do you convincingly put God into a fantasy world? Clearly God would want to save all fallen worlds. C.S. Lewis answered this question in two different but equally valid ways: in Narnia,

---

he assumed that God would choose another incarnation in order to redeem that world's sin; in *Perelandra* he assumed that the incarnation of Jesus was valid for the whole universe.

Some Christian fantasy writers have appealed to both Christians and non-Christians by a certain indirection. The name of God is never mentioned in *The Lord of the Rings*; you have to read Tolkien's other works to understand the couple of references to 'the One'. Diane Duane uses the same term, with the 'Lone Power' standing in for Satan. Of course there's nothing wrong with being direct, but you may end up preaching only to the converted.

I recommend Chesterton's *The Everlasting Man* as a overview of religions from a Christian perspective, full of unusual insights, and Dorothy L. Sayers' *The Mind of the Maker* as an essential exploration of both the Trinity and the nature of artistic creation. J.R.R. Tolkien's essay "On Fairy Stories" is a spirited defense both of fantasy and of subcreation.

For atheists: How to create something you despise

My advice to atheists is about the same as for Christians: avoid cheap caricatures. Religions are not just cabals of nasty old men plotting the enslavement of others. I admire the amazing invention and rip-roaring pace of Philip Pullman's fantasies, but his Magisterium has a bit too much of the James Bond Villain about it. (On the other hand his Marisa Coulter is a model for how to create villains; she's a genuinely threatening character but her relationship with the main character, Lyra, is as much love as antagonism.)

Beyond that, just read the chapter, especially the next section, which goes into much more detail on what belief systems are and addresses some common misconceptions about them.

What are they for?

Let's start by looking at what belief systems do. They go far beyond telling stories about God or the gods.

Framework for thought and action

Above all, a belief system is a mental framework— that's why I compared it to a skeleton. It provides a model or sketch of the universe we live in, sets out the laws of that model, and suggests how it affects us and how to affect it back. It tells what our purpose is, how people should treat each other, when we're messing up and what to do about it.

It's silly to say that atheism is a religion, but an atheist has a belief system. A commitment to "science" is a value and requires a strong belief (which any philosopher since Hume could easily tear apart) in the objectivity of the outside world and in its freedom from meddling deities. Very likely— indeed, hopefully— the atheist also has moral values, some of which are moral axioms which can't be reduced to any other moral principle.

Most belief systems go far beyond this, of course. Think of a fundamentalist Christian, or a Communist, or a talk radio host. They have an answer for everything, and everything can be put in its place. Don't think of belief systems as extreme, however. Mild Anglicanism, or a bemused eclecticism, are also perfectly valid belief systems, and more typical of belief systems worldwide.

Why not have the minimum possible framework and work out everything else as you go? Well, this is like saying everyone should build their own cars and write their own operating systems. Following an existing system— especially the one that's a norm in your community— is an immense time-saver. Most people don't want their metaphysics and morality up in the air.

Support for the social system

Belief systems provide a justification for the prevailing social system— indeed, the two are hard to disentangle. In general, religions are going to be big on obedience to authority, property rights, respect for holy things, treating people peacefully, not stealing other people's sex partners, not running with scissors, etc.

If you have a dramatically different society, its belief systems should match. On Almea, for instance, I have ktuvok empires, where one sapient species, the ktuvoks, dominates a much larger mass of humans. Naturally the religions of these realms depict the ktuvoks as holy and superior creatures, preach obedience to them, and warn about the dangerous lies of humans who think they can govern themselves. Less dramatically, if a culture oppresses women or holds slaves, its belief systems will explain why that is just and true— just as most modern belief systems explain why it's not.

I should that add that a reflexive conservativism isn't an entirely bad thing. Most new ideas are bad, and sticking to the old ones saves the time needed to prove them wrong or to try them and have them fail.

Call for change

I must immediately add that belief systems also justify change, and sometimes rebellion. This can happen in several ways:

- A society which has drifted far from its ideals will find its very belief system exhorting reform, or even revolution. Societies rarely live up to their ideals; a religious case can always be made for change.

- The belief systems started in historical times all have origin stories— they had to challenge existing society. Jesus was crucified, Muhammad was chased out of Mecca, the Shi'ites began when the descendents of Ali were denied power, the Communists wished to sweep away the bourgeois who had only just elbowed their way into power themselves. All these belief systems therefore have, not far buried in their DNA, models for rebellion.

- Society can change, and the religion changes in response— despite itself, perhaps, but sincerely. Catholicism eventually made its peace with Galileo (and indeed with Darwin).

In the U.S., churches were at the forefront of abolition and the civil rights movement— Martin Luther King Jr. was a pastor. When Britain threw out its king, a hundred years before the French Revolution, zealous Protestants were the firebrands. Peasant rebellions often coalesced around a charismatic religious leader. The

Messianic hopes in 1st century Palestine, part of the background of Christianity, were in part driven by the desire for liberation from Roman rule. The founder of the Míng dynasty, Zhū Yuánzhāng, belonged to a Buddhist secret society, the White Lotus.

There can be retrogressive religious movements too, of course. But before modern times, if any group was agitating for peace, justice, or national liberation, it was more likely than not to be a strong religious movement.

Difficult social values

Marvin Harris has argued that belief systems provide support for difficult social values— those that don't come naturally. Religions don't have to urge men to look at pretty girls, or to eat chocolate. Examples:

- Hinduism urges poor peasants to worship their cows. This seems irrational to Westerners, but in fact it's quite sensible: the cow is the basis for the peasant's prosperity— it provides milk and butter, dung for fuel and fertilizer, and bears the oxen needed for plowing— but all that is easy to forget if the monsoons fail and there's a drought. It's mighty tempting to eat the cow then— but if he does so, the peasant is ruined. Religious sanction helps reduce the temptation.

- Judaism and Islam ban the eating of pork. This doesn't make much sense in Europe, but it does in the arid Middle East, where pigs would compete directly with human beings for food, and where their instinct to keep their skin wet assumes unsanitary forms.

- Among the Bushmen of the Kalahari, excessive ardor for hunting is discouraged. "When a young man kills much meat he begins to think of himself as a chief... we cannot accept this," one explains. "We refuse one who boasts, for someday his pride will make him kill somebody. So we always speak of his meat as worthless." The reason for this cultural more is not hard to find: the Kalahari is a desert. Overhunting would produce a short-term feast and then starvation.

- Why do so many religions have strictures about sex? There are many answers, but some of the best are the most obvious:

venereal disease and pregnancy. Both are highly dangerous in a premodern society and sufficient justification for putting a lid on our natural desire for free sex. It's not coincidence that we've rebelled against these strictures precisely in a period where antibiotics and birth control have fundamentally changed the danger level.

Practical help

Much of this so far is abstract. People want practical help too, in areas where medicines or machines are of no use. They want to cast or counter curses, to get healed, to meet lovers, to have babies, to have rain, to find lost objects, to protect their homes, to hear from the dead. And where needs exist, providers will come.

No one likes disappointment, and belief systems will go to great lengths to deliver on what they promise. In some American Indian religions, for instance, all boys coming of age must experience a spiritual vision. A matter of such importance is hardly left to chance; drugs, hunger, and physical exhaustion help ensure that that vision will come.

In a fantasy world, such beliefs may not be illusory. This raises an interesting question: would the religions look any different? I suspect the answer is, not much. Actual believers don't feel that they lack for evidence or that their gods are unresponsive.

The requested aid need not be supernatural. In the slums of Brazil, evangelical and charismatic churches expand by addressing people's immediate needs— how to deal with alcoholism or drug addiction, how to get jobs and get along with their families. Islamic fundamentalists build support by running schools and charities. Many universities and hospitals in the West had their start as religious projects.

More abstractly, the belief system offers **heuristics** for mental and social life. Richard Feynman gives an example of a scientific heuristic: distrust the first or last data point in a series. If that data was better, there'd be more points beyond it. It's not a physical law, it's just a rule of thumb backed by lots of experience. For examples of moral heuristics, consider the idea of forgiveness, or the notion that hubris will lead to disaster, or the idea that radical renunciation fosters enlightenment.

Personal growth

On a more personal level, belief systems can offer disciplines for **personal growth**— meditation, introspection, confession, prayer and fasting, visions, the interpretation of dreams, recovery from neurosis, the perfection of virtues.

This shouldn't be hard to understand, as these are fascinations even today— though traditional religions aren't the only suppliers in the market. If these things still seem odd, think about it this way:

- Mental peace really helps. It's useful to still that inner voice that insists on worrying, resenting, or replaying painful memories. To put it bluntly, our culture abounds in other ways to relax. Premodern cultures didn't have iPods, DVDs, mystery novels, TV, video games, and sleep pills.

- We still believe in the cultivation of will— if you want to give up smoking, maintain an exercise program, learn a language, or run a marathon, you must learn discipline and a certain acceptance of pain for future good. "No pain, no gain", we say. Once you start down this path, it's not hard to feel that with even more pain you'll get even more gain.

Worship and wonder

Belief systems in general satisfy the sense of wonder— in religions per se, this may take the form of worship. A healthy religion appeals not merely to the conscience but to the heart; it offers marvels and poetry as well as duties and laws; it stimulates love and creativity. In cultures racked with violence, pestilence, and injustice, it is a refuge for contemplation, gentleness, scholarship, and art.

Memetic effects

There's very little to be said for memes— for why, see the essay on my site, zompist.com— but memetics offers two genuine insights.

First, belief systems develop an **immune system**. Among the beliefs are a set designed to counter backsliding and skepticism. There are explanations why other beliefs are wrong, warnings that temptations will come, and predictions of unhappiness outside the fold. Socially, the believers have a tendency to isolate themselves, avoid outside messages, and ostracize heretics.

Thus Christianity explains that all other gods are false. Atheism simplifies further by deleting the word 'other'. Communism posits the dialectic, which elaborates ideologies of greater and greater complexity— ending in communism itself, where the process stops. Movement conservatives turn harshly on anyone who criticizes any aspect of movement doctrine or its most popular adherents. Bahaiism more subtly declares that any truth found in other religions is already incorporated in itself.

Such doctrines are hardly intellectually defensible; they exist to protect the belief system from deterioration. A religion just isn't going to last very long if it says "believe as you like, it's all good."

Memes also offer an explanation for **zeal**. Extreme beliefs have an advantage, because they provide motivation for propagating them. It's the zealots who look for converts and punish apostates. Above all they expend considerable effort to pass their beliefs to their children.

A denomination can become moderate and tolerant, and that may keep its members happy. But their very moderation makes them unlikely to look for followers and diffident about keeping wayward teenagers in the faith. Thus the slow decline of moderate denominations in the U.S.

At the same time, there are factors that mitigate zealotry— the principal one being the general cussedness of human beings. Zealots can intimidate an entire population (cf. Saudi Arabia, or Stalinism); but most people are not interested in being zealots. The normal state of a religion is fervor on the part of a few, quiet acceptance on the part of the majority.

The evidence of narrative

Most belief systems, including non-religious ones, do have one fatal flaw: they're not falsifiable. This is the secret motor of science— scientists ideally highlight contrary evidence, and disdain a hypothesis that can't be tested. The crackpot, by contrast, only looks for confirmation. He not only ignores or denies evidence against his theory, but modifies his theory such that it can never be disproved.

Some beliefs in a belief system may be derived and debated rationally. Others can't be, because they're axiomatic— basic morality can't be derived from logical propositions, for instance, because no logical operation can turn an *is* into an *ought*. But a large chunk of a belief system isn't designed to be falsifiable.

Belief systems are evaluated by another standard, which we may call **narrative coherency**. Does it make a good story? Does it hold together, does it shed light on the world and inside our heads, does it satisfy our sense of wonder and our sense of justice? Stories are still appreciated this way; also much of politics, and even philosophical arguments. No one can prove that libertarianism or Buddhism or free will are right or wrong— all we can do is provide the best possible narrative.

In some ways that's what this book is about: creating a conworld with narrative coherency.

To a modern ear, myths are obviously false because they're made-up stories. To their original hearers, I think they seemed true for almost the same reason: how can someone tell a story at all unless it was dictated by a god?

Easy assumptions

Many conreligions are too closely modeled on Christianity— whether as it is or as it's perceived by outsiders.

Religion = Catholicism

Catholicism makes a great model: a powerful centralized organization, gorgeous stone cathedrals, holy water, incense and chanting, priests in distinctive robes and funny hats. If you like it, it's solid, homey, and grand; if you don't, there's a sinister undercurrent to draw on, from self-mortification to the Inquisition.

But just as fantasy writers again and again end up with pseudo-European monarchies, they keep imitating Catholicism. The only religion that's like Catholicism is Catholicism; religions don't have to share *any* of its attributes.

Exclusivity

The Abrahamic God is a jealous God; his believers aren't just prohibited from worshipping other gods; they're not supposed to believe they even exist. Mixing your religions is a decided no-no.

The atmosphere is far different in East Asia, where people have no trouble following multiple religious traditions at once. The approach of Chinese intellectuals was to look over everyone's ideas, from all the major schools, and select the best of each.

This should put into perspective intriguing events such as Kublai Khan asking for a hundred Christian scholars to come explain their doctrines in Yuán China. Christians hearing about this regret the lost opportunity: China could have become a Christian country! Not likely; Kublai was simply inviting more viewpoints to the table.

Ancient Greece and Rome were much more like the East than like our culture. There was always room for one more cult.

The nature of faith

Unbelievers often misunderstand the nature of faith. To admire faith as a virtue seems repellent to them— it sounds like a glorification of believing things against the dictates of reason and evidence. But this is a parody of faith, and entirely irrelevant to the premodern world.

Paul's letters show some tension between Greek rationalism and Christian belief, but this was not a war between "science and religion", more a reflection of a cultural gap: like the Chinese, the ancient Greeks just didn't get the mindset of uncompromising, exclusive declarations about God.

In the 13C, Thomas Aquinas devised a brilliant synthesis of Christianity with Aristotelian rationalism. Reason was a godly virtue; its Greek name, *logos*, was associated with Jesus. The universities of the Middle Ages revived ancient learning (much of it via Arab intermediaries); the Scholastics' use of dialectical reasoning, heuristics such as Occam's Razor, and the empirical focus of clerics like Albertus Magnus and Roger Bacon, all prepared the ground for modern science. (Academic robes even derive from ecclesiastical ones.)

It's a commonplace that science makes belief harder. But it doesn't— for believers. The believer has made his peace with the apparent conflicts. Some just deny them; some do their best to accept scientific facts without denying their faith; some have elaborate answers; some just don't care. But what's quite wrong is to imagine that believers must constantly beat down or suppress contrary evidence. Quite the opposite: for a believer, the world is full of confirmations of their beliefs and reminders of unbelievers' foolishness. Neil Gaiman explains this nicely:

> I noticed a long time ago that the Universe rewards belief systems. It doesn't really matter what you believe— it'll be there and waiting for you if you go and look for it. Decide the universe is, say, run by secret enormous teddy bears, and I can guarantee you'll immediately start running across evidence that this is true.

It's probably just confirmation bias; but if you want to dismiss people's ideas because of that, remember that it applies to whatever *you* believe, too.

C.S. Lewis gives us a good way to think about faith: it's the same thing we offer our friends or lovers. Once you decide to make a friend, or get married, you don't subject them to careful laboratory tests, even if you're a positivist. You give them the benefit of the doubt. You can take all the care you want converting, but once you've accepted your God or god, you give them the same trust.

At the same time, Christianity tells us that faith must be *practiced*, that if you don't make an effort to keep your beliefs straight in your mind, you'll lose them. This is a heuristic, an observation made from generations of spiritual experience. Acquiring a belief system is like learning a language: you have to keep it up, not because it's inherently hard to swallow but because it's a complicated set of beliefs and practices. Unbelief, by contrast, requires no maintenance, just as if you don't know French you don't have to practice not knowing it.

Beliefs never change

Another commonplace, both among believers and unbelievers, is that belief systems never change. Believers are proud of their constancy, unbelievers disdainful of it. But they're both wrong: belief systems constantly evolve, albeit slowly.

- Political changes are easily swallowed. In 1776 the Anglican church in America fairly painlessly changed into the

Episcopal church, giving up its allegiance to the Crown and indeed its belief in crowns at all.

Early Christianity went from a sullen hostility to the Roman Empire (which after all had crucified its founder as a rebel and periodically persecuted it), to a thorough intertwining of church and empire. No one seemed to remember the "Rome is Babylon" message once the emperors were painting Christian symbols on the army's shields.

- Scientific challenges are accepted, sooner or later. Copernicus was at first accepted as a methodological convenience, then rejected as an offense against scripture, and finally quietly accepted— the fundiest fundamentalist doesn't insist on an unmoving Earth today.

- Social changes are accepted too, though it may take generations. Slavery was fully accepted by every writer in the Bible and by Christians for many centuries; it's been entirely rejected. Racism used to be justified by the story of Ham, son of Noah, but racism is no longer part of theology. In the last half century or so, conservative Christians have accepted things their predecessors shuddered at: female pastors, rock music, makeup.

It goes deeper than that: read the Mosaic Law, and it's striking how much of it Christians don't even dream of applying. Even if they believe it's the Word of God, they're not going to stone adulterers, keep kosher, worry about mixing cloths, forbid interest, forgive all debts in Jubilee years, sacrifice animals, or check for leprous walls. For that matter, not many will follow the New Testament and eschew violent retaliation, never utter verbal abuse, avoid marriage, have multiple elders in a house church, keep their money in common, give all they have to the poor, or have women keep silent in church.

Don't make the opposite error and consider that belief systems are fickle and quickly jettison anything inconvenient. Many of these changes occasioned much struggle and debate, and were solved not so much by people changing their mind as by the previous generation dying off.

Beliefs = practice

I once read a book which asserted that religious taboos against masturbation, birth control, and oral sex led their adherents to vaginal sex only and the resulting high birth rates. The author forgot that religious prohibitions aren't always obeyed, and that beliefs don't always translate into action.

Frequent and fervent admonitions, in fact, are pretty good evidence that the precept is frequently violated. We use this in linguistics, in fact— prescriptivists' complaints about some pronunciation or word misuse may be the first evidence that the pronunciation or the meaning has in fact changed.

Sometimes an explicit rule has the **opposite** of its intended effect. The abortion rate is far higher among U.S. Christians than among atheistic Swedes. There are many reasons, but one is that believers overemphasize the easiness of following rules. In theory they disapprove of abortion more than fornication. But they get so hung up on the "no sex" rule that they reject attempts to reduce abortion by providing information about sex and birth control. They believe so firmly that the abstinence message *should* work that they can't face why it doesn't.

Don't just invent the rules of your religion; think about which ones are *really* followed. This can vary by sex or class... often in eccentric ways. Don't assume the lower classes are always laxer; sometimes they're shocked at the wild ways of their betters.

The dustbin of history

S.f. is often written by technophiles who think religion should have disappeared long ago. But religion is still hovering around. without making any definitive move toward the exit.

It's human nature, in part— we have a spiritual side that keeps coming out. In American society, strong forms of Christianity are still with us, but there are plenty of alternatives— Buddhism, pagan revivals, reverence for the Earth, crystals, aliens.

To a large extent, the destructive fervor that once attached to religions now attaches to politics. Fascism and communism are the big examples and the big killers. But the unrestrained anger of contemporary politics shows that belief systems are alive and well.

More respectably, it's hard to picture a prosperous and progressive society that isn't supported by a belief system— or several of them. Consider the following propositions:

- Human beings aren't bags of meat; they're persons, with a right to exist and be prosperous.

- Social systems should produce prosperity and happiness for their citizens.

- People should be free from injustice, oppression, and arbitrary interference. The community may impose rules, but greater intrusions require greater justifications.

- The common habitat— our Earth, while we're restricted to it— must be preserved, both to support the human population and for its own sake.

- Truth should never be feared, and we wish to know as much as we can about the universe. The scientific method is the best guide to the physical world.

These are all moral propositions, completely unprovable by science. But a society which explicitly rejected them in belief or in practice would be miserable and ultimately destructive.

And because humans can be dunderheads, it would be better to go beyond the minimal beliefs necessary. These propositions should have a wide margin of error: maximal definitions of "human beings", "happiness", "science", etc. That's why we have things like burial customs. Humans shouldn't become bags of meat the moment they die; that's too close to deciding that some of them are meatbags while still alive.

Beliefs

To describe a belief system you'll want to describe its beliefs. This may be a bit Christocentric: not all religions have a systematic theology. What teachings they do have might be given only to an elite, or might not be very important to the believer— arguably paganism is more about what you *do* than what you think.

Still, the belief system is likely to have at least a strong opinion on the following topics.

Cosmology

What's the overall structure of the universe? What are those bright lights in the sky? What is under the ground and behind the clouds? What other planes are there?

Religions often feature at least one '**other world**', close enough to our world to affect it, with its own laws. Christianity has heaven and hell. Some Native American religions have a series of worlds arranged vertically... at some point humanity climbed out of the previous world from a cave, and when we die we ascend to the next one.

Speaking as a conworlder, the visualization of these worlds is on the whole unimpressive. They're either foggy (because spirit is a little like the airiest visible substance we know, smoke or fog), or a preternaturally bright and summery copy of the natural world.

Well, it's hard to describe what we've never seen. But here's some different approaches:

- Add a dimension. The supernatural world should be deeper and richer than our own, as our 3-D world is richer than a flat picture.

  (The classic description of 2-D life is Edwin Abbott's *Flatland*; an excellent evocation of the fourth dimension is Rudy Rucker's *Spaceland*.)

- Spirits are minds, so the spiritual world should have the attributes of mental thoughts and images: infinitely malleable, often wild and lawless, able to switch locations instantly, easily lost. My dreams, at least, come with meanings attached, with no need of exposition: I just know who everyone is, what the shadowy threats are, what the evil ones are after.

- Perhaps the imagery of a spiritual world *is* based on spirits' recollections of the natural world; but as spirits from all worlds interact, they share images, so the spiritual world has aspects of highly alien worlds.

- Physics suggests that energy is quantized, and possibly time and space as well; I wonder if the universe is a cellular automaton run on a hyperdimensional supercomputer by some bored grad student. If we don't generate some interesting patterns soon he's going to turn it off.

Premodern religions' attitudes toward **matter** are generally negative. This was not a matter of dour Christians and carefree pagans; if anything orthodox Christianity was unusually pro-matter, asserting that as God created the world, the physical world was good. More typical was the Gnostic position that matter is evil. The Hindu view that the world is *maya* (illusion), and the Buddhist rejection of desire, are along the same lines.

This does much to explain why many religions exalt ordeals, physical deprivation, even self-harm: the attachment to base matter must be attacked.

Religions may also classify matter into clean and unclean, and establish elaborate rules for dealing with and eliminating uncleanness, a concept both physical and moral. Isabel Fonseca's description of Gypsy customs is relevant here— Gypsies have a very strong sense of cleanliness, are obsessed with washing, and disgusted with non-Gypsy customs like keeping pets in the house. Yet their horror of uncleanliness is not at all triggered by squalid clothing.

Historicism

Cosmologies may extend over time as well as space, giving an outline of the history of the universe: how it was created, what sort of times preceded our own, what comes next, how everything ends.

Creation myths face the metaphysical question of how to make something out of nothing; the usual expedient is that *something*, probably something bland and seemingly worthless, must have already existed. (Modern science achieves the neat trick of allowing particle-antiparticle pairs to arise from literally nothing; the vacuum boils with detectable energy. The whole universe may have arisen from one super-expanded blip. But this only pushes the question back one step: where did the physical laws come from that allow this?)

Many religions posited a Golden Age at the beginning and a slow decline afterward. This may sound depressing, but C.S. Lewis thinks otherwise:

> Historically as well as cosmically, medieval man stood at the foot of a stairway; looking up, he felt delight. The backward, like the upward, glance exhilarated him with the pleasures of admiration. ...The saints looked down on one's spiritual life, the kings, sages, and warriors on one's secular life, the great lovers of old on one's amours, to foster, encourage, and instruct... One had one's place, however modest, in a great succession; one need be neither proud nor lonely. (*The Discarded Image*)

Our own belief systems assume progress— a steady march from the amoeba to the australopithecus to the agnostic. Christians more than ever seem fascinated by eschatology, compiling prophecies and writing fantasy about the end times.

Cyclical cosmologies have a certain romantic appeal, though if the cycle is long enough it's hard to get any narrative use out of it. E.R. Eddison's *The Worm Ouroboros* in effect presents a four-year cycle.

The soul

Consider these two sets of phenomena:

organs and flesh	thoughts and memory
death, decay, and pain	meaning
growing plants	ideas, facts, and arguments
preparing and eating food	love
gravity	anger, fear, and other emotions
weather	stories
earth and water	poetry

All of these are everyday human experiences, yet the two columns are like two different and incommensurate worlds. Very little that we know about the first column, even today, sheds any light on the second, except by analogy.

Not surprisingly, many belief systems separate these two aspects of our lives as *body* and *spirit*. The soul or spirit is usually judged to be superior, partly because it seems to be **us**— we have a picture of *living in* the body, which the soul controls much as a driver controls a vehicle. The native Germanic word was *ghost*; which thus become the name for the thing that sticks around after death minus its body; also cf. *Holy Ghost*, the older name for the Holy Spirit.

Religions may elaborate this picture, telling a story about where the spirit comes from (if it's separate from the body, either it had to enter the body or be created there between conception and birth) and what happens to it after death:

- it's lost

- it stays around as a sad little incorporeal thing— the Greek 'shades'

- it is transferred to a new body (reincarnation)

- it hangs around till God creates a new body in a new perfect world (the Christian Resurrection)

- it moves on to another plane, with or without a new body to match; some spirits may hang around our world to see to unfinished business

- it's reabsorbed into the Universal Soul (the ultimate goal in Buddhism)

- aliens capture it just before death, keeping it in an enormous library, or perhaps giving it a virtual world to roam in

Once you have the idea of the spirit, it's easy to imagine purely spiritual beings like angels, creatures who either have no body or can temporarily manufacture one when they must interact with the physical world.

Medieval Christians actually distinguished three levels of immaterial soul:

- the Vegetative, which as its name implies is shared with plants; its powers include nutrition, growth, and propagation

- the Sensitive, which is shared with animals; these add the senses and the power of movement

- the Rational, which man alone among the animals has

A strict separation of body and soul— *dualism*— is no longer respectable in philosophy. It seems all too likely that our minds are only a very strange epiphenomenon of our brains. We can largely blame this on science, which has found most of life explainable without recourse to spirits or creators. It's well to remember sometimes that science can't yet explain everything about our minds. Its track record is good; on the other hand, the feeling that science already explains 99% of phenomena and the rest will turn out to be trivial was maintained by Victorian physicists and turned out to be quite wrong. That last 1% always proves larger than it looks.

As a corollary, cultures without modern science are less likely to have materialistic or monistic philosophies. Philosophy alone can't convincingly explain why a corpse is different from a living animal.

Ethics

One of the major purposes of a belief system is to provide a moral framework... especially for those things that get in the way of our baser desires.

We often evaluate belief systems morally... but that only means that we judge them according to *our* belief system. If we find earlier systems cruel, racist, sexist, authoritarian, and superstitious, that's because they conflict with our own values. From their own point of view, we'd seem to be arrogant, libertine, appallingly materialistic, full of disrespect and blasphemy.

If you want to outline a moral system, the most convincing method is probably to give your own. You don't have to feign anything, and your invented sages can speak with your own passion. But obviously you can make them disagree with you too— even explore a set of positions you abhor.

Marvin Harris makes a provocative point about **universal ethical religions**, such as Christianity, Confucianism, and Buddhism: all appeared and flourished in empires, and made them function more smoothly. Spiritualizing poverty— e.g. Buddhism "convert[ing] the de facto vegetarianism of the semi-starved peasants into a spiritual blessing" as Harris puts it— reduced demands to actually improve living standards. At the same time, a call for compassion and mercy towards the weak would to some extent reduce their grievances and sense of oppression.

Don't just list rules; think about how they **conflict**. The ordering of rules can have a large impact on the system. George Lakoff (in *Moral Politics*) has analyzed the disagreements between liberals and conservatives as due in part to a different ordering of the virtues of *compassion* and *obedience to authority*.

How much are your rules actually **followed**? Which rules are insisted on but widely violated? Which ones are winked at?

Let's look at some examples.

Confucian morality

Confucian morality can be organized by three key concepts:

- *Rén*, compassion or humaneness. It was specially concerned with person-to-person relationships, especially father to son, elder to younger brother, husband to wife, elder to junior, and ruler to subject. The junior partner is expected to be respectful and loyal; the senior to be kind and benevolent.

- *Lǐ*, ritual or social norms. A Ministry of Rites was one of the six ministries of imperial China, in charge of state ceremonies, but the word also applied to everyday behavior. The basic idea was that training the body to do things correctly would also train the mind.

- *Yì*, righteousness or correct action. Confucius recognized that this might conflict with *rén*; he gives the example of a man who reported his thieving father to the authorities— correct according to *yì*, but a violation of *rén*.

Endajué

In Endajué, a religion of Almea, the vices are organized into opposing pairs:

- theft (*gonaudo*) vs. avarice (*dusrosmeludo*)
- perversion (*payjuacudo*) vs. puritanism (*xezidaudo*)
- aggression (*xwemeludo*) vs. cowardice (*dzismelic*)
- tyranny (*jusudo*) vs. lawlessness (*kuvetudo*)
- servility (*edemudo*) vs. disrespect (*xaušmelačudo*)
- selfishness (*dzuxešudo*) vs. conformity (*dzurodudo*)
- foolishness (*bodusaudo*) vs. cynicism (*ezešindudo*)

Righteousness consists of navigating a path between the errors on either side— a more sophisticated attitude than creating binary oppositions.

Jippirasti

In another Almean religion, Jippirasti, the overriding concept is uncleanliness, *istuja*, which is prototypically physical dirt, but also includes spiritual or moral dirt. The prophet Babur provided 35 categories of *istuja*:

- Blood
- Excrement
- *Huj*: phlegm, snot, vomit, discharges from disease, etc.
- Contact with a corpse, including its clothes; eating one, of course, was right out
- Sleeping in a room where animals are kept
- Eating the intestines, bones, or feet of animals
- Eating insects, shellfish, frogs, or animals which eat carrion (e.g. crows, coyotes)
- Killing an animal or a human "slowly enough to cause pain" (the killing blow or stroke must be quick and smooth)
- Malformed animals or children (e.g. multiple limbs, hermaphrodites)
- Indecent language
- Rudeness
- Ingratitude
- Attending a pagan ceremony, or entering a pagan temple
- Eating food sacrificed to pagan gods
- Magic
- Tattoos, earrings, body paint, and other bodily modification (abominable because the Munkhâshi favored these)
- Betraying a comrade, or running away in battle
- Dropping one's weapon
- Fighting with a *fsava* member
- Theft
- Disinheriting one's sister
- Drunkenness
- Rape (literally *igejruda,* sex with a woman outside her bed, thus, uninvited)
- Sex with children (defined as under 12) or animals

- Sex with more than one woman at once
- Sex with a woman in one's own *fsava* (clan)
- Sex between men, except during war, or as part of an expiation
- Sex with a pagan
- Mixed-sex nudity, except in the course of licit sex
- Bigamy
- Gossip
- Causing division in the *tej* (the Jippirasti community)
- Violating a fast
- Blasphemy
- The entire period of expiation (*igosota*)— that is, a person undertaking an *igosota* is unclean

Jippirasti was developed among nomads, and therefore says little about the sins of urban and agricultural peoples. When it conquered such people, theologians adapted the 35 categories to cover new offenses; e.g. tax evasion fell under 'causing division'; commercial fraud under 'rudeness'. There was also trouble with strictures which were easy to follow on the steppe but less so in the city (e.g. keeping animals outside, avoiding shellfish).

Supernatural beings

Most religions come with a roster of supernatural beings. These can be classified by accessibility.

- **Remote** father figures. In some religions the creator is so remote or so lofty that he's effectively gone. People may treat God or the gods like kings— unlikely to be interested in their problems.

- **Benign** helpers. These are your go-to guys for requests, because they've got time for you. In traditional Catholicism this role was fulfilled by the saints. The Evangelical God is like a friendly CEO with an open-door policy.

  People can get very familiar with these— they can be yelled at or cajoled; idols can be punished for not coming through.

- **Mercurial** powers. These are beings with their own agenda, like satyrs or the Fae. If you run into them, the results are unpredictable but rarely are simply good.

- **Antagonists**. These are hostile to humanity and to the gods. At the same time there's a tradition of magicians being able to control them.

  Writers who don't believe in traditional devils and monsters tend to move them into the previous category, and tone down the gods as well. Thus numinous and alarming magical beings become cute little fairies; monstrous vampires become troubled romantics; brutal and irredeemable orcs become gruff tough guys.

Several writers have played with the idea that belief *creates* gods— that strong belief systems create powerful deities, and as worshippers disappear, the gods wane as well. I find the idea rather annoying, partly because it seems to both deny and accept the gods (the gods are real, but somehow not real in the traditional way), partly because it trivializes them— Yemaya no longer controls the sea, she's merely a sort of supernatural maritime MP for Yorubas. But the idea has been done very well by Neil Gaiman in *American Gods*.

On the other hand, I rather like the idea used by Georges Pichard and Jacques Lob in their version of *Ulysses*, that the Greek gods were extraterrestrials whose wonders were all advanced technology— e.g. when Aeolus gives Odysseus the North Wind to propel his ship, it's actually a powerful jet engine. It adds a nice sense of irony to the old story. Roger Zelazny's *Lord of Light* uses a similar idea based on Hinduism.

The Greek and Roman gods had strict portfolios— e.g. Venus/Aphrodite was the goddess of love. But gods can be characterized in other ways: types of animals, the elements, stages of life, planets. Or perhaps they simply have different personalities, and you worship the most compatible one.

Practice

What do people *do* following your belief system? Here's some possibilities:

- **Worship services**. These are the quintessential activities of Christian churches, but not all religions get their believers regularly into a room.

- **Sacrifice**. These may be public events; but descriptions of ancient religions (including ancient Judaism) indicate these might be individual too, or provided as a service by priests.

- **Prophecy**. This was a major function of the oracles of Greece, and the prophets of Israel.

- **Healing**. One of the most useful powers of the gods.

- **Festivals**. These are more freewheeling than a worship service. They may be organized around a meal, or games, or a performance, or a procession; the mood may be festive or repentant or erotic.

- Ceremonies marking **life transitions**: birth, puberty, marriage, death. In Caðinorian paganism I posited that the major celebration was of *second* births... you didn't want to draw unneeded supernatural attention to your first child.

- **Discussion**. People from the Greek philosophers to Jewish rabbis to Chinese scholars to Quakers like to meet together to talk or argue about their beliefs.

- Individual **prayer**— personal communion with one's god, whether for worship, thanksgiving, confession, or supplication.

- Rituals of **cleanliness**. Some religions seem obsessive about cleanliness— literally. Robert Sapolsky suggests that such rituals may have started when some hand-washing obsessive, normally ignored by the tribe, was suddenly seen to be proved right by some disaster.

- Spiritual **disciplines**: special practices to train the body or the mind— anything from exercise to martial arts to pilgrimages to meditation to self-mortification.

- **Education** is often a religious duty— after all, the beliefs and practices must be transmitted to the young, and you might as well teach them other useful things while they're at your mercy.

- **Renunciation**. The easiest way to distinguish yourself from the greedy masses is to give up something. This can range from minor inconveniences to a simple but comfortable life (à la Ben Franklin) to a life of poverty.

- **Evangelism**, which is characteristic of universalistic religions, such as Christianity, Islam, and Buddhism. Traditional religions generally don't see the need.

Priests and monks

Don't assume that all these functions are performed by the priests. Families often have built-in religious roles, so rites can be performed at home. Kings may have religious powers separate from those of the official clerics. Other functions might be performed by isolated, self-selected hermits or eccentrics.

Even if the larger nation follows your religion, it can be useful to retire to a small community dedicated to it. These often begin with a particular holy person and their followers, and can grow into powerful and rich institutions.

Religions may or may not be organized above the level of a single holy place... indeed, Christianity is unusual in striving to keep its clerics and doctrines under central control. Even Islam has no such hierarchical organization.

In perhaps all civilizations, holy people inspire gifts from the rich and powerful— which can lead to temples or monasteries becoming wealthy businesses and landowners. This may in turn tempt the avarice of kings.

Scriptures

A religion in a civilized country will generate an enormous and growing body of literature. At some point it becomes useful to distinguish one or more works as canonical. These may be the works of founder(s), or those works considered earliest and most authentic.

Someone will disagree; indeed, the need for a canon pretty much implies disputation. The Christian canon marked the victory of one faction of the early church, and the rejection of the other factions' literature. The Protestants rejected a large chunk of the Catholic Old Testament.

Zhū Xī (d. 1200) codified the Confucian canon (choosing four books and deemphasizing the *Book of Changes*) and wrote extensive commentaries; in 1317 both became the basis for the imperial examination system and thus for scholarship and government in China.

A new religion may accept all or part of an existing canon and add new works, as for instance Mormonism does by adding the Book of Mormon to the Christian Bible.

Ancient enough commentaries or other literature may become important enough to be 'near-scripture'; e.g. the Talmud in Judaism and the Hadith in Islam.

The physical form of scriptures may receive special veneration, and the very language may become holy, and believers of other lands expected to learn it to properly study them.

Future belief systems

Future religions might of course resemble past ones. But let's look at some of the ways they might not.

- From the French Revolution on, we find mass movements: political ideologies with doctrines and foundational works, proselytism, zeal, and persecutions. Eric Hoffer's *The True Believer* is an excellent survey. These have their downsides— there's that little matter of World War II— but they're undeniably modern, and are likely to be with us for a long time.

- The least convincing s.f. religions are those attached to mundane things: atoms, rockets, spaceways. Marvelous as they are, we don't worship our refrigerators. But spiritual feeling can attach to things out of the ordinary, e.g. the recent fad for crystals.

- There are always unexplained things in life; and probably because our brains developed to understand social interaction, we assign these to actors. It used to be ghosts or fae; now it's aliens. When aliens are a matter of everyday life it will be something else— post-singularity essences?

- Religions affect culture, but also broadly reflect it. God in many ways resembles a king; the Chinese pictured a Celestial Bureaucracy. The individualism of Western culture gives us religious movements that emphasize personal development.

  Look at the overall nature of your culture. A new colony on a garden world might gravitate toward a freewheeling individualism; a tiny space habitat might need strict disciplines to preserve its fragile ecosphere. But there's likely to be a lag, with interesting consequences during a time of transition— e.g. the garden world is settled from the space habitat.

- Westerners have seen so many well-meaning systems lead to catastrophe that an extreme distrust for authority becomes compelling. Perhaps this becomes the prevailing ethos: a punk rock culture. I'd imagine its people quick to resist impositions and ready to violence, but hard to organize.

- Religious communities sometimes withdraw from the world. Space travel might let them do so permanently: move to an asteroid or a new colony and build a society in complete conformance to their beliefs.

- From the beginning (e.g. Wells's Eloi; E.M. Forster's "The Machine Stops") s.f. writers have worried about humans having it too good. Like Calvin's dad, they believe that adversity builds character. This may be so; but generally adversity just creates misery. If we have a deficit of character, should we bring back the Black Death or slavery?

  I expect it's a moot point, though; if we eliminate one evil, like slavery, we invent a new one, like totalitarianism. If your fictional world is getting too soft, throw a crisis at it.

Controversies

Your religion isn't done till your people can argue about it. Not even the strictest religion can force agreement on everything; and it gives a much better idea of what people actually talk about.

Here's some ideas to get you started:

- **Popular vs. scholarly** religion. The people are likely to understand things differently from the philosophers. They're less interested in fine theology and more likely to take things literally. They may be more or less lax than the clerics. They may keenly resent lapses in the clergy.

- Attitudes toward **authority**. A religion is likely to have a complicated relationship with rulers. It might have been persecuted once; the state's aims are likely to conflict with religion at some point. Clerics may expect the king to act as a humble worshipper— a view the kings will ultimately resist. The Sunni-Shi'a division in Islam was originally a dynastic dispute; the fact that the Shi'ites lost has colored their attitude toward authority ever since.

- **Church vs. state**. There's no conflict if the religion is state-controlled or vice versa, and not much more if the religion isn't organized. If church and state have separate, powerful leaders, there will be a fight for authority, complicated by mutual dependence. The situation may dramatically change if one side is removed (the church fragments, the empire collapses).

- **Religion vs. science**— a conflict which can really only start when science starts questioning key dogmas. And then it will probably go through stages of wariness, furious reaction, rear-guard fundamentalism, and acceptance.

- **Fundamentalism** is not the original state of a religion; it's a reaction against a perception that people are watering down the faith in response to modern scholarship or cultural laxity. Factions may differ in what beliefs and especially what practices are considered fundamental.

- Attitudes toward **novelties**, technological or cultural. Can your prayer wheels be moved by electric motors— or magic? Is electricity subject to rules about fire? Are the novel foods of a new continent clean or unclean? Are new intoxicants allowed? What happens if the ecological reasons for a practice (p. 193) change? What happens to strictures on sex if an effective condom is invented?

- **Rivalries** with other religions. An older religion may strive to adopt the attractive characteristics of the new, as paganism acquired a trinity (the One, Mind, Soul) and an ethical cast under the influence of Christianity, or as Orthodox Christianity rejected icons once it competed with icon-less Islam. Confucianism and Daoism both adopted some features of Buddhism. Such changes can of course cause a counter-reaction, as the policy of iconoclasm did in the West.

- **Regions** may develop variant beliefs. This may be due to difficulties of travel and translation, as in the divergence between Indian and Chinese Buddhism; or to the popularity of a local leader— e.g. Arius in the 4C. A region may seize upon a religious difference to justify a move toward independence.

- Pick a group **condemned** by the orthodox— anything from pagan minorities to merchants to wizards to women. Give them some quill pens and parchment and see what their reply is. Do they eventually overcome the condemnations, or at least moderate their tone?

A **cult** is a dissenting faction large enough to attract persecution. Excessive behavior— free love, nudity, raucous celebrations— may be enough to invite repression, but there's likely to be some theoretical challenge to orthodoxy, even if it's as simple as defying the existing authorities.

Magic

What's a fantasy world without magic? A relief, if you ask me. But fine, let's put some magic in.

Techno or spiritual?

In older fantasy, magic is a dread discipline, pursued by creepy old men in symbol-bedecked robes and overgrown beards, and wild women with wilder hair. They're solitary and distrusted— likely as not they cavort with evil spirits and do their bidding— and they richly return the disdain of the masses.

Gandalf has the shadiness and the facial foliage, but he's on the side of Good. But magic in *LOTR* is still a spiritual force, not a type of technology. We never really learn what Gandalf can or can't do. He sometimes does some spectacular magic, but for most problems, from trolls immobilizing all his friends to opening a locked dwarven gate, he relies only on mundane cleverness.

In fact Gandalf is a *maia*, more or less an angel, sent to oppose Sauron not by the direct use of supernatural force, but by stirring up men and elves. His reticence to use great magic thus has a spiritual point— opposing evil is something men are supposed to do, not something greater powers will do for them.

It can be very effective in stories to have magic be limited, and used more by personal whim or urgent necessity than rational calculation. If you're after the sense of wonder, it can be fatal to explain too much. Neil Gaiman is very good at getting this right; e.g. *Neverwhere* is all the better for not explaining its magical powers.

On Almea, magicians are those who can speak with Powers, supernatural beings— who however have no interest in doing menial tasks for human societies. Rather, they view the wizards as amusing pets, or as useful servants in otherworldly schemes of their own; they are likely to drag the wizard into their own world permanently sooner or later. But a wizard of strong character and diplomatic

218

nature can get the Powers to favor them with abilities of use in the physical world.

Many writers prefer to take a more s.f. approach, and treat magic as a form of technology. J.K. Rowling's *Harry Potter* books are the best known example: magic is something you learn in school, by hard study and constant practice; you can use it grandiosely and routinely to light your halls, send messages, fight your enemies, or just get around.

In games, on tabletop or computer, it's hard to deal with magic in any other way. If you're going to use it in combat, healing, and dungeon exploration, it needs to work every time and in set, specified ways.

There's some room in between these extremes. In sword & sorcery stories, for instance, like Fritz Leiber's, there may be isolated mighty warlocks of unpredictable power, but there are also guilds of mages who presumably offer their services as reliably as physicians or assassins.

Magic systems

If you want magic as technology, I'd urge a couple of things on you.

First, divide it into rationalized **subsystems**. These might be based on the elements (earth, air, fire, water), on function (e.g. *Oblivion*'s Alteration, Conjuration, Destruction, Illusion, Mysticism, and Restoration), on spiritual source (heaven, hell, chaos), whatever.

This isn't just because systematization is neat; it's to impose limits and predictability on the system. A system where you can do *anything you want, any time* is not going to be challenging— nor ultimately any fun. It's better to choose a narrower set of powers and explore those.

Second, **apply it consistently to society**. What will happen to a society if such skills are commonplace? It doesn't make much sense if magic is an everyday thing, and yet the rest of the world is strictly 13C England. I'd expect developments such as these:

- Light spells illuminate private and public spaces; as a corollary most people no longer go to bed at dusk.

- Healing spells take the place of medicine. (A corollary might be a lack of anatomical and medical knowledge: why learn how the body functions if the spell does all the work?)

- Magical fire supplies heat, powers steam engines, clears forests.

- If you can create food, no one needs to engage in agriculture. Assuming magic isn't a new thing, that means most people do something else: craftwork, scholarship, war.

- If you can create or even just purify water, many diseases and plagues will be cured. Expect a population explosion.

- Messaging spells allow instant communication across the realm— at least as much of a revolution as telephones and the Internet. Local lords, tiny workshops, and weak kings would give way to modern states and corporations.

- Telekinesis spells would replace water and land transport, enabling large-scale trade and industry.

- War, of course, would be waged by battlemages. In effect armies all have cheap, powerful ranged weapons; the results should be comparable to the gunpowder revolution.

- Spells affecting other people would transform interpersonal relationships and government. Why argue with people if you have a Persuade skill? You can toss away the rack if you have Truthtelling.

Some writers have embraced all or most of this, notably Rowling; also see Susannah Clarke's *Jonathan Strange and Mr Norrell* which finds fascinating uses for magic in 19C England. If you still want a medieval world, you'll need to limit magic in some way.

A couple ideas that don't do the trick:

- Limit magical abilities to 5% of the population. That's like saying that you'll limit the power of airplanes by having no more than 15 million pilots. Maybe magic is no longer widespread enough to replace agriculture, but how many mages do you need to run a telegraph agency or a transport firm?

- Mana is a nonrenewable resource that can be used up in a given area. Larry Niven got some good stories out of this, but he also depicted what would happen: people would exploit the mana fully till their magic-based civilization collapsed.

Here's some better ideas:

- Magicians can only be highly exceptional individuals— a handful in the entire kingdom, rather than a pair in every adventuring party. Of course, this idea pretty much makes all wizards into valuable state resources.

- Put a principled restriction on what magic can do. For Almea, I took an idea from Ariosto: magic is like having a legion of invisible, fast, yet stupid trolls. So you can only do what could be done with such a tool. You can build a mansion, search a town, or attack an army; but you can't create light, heal, or persuade.

  Or restrict magic to local and temporary effects. This would eliminate the most society-changing spells— long-range communications and transport— and prevent routine, mechanical use of magic: you can only light your street if the magician stands there flicking his wand every twenty seconds.

  Or let's say magic is a largely energetic phenomena, resisted by large masses. The easiest things to affect, perhaps, are minds and the air: illusions and light shows are easy, but powering a boat is a challenge, and knocking down a castle wall is quite impossible.

- Magic could have certain vulnerabilities. The classic one is that armor blocks magic, so the spellcaster is vulnerable to physical force. Perhaps magical communication and transport are fairly easily diverted to other destinations, making them unreliable or benefitting the wrong people. Maybe a skilled battlemage can send magical bolts back where they came from... another reason to hedge your bets and recruit traditional pikemen and cavalry.

- Magic has a cost to it. Perhaps to create the positive energy to cast a spell, negative energy is also released and causes damage to the spellcaster or to the environment. Perhaps it consumes ordinary resources or requires energy that could be devoted to other things. Perhaps it ultimately reduces the spellcaster's lifespan. Maybe it seeds the material world with instabilities so that overuse of magic degrades the environment.

- An extension of this: maybe magic is tied to demonic forces... perhaps one in a hundred magicians becomes a monster. The type and degree of danger would determine whether it's viewed as a noxious but necessary nuisance, like a tanning factory, or a criminal activity.

- A goth extension of "no pain no gain": the power to do magic comes from destruction. Sacrificing an animal or destroying a valuable object is enough for everyday spells. Harming a person— cutting off a finger, for instance— generates even more power, and the strongest spells are powered by murder.

You have something of a meta-narrative excuse, of course, in that if there are *any* magicians in the society, your story can center on them. (The James Bond stories don't require that every Englishman be a spy.) But it's the other details in your story or world that really show how widely magic is used. If you have magicians' guilds, magic shops, healers in every temple, and magic items in every hidden chest, then you have a magic-ridden world.

Magic, herblore, ancestors

Wizardry need not be the only type of magic around. A premodern society might have a number of disciplines and people that aren't even viewed as one thing:

- **Herblore**— the use of plants with special properties, something everyone might know something about, with more accomplished practitioners to be found in every village. It's also easy to imagine a few canny old women and men who've pieced together a few useful cantrips— things that ease life a little without greatly changing it.

  Some very alarming mixtures were used as cosmetics. Táng manuals suggest bats' brains to remove blackheads and lead oxides to whiten the skin, and powdered coral blown into the nose to stop nosebleeds. (But then, you may not want to learn too much about the ingredients of present-day personal hygiene products. It's not all flowers.)

- **Alchemy** in our world was just the early form of chemistry; ideas like the transmutation of elements followed the best scientific theories of the time. Things like distillation and the ability to dissolve gold made it seem like they were on the right track, and playing around with liquid mercury was always a good party trick. No wonder many fantasy worlds allow alchemy to produce all sorts of wonders. (In video games, there's something very satisfying about being able to make use of bits of defeated enemies— imp gall, troll fat.)

- **Spiritual arts**— martial artists, hermits, mendicant orders, wandering tinkerers. In our world these have special powers only in that they have exceptional discipline, or knowledge beyond the usual. But in your milieu perhaps they attain more spectacular powers. A *wuxia* world where adepts dash between arrows, defeat armored opponents with bare hands, and make hundred-foot leaps, is a hell of a lot of fun.

  (Tinkerers? For a memorable portrait of such, see Melquíades the Gypsy in Gabriel García Márquez's *One Hundred Years of Solitude*. If a community is isolated enough, someone coming from outside showing off the latest mechanical marvels may seem to have occult powers.)

- Perhaps the **dead** don't wander too far from the world, at least at first. They can be given some interesting abilities through not being tied to a body: movement through solid objects, invisibility if they choose, direct effects on people's minds (e.g. fear).

See also...

Cosmology (p. 203), magic in warfare (p. 272); and of course almost any aspect of your world— creatures, sustenance, economics, travel, government— can include fantastic and magical elements.

Technology

Wait, what? If you're writing s.f., your culture already includes all past technology, and if you're writing fantasy, you hate technology anyway, right? There's still reason to work out the tech.

First, **consistency**. Even if you're just doing one culture, it should have a believable and coherent level of technology. It doesn't make a lot of sense to add steam engines to ancient Rome (which couldn't produce cheap strong steel), or throw a printing press into a feudal society with no social effects.

Second, **accuracy**. This is especially so in military matters, such that I've devoted a whole chapter to war (p. 243). But it comes up in other areas too. A Roman atmosphere is impaired by spinning wheels, spectacles, and windmills; a medieval atmosphere by ironclads, pendulum clocks, and gas lighting.

If you want a **complete** world like Almea, it shouldn't be static. Many a conworld doesn't ever seem to change... even Middle Earth doesn't seem to have any technological development over the millennia, and don't get me started on *Star Wars*.

Once you look at technology, it's evident that human beings are constantly modifying their culture and environment. In dark times maybe there's only one major advance per century, but things aren't stagnant. Medieval Europe was changing constantly and spectacularly— 1400 was very different from 1100, which was very different from 800. Technological change didn't begin in the Renaissance.

Finally, even in **s.f.** you're likely to need some primitive cultures— for aliens, or new colonies, or after the apocalypse. For that matter, the technology of the future should keep changing; indeed, there should be a few technological revolutions that transform society.

A timeline

Here's a fairly broad list of technologies and discoveries, sorted by the date they emerged on Earth.

I realize it may look intimidating, but it's intended to be detailed enough for in-depth conworlding. The most significant entries are bolded. There's also an **interactive** version of this chart on the web resources page which may be more approachable.

Round numbers for **dates** are intended to signify uncertainty, and in the early period should be taken as a lower bound; e.g. -7000 indicates the entire 8th millennium B.C.

Archeology can be competitive, and claims for primacy may be provisional or disputed. I've preferred to cite fairly sure dates; this may merely mean that at the cited date the technique was common enough to be preserved in the archeological record.

Researching just about any bit of technology, it's striking the **number of steps** involved in any advance. Lists like this one can give the impression that some inventor of genius, known or unknown, created a revolution. Sometimes they did, but more often there was a dizzying array of early suggestions and minor improvements. I've tried to include some of these below, but for each entry, imagine half a dozen more not listed.

Many inventions or discoveries are made **simultaneously by different people**; classic examples include calculus and the electric light. This is a corollary of the previous point— a number of people are working at the state of the art, and several will be poised to advance it.

-2.5M	Stone tools, used mainly in scavenging	East Africa
-1.8M	Hunting	East Africa
-400K	**Fire**	Africa
-200K	**Language**	East Africa
-200K	Spears tipped with stone points	Old World
-90K	Burial with evident **ritual** meaning	Fertile Crescent
-50K	Clearly **differentiated tools**: points, engravers, knives, drills, piercers, needles	Africa
-50K	Dogs domesticated (from wolves)	Old World

-40K	Australia settled	Australia
-33K	Sculpted figurines	Europe
-30K	Cave paintings	Europe
-25K	Fired pottery figures	Central Europe
-15K	Humans reach the Americas	North America
-10K	Pottery vessels	China
-9000	**Agriculture**	Fertile Crescent
-9000	Copper (which appears naturally as a pure metal) mined	Fertile Crescent
-8000	**Bow and arrow**	Europe
-8000	Clay tokens (precursor to writing and accounting)	Fertile Crescent
-8000	Sheep, goats **domesticated**	Fertile Crescent
-8000	Pig domesticated	Mideast & China
-7000	Maize domesticated	Mexico
-7000	Warp-weighted frame loom	Anatolia
-6000	Cattle domesticated	Fertile Crescent
-6000	Rice domesticated	Yangtze valley
-5500	Irrigation	Mesopotamia
-5500	Copper smelting (refining from compounds)	Anatolia
-5000	Chicken domesticated	East Asia
-5000	Plow	Mesopotamia
-5000	Lacquer	China
-5000	Cotton domesticated	Indus valley
-4000	Barrel vault (like a long extended arch)	Sumer
-4000	Potter's wheel	Mesopotamia
-4000	**Urbanization** (~1000 residents)	Mesopotamia
-4000	**Wine**	Near East
-4000	Donkey domesticated	Egypt
-4000	Water buffalo domesticated	China
-3500	Beer	Iran
-3500	**Horse** domesticated	Central Asia
-3500	Alpaca domesticated	Andes
-3300	Gypsum (used as plaster)	Egypt
-3200	**Writing** (logographic)	Sumer
-3000	**Kingdom**	Egypt
-3000	Arsenic **bronze** (copper alloyed with arsenic, making it stronger)	Anatolia
-3000	Crude distillation used for perfumes	Middle East

-3000	Silk	China
-3000	**Wheeled** vehicles	Near East/Europe
-2800	City-states (population reaches 5000)	Sumer
-2800	Soap	Babylonia
-2600	Large-scale warfare between cities	Sumer
-2550	First structure over 100 m (a pyramid)	Egypt
-2500	Seagoing ship	Egypt
-2500	Tin bronze (copper alloyed with tin— stronger, easier to use, and safer than arsenic)	Mesopotamia
-2500	Glass	Middle East
-2500	Iron smelting; produces wrought iron	Anatolia
-2500	Lime	Mesopotamia
-2500	Parchment (prepared animal skins)	Egypt
-2500	Camel domesticated	Central Asia
-2400	Rudder (adapted from a steering oar)	Egypt
-2400	Scaling ladder (for attacking walled cities)	Middle East
-2400	Beekeeping	Egypt
-2250	First **empire**	Akkadia
-2000	Brass (alloy of copper and zinc)	Middle East
-2000	Papyrus (made from cut strips of the plant's pith)	Egypt
-2000	Quadratic equations	Mesopotamia
-2000	Written **legal code**	Sumer
-2000	Grafting of fruit trees	China
-1900	"Pythagorean" theorem	Mesopotamia
-1900	Battering ram	Egypt
-1800	Banks (referred to in Hammurabi's laws)	Mesopotamia
-1700	**Consonantal alphabet** (drastically reduces symbol set needed for writing)	Palestine
-1700	Syllabary	Crete
-1600	Chariot	Aryans
-1600	Water clock	Middle East
-1500	Fresco painting	Crete
-1500	Glazing applied to pottery	Middle East
-1500	Compound bow (made of composite materials, much more powerful than simple bow)	Middle East

-1300	Bow lathe (turned with a rope; a second worker cuts the wood)	Egypt
-1000	Carburization (heating iron with charcoal, which adds carbon, then quenching in water, making the outer layer into steel, allowing lasting **iron weaponry**)	Middle East
-1000	Tea	China
-900	Cities reach 10,000 population	Assyria
-800	Letters of credit	China
-750	Alphabet	Greece
-700	**Cavalry** (effective fighting from horseback)	Eurasian steppe
-700	Ram (on ships)	Phoenicia
-600	Coins; **market economy**	Anatolia
-510	Senatorial rule (without kings)	Rome, Athens
-500	Abacus	Egypt
-500	Cast iron	China
-500	Stirrup	India
-450	Atomism	Greece
-450	Irrational numbers	Greece
-475	Crossbow (bow with mechanical assistance to pull string)	Greece
-400	Torsion-powered catapult	Greece
-385	Academy	Greece
-300	Traction trebuchet (sling pulled by men)	China
-300	Zero (used only between symbols)	Babylonia
-250	Water mills (with waterwheel and gears)	Greece
-200	Cam (translates between rotary and linear motion)	Greece
-200	**Moldboard plow** (lifts and turns a strip of soil— faster, and moves more earth)	China
-200	Towns reach 100,000 size	Hellenic Egypt
-150	Astrolabe	Greece
-125	Precession of the equinoxes	Greece
-100	Lateen rigging	Hellenic Egypt
-100	**Paper** (first used for packing)	China
-100	Porcelain (pottery fired hot enough to vitrify)	China
1	Glassblowing	Middle East

1	Magnetic **compass**	China
10	Towns reach 250,000 size	Rome
50	Austronesians reach Polynesia	Polynesia
100	Clear glass	Hellenic Egypt
100	Groin vault (intersecting barrel vaults; allows covering a wide span)	Rome
100	Improved distillation apparatus	Egypt
100	Treadwheel crane	Rome
100	Wheelbarrow	China
200	Crucible steel	India
400	Austronesians reach Madagascar	Madagascar
400	Padded horse collar (allowing full strength of the horse)	China
400	Pure alcohol distilled from wine	China
500	Chess	India
500	Toilet paper	China
600	**Windmill**	Persia
600	Civil service examinations	China
700	Woodblock printing of text	China
800	**Positional** decimal numbering system	India
800	Pure distillation	Islamic empire
800	**Three-field agriculture**	Europe
820	Algebra systematized (many specific methods date back far earlier)	Persia
900	Coke (purified coal used as fuel)	China
1000	Paper money	China
1000	Silkscreen printing	China
1040	Moveable type	China
1050	**Gunpowder**	China
1088	University	Italy
1100	Counterweight trebuchet	Byzantium
1100	Rib vaulting	Europe
1200	Nitric acid, sulfuric acid, hydrochloric acid isolated	Europe
1200	Pole lathe loom (foot pedal allows one-person use)	Europe
1200	**Spinning wheel**	China, Iraq
1200	Wine press	Europe
1250	Joint stock company	France
1270	Eyeglasses	Europe

1290	**Cannon**	China
1300	Hourglass	Europe
1300	Weight-based clock	Europe
1350	Double-entry bookkeeping	Italy
1350	Arquebus (early rifle)	China
1375	Granular gunpowder (more efficient and reliable)	Europe
1400	Coffee roasting and brewing	Arabia
1400	Full plate armor	Europe
1400	Perspective	Italy
1400	Intercontinental exploration	China, Portugal
1420	Patents	Italy
1430	Intaglio printing	Germany
1440	**Printing press**	Germany
1490	Cast cannon— far stronger than earlier forms, able to fire iron balls, and above all mobile	France
1492	**Transatlantic colony**	Spain
1530	Footpedal for spinning wheel	Germany
1543	Heliocentrism mathematically demonstrated	Poland
1550	Spring-powered watch	Germany
1590	Microscope	Netherlands
1600	Constancy of pendulum	Italy
1602	Stock exchange	Netherlands
1605	Printed newspaper	Germany
1609	Elliptical orbits of planets	Germany
1610	Telescope	Netherlands
1610	Jupiter's moons, phases of Venus observed	Italy
1614	Logarithms	Britain
1620	Slide rule	Britain
1650	Air pump	Germany
1654	Pendulum clock	Netherlands
1654	Probability	France
1660	Royal Society	Britain
1663	Static electricity generator	Germany
1671	Hydrogen	Britain
1676	**Microorganisms**	Netherlands
1680	Ring bayonet	Europe

1682	Boiler safety valve	France
1684	Calculus	Britain, Germany
1687	Theory of **gravity**; laws of motion	Britain
1700	Analysis of prisms and the spectrum	Britain
1712	**Steam engine**	Britain
1730	Octant	Britain
1733	Flying shuttle	Britain
1735	Linnaean taxonomy	Sweden
1740	Electric wire	France
1744	Leyden jar (capacitor jar; stores static electricity)	Netherlands, Germany
1749	Lightning rod	British N. America
1755	Carbon dioxide	Britain
1762	Marine chronometer	Britain
1764	Spinning jenny (multiple spindle machine)	Britain
1767	Lightning shown to be electric	British N. America
1772	Nitrogen	Britain
1772	Oxygen	Sweden
1775	Separate condenser for steam engine	Britain
1781	Iron bridge	Britain
1781	Uranus discovered	Britain
1783	Hot air balloon	France
1785	Non-blackening oil lamp	USA
1785	Power loom	Britain
1789	Conservation of mass	France
1790	**Chemical element theory**	France
1790	Water understood to be hydrogen + oxygen	France
1792	Gas lighting	Britain
1793	Cotton gin	USA
1795	Dinosaur bones understood as reptilian	France
1796	**Smallpox vaccine**	Britain
1800	Card-controlled loom	France
1800	Electric battery	Italy
1800	Towns reach 1,000,000 size	Britain
1801	Ceres discovered	Italy
1804	Canning	France
1807	Steamboat	USA

1808	Self-loading cartridge, allowing practical breech-loading rifles	France
1822	**Photography**	France
1825	**Railroad**	Britain
1830	Old earth theory in geology	Britain
1837	**Telegraph**	USA
1843	Iron-hulled ships	Britain
1852	Elevator	USA
1855	**Mass industrial steel** production	Britain
1858	Theory of **evolution**	Britain
1859	Spectroscope	Germany
1861	Reconstruction of Proto-Indo-European	Germany
1862	Machine gun	USA
1865	Dominant and recessive genes	Austria
1866	Transatlantic cable	USA
1867	Typewriter	USA
1869	Periodic table	Russia
1873	Laws of electromagnetism	Britain
1876	**Refrigerator**	Germany
1876	Telephone	USA
1877	Phonograph	USA
1879	**Electric light**	USA, England
1887	Mechanical adding machine	USA
1888	Radio waves	Germany
1895	**Automobile**	Germany, USA
1895	Motion picture	France
1895	X-rays	Germany
1897	Electron observed	Germany
1902	Air conditioning	USA
1903	**Airplane**	USA
1905	Relativity	Germany
1909	Plastic	USA
1910	**Antibiotics**	Germany
1911	Proton	Britain
1912	Continental drift	Germany
1916	Tank	Britain
1925	Quantum mechanics	Germany
1929	Expanding universe	USA
1929	Instrumented rocket	USA
1930	Jet engine	Britain

1931	Electron microscope	Germany
1931	Incompleteness theorem (an epistemological shocker)	Germany
1931	Radio astronomy	USA
1932	Neutron	Britain
1939	**Digital computer**	USA
1939	Helicopter	USA
1945	Atomic bomb	USA
1947	Holography	Britain
1948	Big Bang theory	USA
1948	Programmable computer	Britain
1948	Transistor	USA
1953	DNA decoded	USA, Britain
1957	Laser	USA
1957	Satellite launched	USSR
1958	Nuclear power plant	USA
1959	Industrial robot	USA
1961	First **astronaut**	USSR
1962	Communications satellite	USA
1969	Landing on the moon	USA
1973	Space station	USA
1975	Personal computer	USA
1982	Compact disk	USA
1989	GPS	USA
1990	**World Wide Web**	Europe
1997	Quantum entanglement	Austria, Italy
1997	Sheep cloned	Britain
2000	Human genome sequenced	USA

How do I use this?

You can create a technological timeline for your conworld, as I did for Almea. If this sounds like work— and it is— skip to the next section, where I describe a simplified approach.

I included the region where each discovery was made; note the rough movement of the **most advanced region**: roughly, the Middle East, then China, then continental Europe, then Britain, then the USA. That underlines that you need at least an outline history (p. 100) so you know where and when to locate these pockets of innovation.

Civilizations can go **backwards**. Quite a few Roman technologies— mills, geared machinery, treadmill cranes, stone houses, standing armies, large cities, long-distance trade— were lost after the fall of the western empire, and were only slowly rediscovered.

Think about the geographical situation of your cultures, who their neighbors are, what resources they have. Some inventions depend on animals: the wheel and the moldboard plow could only be exploited using traction animals. The highly convoluted Greek coastline encouraged maritime exploration in a way that (say) the Nile didn't. Mining technology is likely to start in nations with mountains. The location of England, the Netherlands, and Portugal on the seacoast, obstructed from grand continental ambitions, must have helped produce a focus on exploration and trade. The Islamic caliphate was a natural crossroads, inheriting Greek knowledge and coming into contact with India and China.

Pure science is rarely a priority; scientific insights in premodern times are driven by practical concerns: surveying, navigation, time-keeping, ballistics, medicine. Adornment has been a surprising driver for progress in metallurgy, textiles, and long-distance trade.

The **order** of developments may be quite different even in terrestrial civilizations. China had paper, silk, porcelain, moldboard plows, the compass, and cast iron a millennium before Europe, while it lagged in other areas, such as navigation, glass-making, alphabetic writing, jurisprudence, and republican government. If you have several major civilizations you may need a timeline for each.

However, there's a natural order to certain discoveries. For instance:

- Gutenberg's **printing press** was an adaptation of the agricultural screw press; the use of moveable type required knowledge of metal casting; the idea of printing built on existing woodblock and intaglio printing; its commercial success depended on a literate population hungry for things to read.

- Progress in **metallurgy** depends on reaching higher and higher temperatures. Copper melts at 1100° C; the timing of the Bronze Age is tied to the fact that a pottery kiln reaches about this heat. (Smelting copper ores requires a lower temperature, 800° C. Even this is above the heat generated by an open wood fire.) Iron melts at over 1500° C, which requires more advanced methods— e.g. increasing the heat using a bellows, or adding carbon to lower the melting point.

- Metallurgy is also driven by the ease of purifying the metal. Gold and silver are unreactive, so they only have to be chipped away from their matrix. Most metals need to be refined from ores. Moreover some metals need to be alloyed together for strength— e.g. copper is too soft to be used for tools, and is alloyed with tin to form bronze, or with zinc to form brass. As many copper ores contain arsenic, smiths were subject to arsenic poisoning, which may explain the prevalence of lame smith-gods in many mythologies.

- Europeans began to build **mills** in large quantity around the 10C. These were great for large-scale machinery; but new advances in metalworking were needed before smaller machines such as the spinning jenny could be created. Clockmaking was one of the missing links.

- **Steam engines** at first only provided linear motion; this was suitable for creating pumps— their first major use was in pumping water out of mines. The key step in making them more generally useful was to deliver rotary motion, which allowed them to power mills, lathes, and railroads. Steam engines were only made efficient with the invention of the separate condenser, and safe with that of safety valves and steel boilers, all reasons not to make too much of the steam toys of 1C Alexandria.

Think about the social effects of any advance.

- The printing press allowed an enormous democratization of knowledge, much as the Internet has. The difference between a library of a dozen books, all chained to the shelf, and one of thousands is more than just quantity.

- Discoveries that disprove the reigning cosmology may have a profound disordering effect. In technical areas, this may simply remove roadblocks on the mind: Lavoisier's chemical theory destroyed the last remnants of the classical four elements; novas and comets showed that the heavens were not changeless; Jupiter's moons showed that the earth was not the center of all rotation in the solar system. But touch a sensitive enough spot and the whole edifice shudders; the theory of evolution is the obvious example.

- The industrial revolution in effect stole the clothing industry from women. Contrariwise, the traditional role of Native American men as warriors and shamans was destroyed, with immense social effect, by restricting Indians to reservations and discouraging Indian religion.

- Wine and beer may be more than a diversion. In large towns, getting unpolluted water becomes a problem, and the easiest solution is to drink alcoholic beverages instead. There's some evidence that cultures which have been urban for millennia have developed a larger tolerance for alcohol.

Technological epochs

You can skip the details of technology by focusing on a particular technological epoch— basically a package of technologies.

For more information you can read up on the particular cultures named, or look in the timeline to see what had been invented and what hadn't.

I give a few models for each; I assume you're smart enough to understand that fiction may or may not aim at historical accuracy.

Babylon, 1200 B.C.

Agriculture, the domestication of animals, and writing are already old technologies. The denser agricultural regions are ruled, and not with a light hand, by kings and occasionally empires. Economic enterprise is largely under the control of the state— there are no markets or coins, though there are private merchants and even banks. Towns reached about 7500 souls. Less populous areas are held by farmers and peasants organized into small tribes, sometimes precariously free, sometimes controlled by the nearest empire.

Priests were important figures, as religion was an important prop of the state.

Warriors are only lightly armored, and wield swords, spears, and bows. Horses could only be exploited in combat using chariots— even the nomads hadn't learned how to fight from horseback. Bronze was still widely used for weapons, but states that could afford it used wrought iron.

There were sophisticated pleasures: fine jewelry and metalwork, decorative pigments, perfume, incense, wine and beer. The educated were already advanced in astronomical observation and geometry, and some claimed to master mystical powers.

A few good **models**:

> The Old Testament: the Israelites were a marginal people in between the major powers of Egypt and Mesopotamia
>
> Homer, *The Iliad* and *The Odyssey*
>
> My own *In the Land of Babblers* is largely Bronze Age in technology
>
> Robert Howard's *Conan* stories have a pre-Roman feel to them

Rome, 1st century A.D.

After centuries of struggle, the bulk of the known world was united under one empire. The empire had till recently been a republic, and still contained a senate of important (and rich) men, often entrusted with governmental tasks. The empire was a patchwork of conquered states, each with their own language, religion, and laws; those outside it were considered no more than barbarians.

Urban life was thriving— the capital had more than 250,000 people, and many other cities had several tens of thousands. Urbanites enjoyed theaters and baths, a wealth of literature, arenas, philosophical academies, and their choice of temples. Trade was market-based and empire-wide, and individuals could become very rich; but there was no great barrier between the state and the private sector. Rich men would bestow public buildings on their cities, and take office— a path to further riches, as corruption was normal. Very large enterprises, from aqueducts to water mills, were imperial concerns.

The empire maintained a huge standing army; its pay was the major government expense. Soldiers wore banded metal armor, and were divided into infantry, cavalry, and artillery (ballistae as well as siege engineers).

Besides impressive buildings, road, and fortifications, the empire boasted fascinating novelties: blown glass, tiny machines powered by steam, alchemical apparatus.

A few good **models**:

> The New Testament
>
> Robert Graves's *I, Claudius*
>
> All those gladiator movies
>
> *A History of Private Life*, vol. 1

Táng China, A.D. 750

At this time China was the most advanced and prosperous civilization on the planet. Perhaps its most distinguishing feature was that its aristocracy depended not on blood, but on educational achievement: advancement in government was based on an elaborate nationwide examination system. This concentrated on the ancient classics, but there was a constant debate serving to apply old precepts to modern situations.

The classics defined the ancient religion of the people, but there was an openness to new and even foreign ideas; the best thinkers rarely declared for just one ideology, but reviewed all the possibilities and chose the best ideas from each. The monk Xuánzàng had recently returned from India with hundreds of Buddhist texts to enrich Chinese Buddhism.

Compared to our previous models, China was striking in its longetivity and homogeneity— no regions separated for long, and the system was able to absorb several foreign conquerors.

Warfare was principally infantry-based, befitting a huge sedentary agricultural population. The primary military threat was nomads in the northwestern steppe; these could often be bought off with tribute, titles, and princesses, or hired as mercenaries. The system was secure enough that in most of the country, large cities needed no walls.

There was a steady stream of important inventions: paper, porcelain, the compass, the padded horse collar, steel-making, woodblock printing. Silk had long been an enormously profitable export. Just past our period, the Sòng continued the tradition, inventing paper money, silkscreen printing, moveable type, and gunpowder.

A few good **models**:

> *Journey to the West*, a retelling of Xuánzàng's journey as fantasy
>
> *Wuxia* movies such as *Crouching Tiger, Hidden Dragon* are set in an idealized ancient China
>
> Video games: *Jade Empire*
>
> Luó Guànzhōng, *The Romance of the Three Kingdoms*
>
> *The Tale of Genji*, from Japan, often listed as the world's first novel

Medieval Europe, A.D. 1350.

We've all been down these cobbled streets, seen the knights in plate armor and the ladies in pointy hats. But fantasy isn't so much the West's nostalgia for its own past, as the descendent of the Renaissance and medieval epic— the medieval era's idealization of itself.

What did they leave out? The medieval industrial revolution, for one. Medieval society was as machine-oriented as we are computer-oriented. The Clairvaux abbey, for instance, was built to exploit water power; the water was used for milling wheat, sieving flour, fulling cloth, and tanning; pipes carried water to the kitchen and to the gardens, and cleaned out the drains. There was an explosion of mills: in the department of the Aube in France, there were 14 water mills in the 11C, 60 in the 12C, and over 200 in the 13C. The English *Domesday Book* records 5,624 water mills, one for about every 50 households.

The Romans had water mills, but nothing on this scale. But the Europeans also had windmills and tidal mills; agricultural productivity soared with the three-field system and the wheeled moldboard plow; horses could pull more with the padded collar; Europeans mined gold and silver in areas the Romans believed to have none. The medievals sometimes depicted God as an architect or engineer, measuring the universe with a compass.

I chose 1350 as being just before the gunpowder era— the first cannons (following Arab designs) were appearing in Europe; the first arquebus wouldn't appear in Europe for another century. The typical armor was chainmail, but through the century it developed in the direction of plate, to counter new two-handed axes and swords, thrusting swords, and the longbow. At this stage the powerhouse of an army was the heavily armored mounted knight— though this concept, like the knights, would be decimated at the battle of Crécy (1346).

In intellectual life, great universities had been founded—Bologna in 1088, Paris in 1150, Oxford in 1167. At Paris, Thomas Aquinas had recently systematized the study of theology, reconciling Christian teaching with the reason of Aristotle. The mineral acids had recently been isolated, revolutionizing alchemy. There were other novelties: the spinning wheel, the wine press, eyeglasses, the hourglass, weight-based clocks. New methods for building were developed, less dark and bulky than Roman architecture. The explosion of European power and knowledge at the Renaissance was only the culmination of economic and social forces that had been building throughout the medieval period.

A modern (especially a European) would probably be most struck by the centrality of God. Everyone believed, and no one saw a contradiction between scholarship and science— quite the reverse; Aquinas was canonized. Not that this meant priests and monks were treated with reverence; they were often seen as corrupt and venal.

A few good **models**:

> Geoffrey Chaucer, *The Canterbury Tales*
>
> Barbara Tuchman, *A Distant Mirror*
>
> Shakespeare is only a little later, and was often writing about earlier times anyway (though with ships, pistols, and the printing press his is already a different world)
>
> Tolkien's *The Lord of the Rings*— not strictly medieval, but as all the glorious empires were far in the past it feels more medieval than classical

C.S. Lewis's Narnia series

Comics: Jeff Smith's *Bone*, Hal Foster's *Prince Valiant*, François Bourgeon's *Les compagnons du crépuscule*, Rosinski & Van Hamme's *Thorgal*

The post-medieval epics: Ariosto's *Orlando Furioso*, Spenser's *The Faerie Queene*, Malory's *La mort d'Arthur*

Video games: *Oblivion, Skyrim, Dragon Age Origins, World of Warcraft*

The early steam era, A.D. 1800.

I personally find this era more fascinating than medieval times, and less overdone in fantasy. It was the dawn of the modern world, when its transformations were still largely potential.

The overall theme was the questioning of authority. The first dethroning was of Ptolemy; the earth-centered universe with its crystalline spheres, the outermost pleasantly scattered with stars, was replaced by the modern concept of space. Newton and Galileo had overthrown Aristotle's momentum-based physics; now Lavoisier had systematized chemistry, a new conception of dozens of elements replacing the ancient alchemical dogmas. Adam Smith's economics, like the new physics, worked without a central decider, without even any dependence on the nation-state. Biology had micro-organisms and the smallpox vaccine to think about. The printing press had revolutionized and democratized information.

Most scholars still accepted God, but the universe seemed more and more like a clockwork he had made and set in motion, not a series of miracles that required his constant intervention. Religious authority had fragmented, and the ensuing Catholic-Protestant wars led to the conviction that the state could not impose a belief on the people. (Not that religion was moribund; freed from the sleepiness of state control, fervent popular forms of religion were springing up— Methodism and Quakerism were originally full of supernatural zeal, like Pentecostalism today).

Kings also seemed less necessary than before. France and the British North American colonies had got rid of them; even England had experimented with being a Commonwealth. The sleepy Iberian empires in the Americas would soon be transformed by revolution.

And yet everyday life was not yet a rush of novelties. The industrial revolution was well underway, but few had seen the new steam-powered machines or worked in a factory. The most striking change from medieval times was in warfare: edged weapons had almost entirely disappeared in favor of muskets, pistols, and cannon.

Go a little further, of course, and you can play with steampunk. There's something delicious about the massive boilers and iron girders of Victorian engineering, perhaps festooned with Art Nouveau decoration, and it's even more fun to make them even larger, or float them from enormous airships.

A few **models**:

> Jane Austen's novels evoke the daily life of the period
>
> Charles Dickens's *A Tale of Two Cities*
>
> James Boswell's *Life of Johnson*
>
> C.S. Forester's Horatio Hornblower series, evocations of the sailing ship as far-flung agents of the British Empire, and an inspiration for *Star Trek*
>
> Tim Powers's *The Anubis Gates*
>
> My own conworld Almea
>
> Steampunk: Alan Moore and Kevin O'Neill's *The League of Extraordinary Gentlemen;* Hayao Miyazaki's *Nausicäa*

Modern times

There's no reason you can't set your fantasy in a time like the present, or develop your conworld to modern times and beyond.

A few good **models**:

> Most of Neil Gaiman, especially *Neverwhere* and *American Gods*
>
> J.K. Rowling's *Harry Potter* series
>
> H.P. Lovecraft's stories
>
> R.A. Lafferty's delightful short stories
>
> *Star Wars* is essentially near-future fantasy

War

Most fantasy, and much s.f. too, features war, or at least some deadly fighting. This is probably one of the biggest gaps between writers and the people they describe— few of us are at all expert at killing someone with a sword. So there's a lot to learn.

Most of this chapter is on historical warfare. I'll pretty much skip the modern era— you know how wars are conducted today anyhow, and detailed material is readily available. At the end, however, I'll consider magical and futuristic warfare.

The warrior

War is hell, but there is a temperament that is not displeased to enter its gates. In John Keegan's words:

> It is the admiration of other soldiers that satisfies him— if he can win it; most soldiers are satisfied merely by the company of others, by a shared contempt for a softer world, by the liberation from narrow materiality brought by the camp and the line of march, by the rough comforts of the bivouac, by competition in endurance, by the prospect of *le repos du guerrier* among their waiting womenfolk.

Our earliest ancestors were hunters, close to the animals they hunted, their senses highly trained, their bodies tough and fit, highly skilled in the use of weapons and in wilderness survival, and able to kill quickly when necessary— all qualities that must be cultivated in the soldier, increasingly setting him apart from the office workers around him.

As a character the warrior comes with that most attractive of narrative traits, paradox. Perhaps the best character in the Narnia series, one which survived the disappointing transition to the screen, is Reepicheep the warrior mouse. The combination of courtesy, politeness, and deadly skill remains its interest in the modern age, all the more so when most people no longer face war themselves.

War cultures

As important as the tools of war is the culture that surrounds it, as Keegan demonstrates in *A History of Warfare*. A war culture generally has limits that inhibit excessive violence, much as dominance fights between predators include a signal of submission (e.g. a dog baring his neck) that ends the fight and allows the beaten animal to escape.

Primitive

Tribes vary in warlikeness. One extreme is the hunter-gatherer **Bushmen**, who avoid conflict; one book about them is called *The Harmless People*. But they live in a highly marginal environment— the Kalahari desert— and may not be characteristic of early man.

Daniel Everett describes the **Pirahã** (Amazonian hunter-gatherers) as highly peaceful among themselves, as well as rather sexually egalitarian; at the same time they can be brutal with outsiders they perceive as encroaching on their land.

By contrast, the **Yanomamö**— garden agriculturalists and hunters of Venezuela— have been called "the fierce people"; males are encouraged to be violent, and horribly mistreat their women— beatings and disfigurements are common. Violence between men, however, is highly ritualized. One form is the chest-pounding duel. Two men with a quarrel take hallucinogens to foster aggression. One stands, chest out, and lets the other hit him in the chest as hard as he can. He bears as many blows as he can, then it's the other man's turn. The fight usually ends with the two men making up and swearing friendship.

Then there's the club fight. A challenger plants a ten-foot pole in the ground; the man challenged takes it and gives him a mighty blow to the head, which can then be returned. Such fights can quickly become a nasty general brawl, and fatal wounds are common; they're ended when the headman takes a bow and arrow and threatens to shoot the participants if they don't stop.

Finally there's the raid, where the men of one village run to another, find some defenseless victim, kill him, and run away. The most deadly action however is the treacherous feast: you get a third village to invite your enemies to a meal, then surprise them and kill as many as possible.

There are two take-home points here:

- **Ritual**. Aggression is channeled into set patterns that limit destructiveness; above all there are conventions on when the fight is over.

- **Limiting risk**. You'll get hurt in a duel— showing your toughness is the main appeal— but you'll survive. The raids and even the treacherous feast are by 'civilized' standards cowardly— they avoid a general battle where the defenders can fight back— and kill— on equal terms.

Marvin Harris notes that the perceived need for fierce male warriors leads to widespread female infanticide, which he views as an effective if brutal means of controlling population. (Population isn't limited directly by war: no matter how many men are killed, the remainder can keep the women pregnant. Only limiting the number of women bearing children can restrict population growth.)

The **Maring** of New Guinea are garden agriculturalists who raise herds of pigs. It takes about ten years for the animals to grow to full size, at which point the gardens are strained. The tribe then slaughters the pigs, holds a huge feast, and goes to war. War takes one of four forms:

- 'Nothing fights', which consist of an exchange of arrows. These usually end if anyone is seriously wounded.

- 'True fights', which add a front line where men duel with stone axes and flint-tipped wooden spears.

- Raids, similar to those of the Yanomamö.

- Routs, usually an outgrowth of a 'true fight', a headlong rush at a settlement with much killing of both sexes; the defeated group abandons its settlement entirely.

Again, note the ritual and the limitation of risk. Fights were not always escalated; they often ended in a peace negotiated by allies. But even the routs are not as final as they sound. The defeated tribe's territory is not occupied, as it's considered to have bad magic. The survivors regroup in the territory of allies.

Direct evidence for warfare in the vast majority of human history is rather slim. It's fair to say that our ancestors were neither brutal nor noble savages. Their wars were likely to be limited displays of aggression which allowed the losers a dishonorable but life-saving retreat.

Of course, there was the rare possibility of a near-genocidal rout. These are all the more striking to Westerners because they're the opposite of our military mores, which glorify facing a fully armed opponent; when the enemy is fleeing in terror we consider the battle won and pursuit to the death an atrocity. But in many military cultures it was simply good sense to avoid a battle except under conditions of overwhelming superiority. Those pointy things can kill you, after all.

In some areas and periods, such as the Trojan War, early medieval Europe, and China's Spring and Autumn Period, war was not much more sophisticated; it was a matter of aristocratic heroes whose battles were more an array of individual duels than a mass action. Their codes of honor may greatly influence their culture's idea of what war should be, but for wars that really change the map you need something more.

East Asian

Classical Chinese military theory was elucidated by **Sun Tzu** (properly *Sūn Zi*) in the -4C. Armies at this time were large (in the tens of thousands) and well trained— maneuvers were signalled using drums, bells, and banners. Weapons included steel swords, spears, and powerful and accurate crossbows; horses were used to pull chariots, though cavalry was introduced soon after his time.

Sun Tzu's major emphases:

- **Calculation**. If we picture Alexander charging sword in hand at the enemy's strongest point, Sun Tzu must be pictured with an abacus, evaluating troop strengths and dispositions, terrain, supply, and morale.

- **Professionalism**. Sun Tzu has to emphasize promotion based on merit (rather than nepotism), the use of experience rather than omens, and the freedom of commanders to ignore the king's orders once in the field.

- **Movement**. Quick movement allowed an attack where the enemy was weakest. An army could be divided into *zhèng* 'orthodox'— big solid battalions— and *qí* 'extraordinary', small élite groups sent to attack the flanks and rear.

- **Deception**. "When capable, feign incapacity; when active, inactivity... Offer the enemy a bait to lure him; feign disorder and strike him."

- **Intelligence**. Use spies, diplomats, and local guides to understand and undermine the enemy. He helpfully suggests that disgruntled courtiers can easily be recruited.

- **Avoidance** of wasteful battle: long wars, sieges, direct confrontation with stronger forces. "To subdue the enemy without fighting is the acme of skill."

One could guide the battle rage of soldiers, one's own or the enemy's. The general Hán Xìn smashed his cooking pots, burned his boats, and fought with his back to a river, so his army had to win or die. Another general, after winning a battle, refused to rush after the losers, as that would provoke them to turn and fight; he could do better moving slowly and harrassing them.

Some of Sun Tzu's precepts can be seen in China's perennial struggle with the nomads to the northwest, which emphasized defense (including construction of the Great Wall), co-opting nearby tribes with Chinese titles, bribes, and princesses, and using them if possible against fiercer farther tribes. Though there were great Chinese generals, Chinese culture tended to disdain military action, especially after the military revolts in the Táng period and the failure of a forward policy in western Turkestan, where Arab rather than Chinese influence ended up predominating.

Perhaps the most spectacular demonstration of Sun Tzu's principles was made by Mao Zedong in defeating the Nationalists. He treated his soldiers well, which helped induce large numbers of the enemy to desert to him, and mastered quick movement— he joked that his army was the best in the world at running away. But this allowed him to attack weak points and set traps.

Ho Chi Minh used similar methods in Vietnam against the French and the Americans. Guerrilla warfare proved to be an effective way of countering the material advantage of Western armies.

Japanese samurai warfare was based on the skillful use of swords; but feudal Japan was ended by the general Oda Nobunaga at Nagashino in 1575 using huge numbers of musketeers. This might have led to an age of gunpowder but once unity was achieved, the shogunate made firearms a government monopoly, effectively eliminating them from use and preserving the samurai as a class.

The samurai objected to the indiscriminate nature of gunpowder weapons— a peasant could mow down a highly trained samurai. Similar objections were made in Europe, but no European state was unified or isolated enough to ban firearms. Japan's 250-year renunciation of the gun is a remarkable exception to the usual quick acceptance of new military technologies, of lasting relevance in light of the destructiveness of nuclear weapons.

Nomadic

As noted (p. 92), the nomads of Central Asia were formidable fighters. The entire adult male population was available as a highly mobile cavalry, all expert with the powerful compound bow and, as Keegan points out, even more experienced with dealing death than hunters, due to the necessities of controlling and culling herds and protecting them from predators. Settled states found them difficult to resist. The usual expedient was to hire other tribes to fight back; Europeans in addition learned to cultivate their own class of horse warriors.

Nomads were frightening and frustrating enemies. One of their favorite tactics was the false retreat, which prompted an unwary infantry to pursue, breaking up their line and allowing a devastating counter-charge. They felt no need to offer a firm defensive line— the Persian emperor Darius famously failed to defeat the Scyths because they simply rode away, refusing to face a battle. When they did win a battle they could be notoriously cruel, massacring the inhabitants of a city to punish them for the temerity of resistance, or chasing peasants off their fields.

There were natural limits to their empires, however. One was the perennial difficulty of ruling the settled states they conquered. If they simply plundered and pillaged, like Timur, there was nothing left to loot and they could only seek new conquests. If they settled down as rulers, the trick was to assimilate enough to the agriculturalists to rule effectively, but not so much so that they lost the skills expected back on the steppe.

Few nomadic empires could maintain this balance for long: Attila's empire collapsed after his death; Kublai Khan's dynasty lasted less than three quarters of a century after him. The later Manchus retained power only at the price of a conservativism that became an immense liability in the modern age. Perhaps the only lasting success was the Ottoman Turks, who long remained a formidable military power, and who managed a successful transition to a strong modern state.

Nomads can extend their grazing lands into marginal agricultural areas, as they did historically in Hungary and Anatolia; but not into forests or rich agricultural land, which don't turn into grassland just because the peasants are dead.

Finally, horselords require, well, lots of horses. Marco Polo reported that an average Mongol warrior owned 18 horses. Extended campaigns off the steppe killed horses profusely— probably one reason Attila's attacks on Europe petered out.

Western

In 480 BC, the greatest empire the world had yet produced was stymied by a tiny coalition of city-states one-tenth its size. This was big news and rocketed the winners to the top of the merc market.

What was the secret of the Greeks? There are a few key points.

- Logistics. The Persian force was huge, but it was at the end of a very long supply line; the full resources of the empire could not be brought to bear.

- Naval advantages. The Greeks had fewer ships, but they forced battle in a confined space, the straits of Salamis, where the Persian numbers were thwarted. Persian ships were more maneuverable but less heavily crewed, so in a tight space the Greeks had a great advantage.

- Armor and weapons. Despite what you may have picked up from *300*, the Greeks had heavier armor and longer spears than the Persians.

- Terrain. Greece has few open plains, rendering the Persian cavalry nearly useless. (In more open terrain, such as in Anatolia, the Persians defeated the Greek counter-attacks.)

The army of a Greek city-state was organized as a **phalanx**— an extended rectangle of men, each man holding a round shield and a spear, long enough that those of first three rows pointed out at the enemy. Tactics were simple, as befit a soldiery whose main job was farming: they consisted of charging forward at a trot till the formation burst against the enemy. A Roman observer commented that the advance of a phalanx was the most frightening thing he'd ever seen. Once the armies had collided, the individual soldier could switch to a sword.

Compared with primitive or nomadic tactics, this represented a major change: a phalanx directly confronted similarly armed opponents, with a high risk of death. It's been estimated that 15% of a losing force died in the battle itself, either from wounds or from being picked off by skirmishers as they ran.

What made men willing to run directly into line of enemies brandishing spears? We can identify several factors.

- The greater risk of running away. Better to face a spearman head on; showing him your side or back was far more dangerous. And the tight formation of the phalanx meant that the front rows literally had no place to go but forward.

- Fear of the shame of not fighting. Your buddies were right there next to you; you fought to protect them and to retain their approval.

- Spirits raised by drink, by religious invocations, even by the rituals of insults and shouting that preceded combat.

- Victor Hanson suggests that phalanx warfare allowed battle to be brief and decisive, a desirable attribute for part-time soldiers. Like having your teeth pulled, it was going to hurt, but it'd soon be over.

In inter-Greek struggles, total victory was not pursued— the losers were allowed to run off. They would often drop their armor, which allowed them to outpace the victors. Once again we see the theme of cultural limitation to war. Often the wars were about revenge or points of honor, which were satisfied by victory; occupation of the enemy city was rarely a goal.

Sparta was a partial exception, in that it had enslaved its neighbors in the southern Peloponnese, also in that its army was composed of a professional class of warriors. But even Sparta never pursued an empire beyond its little slice of Greece. It was left to Athens to attempt to exploit the Greek military superiority revealed by the victory over Persia. This ultimately stalemated: Athens's little empire did not have the resources to do much harm to Persia. But all of Greece did if it were united, as Alexander showed in the -4C.

As time goes on, conventional limits to war get stretched and broken. By Alexander's time the army was professionalized; the short campaign season had extended to nine months; and of course the wars were fought for conquest.

The Romans adapted the phalanx into the **legion**, dividing it into smaller sections (maniples) which allowed greater maneuverability. Perhaps more importantly, they added an ethos of fighting to the end that none of their enemies could match. Hannibal of Carthage invaded Italy, soundly thrashed the legions several times, and won away a slew of Italian cities; by the standards of the day the Romans should have sued for peace. They did not; they resisted for ten years, defeated the Carthaginians in Spain and then invaded Carthage itself, forcing Hannibal to return to defend it. They reduced the Carthaginian empire to a remnant and, still not satisfied, eliminated it fifty years later in another war.

Even when they lost, they won: the term "Pyrrhic victory" refers to their wars with Pyrrhus of Epirus, whose defeats of Roman armies were so painful that he abandoned his war.

And this, through many a change in military technology, largely remained as the European idea of war: where men and materials permit, squarely engage the enemy, instill the discipline required to throw soldiers into probable death, and seek the total destruction of the enemy's army.

(The nuance is important; medieval armies, for instance, were hamstrung by the difficulty of raising a large army. Armies were therefore small, and wars rarely decisive.)

For all its brutality, Western culture has its cultural limits—respecting medical units, for instance. There's also the expectation that once your army is defeated, you surrender. The denial of this expectation in the Iraq war was a huge and unwelcome surprise to the Americans.

The ultimate expression of Western military culture was World War II, a conflict so brutal that it largely discredited the very idea of war for the Europeans, at least.

Weapons

For ease of exposition I'll focus on one weapon at a time, but be aware that civilized states rely on combined arms; relying entirely on one type of weapon is generally a mistake.

Spear

If you play a fantasy game, what weapon do you want? A spear? Of course not; spears are for weenies. You want a badass sword.

But primitive and classical warriors preferred the spear. A 2.5-meter-long spear, made of ash with an iron tip, was the basic weapon of the Greek phalanx; the Macedonian *sarissa* was twice as long, which compensated for their lighter armor. A spear can of course reach farther than a sword; phalanx tactics are also relatively simple, suitable for part-time soldiers. Spears are are also cheaper to make than either swords or arrows.

A javelin is a lighter spear that is thrown at the enemy; this was effective to about 20 meters. Peltasts, light infantry armed with javelins, would be used to harrass the enemy. At Lechaeum in 391 BC peltasts defeated a small Spartan phalanx, repeatedly advancing to throw their javelins and then nimbly retreating when the Spartans attacked. (Normally peltasts were countered by other peltasts, but in this battle the Spartans had none of their own.)

Roman legions gave up the thrusting spear in favor of the *pilum* or javelin; they would throw this and then follow up with the sword.

The medieval pike was three to six meters long, and most useful against cavalry charges. The cavalry themselves often used the lance, a stout, long spear whose thrusting power was multiplied by the weight of a charging horse. However, after the initial charge, the horseman would switch to sword or mace for melee.

Sword

Swords require metal, and bronze doesn't allow swords more than 60 cm long, while spears can be far longer. Wrought iron doesn't hold an edge well, but charcoal heating and water quenching, mastered by 1000 BC, produced a hard steel layer on the outer edge.

Around 300 AD India was producing wootz steel, a pure steel with high carbon content and a characteristic swirling grain pattern, which could be used to make hard and tough blades. In Europe, the best steel was produced by heat-layering high-purity Swedish iron with charcoal, until the invention of the Bessemer process in 1858 allowed cheap mass production of steel.

Set designers and video game players love huge elaborate swords with extra sharpened bits, like the Klingon *betleH*. But heavy weapons are hard to control and tire the user, and wacky indentations and protrusions are probably an invitation for the sword to get caught on obstacles. In a rapier vs. *betleH* battle, I rather imagine the rapier would be spearing an internal organ while Mr. Klingon was still figuring out his grip.

The axe was the preferred weapon of the Viking, not least because it was also a useful tool in peacetime, at least in the forested north. Metal tools are expensive and time-consuming to forge and maintain, so greater utility was a real plus.

Swordfighting 101

The golden age of swordfighting, as Arthur Wise points out, was due to the invention of firearms. Plate armor encouraged the use of weapons that would crack it or induce injury despite it: war hammers, maces, axes, flails. Gunpowder eliminated the defense of heavy armor, and personal combat fell back on the sword.

In the 16C, swords were thick and heavy, and often wielded with a mailed gauntlet to protect the hand. The swordsman circled his opponent, sword held out, looking for an opening, preferably on the opponent's left side (i.e. away from his sword arm). Attacks could depend either on cutting or thrusting.

In defense, he might use a small shield, a mailed glove, or a cloak wrapped round his hand: the cloak could be used to brush a point aside, or to attempt to catch it in the cloth, or could even thrown at the opponent. The best defense was a counter-attack: step back, parry, or meet the opponent's blade with his own, in either case making a counter-thrust. Bouts required strength and endurance.

Tripping and kicking were not out of bounds; one could also grasp the opponent's sword (by the blade or by the guard) and wrest it away.

Rapier

The broadsword was replaced in personal combat by the rapier, a thin sword that emphasized dexterity and ultimately the thrust rather than the cut. A thrust was faster, the masters taught, and put the attacker at less risk. The rapier's hilt also evolved curved projections that protected the hand.

The usual defense became a dagger held in the off hand, and eventually nothing at all— the rapier itself could be used for defense. The rapier is held such that the opponent cannot hit merely by thrusting forward, but must move his weapon; and the typical counter to a thrust is to parry rather than counter-thrust.

There is an element of fashion to all this— if your opponent has a rapier that's all you need as well— but the rapier was also considered more effective. "The short sword against the Rapier is little better than a tobacco-pipe," as a royal weapons master wrote in 1617. (On the 17C battlefield, of course, the only edged weapons to be seen were cavalrymen's sabers and anti-cavalry pike; the infantry used muskets.)

Bow and arrow

The simple bow is made from a single piece of wood; a sapling provided the necessary elasticity. Nonetheless it allowed attack at a hundred yards, much longer than the hurled spear.

The composite bow is much more complicated. It was made from five pieces of wood— grip, two arms, two tips— glued together and steamed into a curve, opposite to its shape when strung. Strips of horn were glued to the inner side, tendons to the outer, then left to cure for as much as a year. Stringing the bow required bending it against its natural shape, requiring great strength but greatly increasing the bow's power. The bow's effective range was 250 to 300 yards.

Typically archers wore little or no armor; their role was to use their speed and range to harrass the opposing force. The Persians relied on a standing army of trained, fast archers wielding composite bows.

The crossbow was introduced to Europe in the 16C, though it was known in China a millennium before. It used a clockwork mechanism to store and suddenly release energy; its bolts could easily penetrate armor. It cost more than the ordinary bow and fired slower, but was easier to aim and did more damage.

Horse and Pike

The first major use of the horse was for food. The first animal used for traction was the ox (i.e. a castrated and thus more docile bull); the first riding animal may have been the donkey or its larger relative the onager. These however are stubborn, resist spurs and bits, and lack the wide range of gaits of horses.

The first stage in the use of horses in war was to pull **chariots**, developed around 1700 BC in the borderlands between the steppe (where the horses were plentiful) and the civilized lands (where the metal and wood necessary to build chariots were found). Chariots were not an item of mass warfare— they were luxury items. At the battle of Qadesh in 1294 BC, the victorious Egyptian army had about 5000 men and 50 chariots.

There is some controversy about exactly how chariots were used. Pictures show teams of two or more, one driving the horse, the others firing arrows or throwing javelins. This would seem to be awkward if driving straight at the enemy; rather they must have ridden along the enemy's flank, or better yet, come close and then dashed back: the chariot is one of the few military implements which fights most effectively when retreating,

Horses were **ridden** in the 2nd millennium, though at first the rider was seated over the rump. By the 8th century BC stronger horses had been bred, and horsemanship had improved, so that they were ridden in the forward control position. The Scyths and Cimmerians, both Iranian peoples, learned to shoot from horseback; their intervention in Mesopotamia led to the downfall of the Assyrian empire.

Horses were the backbone of the nomadic armies for the next two millennia, forcing agricultural states to invest resources in either developing or buying horsemen of their own.

Cavalry forces can also be divided into heavy and light, the latter relying on missiles, the former on lances and heavy armor; heavy cavalry was often decisive in Alexander's battles, a lesson absorbed by the Persians' successors, the Parthians.

In the post-Roman period, cavalry was the most efficient use of scant resources, and its power was reinforced by the stirrup, which reached Europe in the 8C. This greatly reduced the rider's risk of falling and increased the power of charges with the lance.

An effective counter was the pike shield; a barrier of pikes could stand up to a cavalry charge if the pikemen stayed steadfast. The Swiss excelled at this; thus their value as mercenaries. The English had their own counter: the longbow, which being constructed from heartwood and sapwood had many of the advantages of the composite bow, though it also required immense strength and training.

Enemies who had never faced horses could be decimated by even small numbers. A typical encounter was the battle of Vilcaconga in 1533, in which Spanish forces numbering no more than 300, including 110 horsemen, routed an Inca army of more than 10,000. The power and the mobility of the horses was of course multiplied by the strength of Spanish steel (as against Inca stone maces) and the near invulnerability of steel armor (compared to the Incas' quilted cotton armor).

The decimation of the Light Brigade at Balaclava in 1854 under rifle and artillery fire may be taken as the battle horse's last whinny. A military historian, with heavy irony, notes that the Polish cavalry of 1939 was perhaps the finest such unit of its time. Horses were nonetheless used in great numbers in both World Wars for transport.

About the only other animal widely used in battle was the **elephant**. (Camels were used for transport, not battle.) An elephant charge is formidable, and not easily stopped by pikemen— stepping aside and throwing javelins is more effective. And the extra height can be used as a platform for archery. But they have disadvantages too; they can panic in battle, and cause as much harm to their own lines as to the enemy. They were used sporadically in classical warfare and even less so in China; but they were a mainstay of Indian armies as late as the 19C; they couldn't stand up to cannonfire.

Gunpowder

Gunpowder is a mixture of crystalline **saltpeter**, powdered **charcoal**, and purified **sulfur**. Sulfur is readily available as a bright yellow crystal found in volcanic regions. Saltpeter, potassium nitrate, can also be found naturally as a white crystalline encrustration on rocks (thus its name, 'salt of stone'), but also produced from a compost of manure, ash, earth, and straw. Gunpowder was discovered by the Chinese by 1050, and used for rockets and cannon.

The first **cannons** don't seem to have been very effective, not least because loose gunpowder was dangerous and prone to separation. In the late 14C Europeans learned how to add liquid to make granular ("corned") gunpowder, which kept better, was safer to handle, and above all burned more efficiently. By the mid-15C cannon were highly efficient at reducing fortification; the French kings used them to burst through English castles, and the Turks finally destroyed the long-impregnable walls of Constantinople.

Early barrels (made of banded strips like their namesake) were liable to burst; in the 1490s the French perfected a long cast barrel that directed the explosion better and allowed the cannon to be attached to a mobile cart.

The earliest hand weapons required touching a lit match cord by hand to the firing pan, a tricky and dangerous maneuver. In the 15C the matchlock was devised— a little clip that held the match and applied it to the touch hole. It was superseded by mechanisms such as the flintlock, which ignited the powder with sparks.

Muskets had become reliable and ubiquitous by the mid 16C, despite their slow rate of fire (no more than three rounds a minute). Their effective range was about 100 meters. They were further improved by rifling (spiral grooves inside the barrel which impart a spin to the bullet, making the trajectory more accurate) and by cartridges, allowing fast breech-loading rather than muzzle-loading. These were invented early but not common till the 19C.

I've mentioned the samurai distaste for the gun as an insult to their skill and elite status (p. 248); Europeans had the same attitude but being disunited had to adapt to it. The gun made metal armor useless and ultimately ended the long domination of cavalry.

Pikemen were still important in the 17C as a counter to cavalry; but by the end of the century they were largely made obsolete by the invention of the ring bayonet, which allowed musketeers to perform their role.

Ships

The predominant warship before the gunpowder era was the **galley**, rowed by oarsmen. Sailing ships were better for trading, but only oars provided the quick maneuvering necessary for battle. Battle galleys were long and narrow (e.g. 24 by 3 meters), and extremely short-drafted; this allowed them to operate in very shallow water and to be beached or even portaged. They were not suitable for the open ocean, however, and couldn't store food for more than a few days; as a result most naval battles were fought within sight of land. For the same reason blockades were very difficult.

From about 700 BC the dominant naval tactic was ramming, though after the -3C it was more common to attempt to board an enemy vessel and engage in melee combat on deck.

Cannon were added to oared galleys in the 15C; due to their narrow width, these could only be added to the bow or stern. In the 16C, however, the advantage shifted to sailing ships with side-mounted arrays of cannon. These were deep-ocean ships which could travel for half a year out of port and arrive ready to fight.

The geography of your conworld will influence what sort of ships are built. The Mediterranean allows small, coast-hugging ships to travel long distances and encounter interesting trading partners or enemies; the Chinese and the Incas had long coastlines but couldn't easily reach states worth trading with or conquering. (Zhèng Hé's expeditions are impressive but underline that China didn't find ocean exploration very rewarding.)

In the 19C the sailing ship gave way to the steamship— though these ships' enormous hunger for coal meant that only those powers which could establish coaling stations worldwide could depend entirely on them. Before WWI ships switched to oil, which being more efficient allowed a greater range without refueling.

Other factors

Terrain

Large swaths of the earth's surface have never or rarely seen a battle. Mountains, deserts, and jungle are bad places for armies, suitable for little more than expensive skirmishing. (Mountain passes can be very important, of course.) Almost all major naval battles took place near the shore.

Commanders prefer large flat plains, perhaps with nearby hills to funnel the invader's army, close to good roads or rivers for their supply line. Men can negotiate hills better than cavalry. A river can serve as a trap, too, preventing a smaller or beaten force from retreating.

Few armies like to fight in the rain, or at night, or in the winter. Peasant levies can hardly be maintained at sowing or harvest time.

The approaches to Moscow are not only protected by generals January and February, as Tsar Nicholas I said, but by the *rasputitsa*, the spring snowmelt and the autumn rains, which turns the region into a morass for a month in each season.

The geographical situation of a country may have an enormous effect on its military fortunes. Ancient Egypt was isolated in the west by desert, in the east by coastal ranges; this channeled its military defenses into two regions, the Nile delta and the cataracts upriver, and probably contributed to its long backwardness as a military power. Japan was protected from the Mongols, and Britain from most of the wars of the last millennium, by their island location. Very likely the many peninsulas of the Mediterranean, each protected by mountains, encouraged the development of separate peoples and nations, while the relative lack of geographical barriers within China encouraged a single administration.

Fortification

Until modern times, the most efficient defense against an army was the wall. Keegan describes three basic types of fortification:

- The **refuge**, a place of temporary safety, only strong enough to deter immediate attack. The pre-contact Maori, for instance, built hilltop pallisades which sufficed to protect a fleeing army, as the attackers had no siege engines and could not operate for long away from their territory.

- The **stronghold** must be able to withstand a siege; it thus needs a water source, room for stores, walls high enough to discourage mounting with ladders, fighting platforms for firing at attackers, and gates for counter-sallies.

- **Strategic defenses**— large-scale fortifications such as Hadrian's Wall in Roman Britain, the Chinese Great Wall, the French Maginot Line, or the series of forts that divided ancient Egypt from Nubia. (Multiple lines are the most effective— raiders who pass one line may be stopped by the next.) Only a strong state can afford to build and garrison these lines, but they may save the expense of garrisoning each city of the interior.

A land dotted with castles, as in medieval France, is associated with weak central authority or endemic raiding. A nation with a strong forward defense, such as imperial Persia, doesn't need walls round its cities— after breaking through the outer defenses, Alexander conquered the empire with three battles fought in open country. Roman cities in pacified provinces were also unwalled; as the Western Empire declined the cities fortified. (Early Sumerian cities weren't walled either, which may mean that large-scale warfare had not yet begun.)

Despite the impression created by the movie of *The Two Towers*, **catapults** were rarely decisive before the gunpowder age. A well-built wall could withstand the glancing blows from hurled stones.

You don't want people walking up to the foundations, or knocking them with battering rams; this could be discouraged with an excavated moat, filled with water if feasible. The moat also provided an open space vulnerable to fire from the defenders.

For their part, besiegers built counter-fortifications as platforms to shoot back at the defenders, prevent sallies, and protect ramps for scaling the walls. Battering rams were built inside mobile wagons, with a steep roof to deflect projectiles and rawhide coverings to resist fire. Besiegers might also tunnel under the walls (mining)— though this could be foiled by counter-mining. The surest methods, however, were surprise, treachery, and starvation.

Mobile cannons, from 1500, made older fortifications spectacularly obsolete. Their great advantage was that they could be precisely aimed at the walls' weakest point, their foundations; worse yet, the higher the wall the greater the destruction. Within fifty years new systems of fortification were devised to resist the cannon. Walls were short but immensely thick, and backed with earth ramparts. They incorporated wedge-shaped bastions which could concentrate cannon and musket fire on the attackers.

Cannons were devastating in open battle as well. A single cannonball could take out more than twenty men. Naturally this focused attention on capturing artillery pieces, or disabling them.

Logistics

Every form of warfare is limited by logistics. War is hell to organize.

A man can carry about 70 pounds of gear— including clothes and armor, weapons, and other equipment that will amount to at least half of this. As a day's food weighs about 3 pounds, a soldier on the march can only carry about 10 days worth of food. As we've seen that amounts to 200 miles (320 km), which wouldn't get a Roman soldier out of Italy.

You can try living off the land— i.e. stealing from the civilians— but this quickly exhausts the base of operations, or slows the army down as it spreads out to forage. A large cavalry worsens the problem; a horse needs about 20 pounds of fodder per day. A large classical force, invading or defending, can't stay in the field without supply for more than a few weeks, a fact which an opposing commander may use to force or avoid battle.

That leaves bringing supplies with pack animals or water transport... but of course oxen have to be fed too, and waterways don't always lead nicely toward the enemy. Few premodern nations were provided with good road systems.

Between armies of the same type (e.g. heavy infantry), retreat is faster than pursuit. For this reason, after Hannibal's initial victories, the Romans under Fabius harrassed and raided the Carthaginians while avoiding battle, denying Hannibal control over Italy. A war of attrition tires the defenders as well; eventually Rome replaced Fabius and sought battle, leading to the disaster at Cannae (p. 266).

The railway revolutionized both logistics and mobilization. In the first two weeks of World War I, Germany mobilized 1.5 million men and transported them ready to fight to the western front. Of course, once at the front mobility dropped to horse speed and then, within the enemy's artillery range, to that of a man walking.

World War II, of course, was fought at modern transportation speeds: Jeeps, tanks, steamships, fighter planes. War between modern advanced states is generally won by the side with the better manufacturing potential, which in recent wars has meant the US.

Communications

Simple communication was an immense hassle before the invention of the telegraph. War suffered all the disadvantages of normal travel (p. 142) with the additional problem that messengers could be attacked. As late as 1815, a major battle of the US-British war was fought two weeks after the peace treaty had been signed.

On the battlefield itself, there was no better communication than horses through the 19C. WWI trenches were equipped with telephones, but these became useless as soon as troops attempted forward movement. Radio was a revolution.

Merely locating the enemy was not straightforward. Scouts could be sent out, or signal fires set; but not a few battles were won or lost depending on who stumbled onto who first, or who could get their reserves to the battle in time.

Death in another form

It's hard to make this look cool in an epic fantasy, but the biggest threat to soldiers is disease and starvation. In WWII, US army hospitals had 17 million admissions for illness or accidents versus a million for combat wounds. In the Civil War, 60% of the Northern war dead succumbed to disease— about half diarrhea and other intestinal disorders, the rest pneumonia and tuberculosis. Sword wounds often killed indirectly, through peritonitis, or by infections caused by forcing dirt into the wounds.

Modern technology has been a double agent, finding new ways to incapacitate and just as quickly improving medical skill. There's been a similar two-step in speed of care. Battles lengthened and the killing zone grew immense— someone felled in the WWI no man's land could lay there for days. But advanced armies have concentrated on quick medical care: in Vietnam helicopters could get the wounded to a field hospital in fifteen minutes.

Armor

Primitive warriors like the Maring generally use no armor at all, a practice maintained till quite late by the ancient Egyptians.

The Greeks— those who could afford it, at least— used bronze helmets, breastplates, and greaves, as well as a wooden shield reinforced with iron. Their weapons were iron; they wore bronze armor because it was not yet possible to make iron plates of sufficient malleability and strength. The Persians by contrast wore light iron scale armor.

Regular Roman legionaries wore chainmail, or a cuirass made of overlapping iron bands. Scale armor was used, though more rarely. Greaves were worn on the legs, and sometimes arm guards. Helmets were iron. The typical shield was rectangular, curved to allow blows to glance off, and a meter tall— large enough that legionaries could protect against a rain of arrows by holding their shields together above their heads, a formation called *testudo* (tortoise).

The armor of the medieval knight was chainmail. After the mid 14C knights switched to plate armor, the famous suits of armor. Though these were not as cumbersome as sometimes depicted, the heaviest suits of armor were intended only for tournaments, where protection was more important than mobility. Medieval states could only fully arm a small army; if a larger force was needed to meet an invasion, much of it would be unarmored and barely trained.

From the 18C, armor was largely abandoned, except for the helmet— due to the power of rifles, as well as the expense of maintaining the era's larger armies.

Modern US soldiers wear lightweight Kevlar helmets and vests.

Ideology

There's nothing quite so dangerous as an army with an idea. The armies that poured out of Arabia on the death of Muhammad were not appreciably better armed or skilled than the Byzantines and Persians they faced; but they were on fire with a new religion.

Ironically, perhaps, once the Islamic empire was divided and most conflicts were between Muslims, religious scruples made it difficult for Arabs to fight wars; they created slave armies or hired Turks instead.

The armies of the French Revolution were just as fired up, first throwing out the invaders who had thought to take advantage of French troubles, then conquering the continent as far as Moscow— an achievement far beyond the dreams of royal France. Similarly Mao Zedong won China by combining the strategic insight of Sun Tzu with the fervor of a mass movement.

Types of armies

Where does an army come from? This might be viewed as the intersection of two choices, how much of the adult male population serves, and how well trained they are. Other things being equal, a big army will defeat a small, and a trained army will beat an untrained one, but both choices are expensive.

	little training	much training
entire population	phalanx militia raw conscripts	nomadic riders experienced conscripts
subpopulation		standing army

In the upper left square we require, or allow, everyone to serve, as an interruption to their ordinary life. Examples include the classical phalanx or the militia that Machiavelli recommended to reduce the Italian city-states' dependance on mercenaries. A part-time army may be well motivated and may supply its own gear, but it can't follow very elaborate tactics.

Conscripts are the male population turned into soldiers; this was the source of Napoléon's million-man army and the huge armies of the two World Wars. These are fairly useless at first, but after a year or so they become a very effective force.

Alternatively you arm some fraction of the population. (It doesn't make much sense to do so and not train them, so I've left that cell blank.) Now the question is the army's standing in society— and how you keep it from assaulting the palace.

- The warriors may also be the ruling class: the medieval knights, the Japanese samurai, the Spartans.

  How do you make sure the elite actually functions as an army? One way is **feudalism**: grant land to successful officers on condition that they supply soldiers on demand. The best that can be said for this system is that it was cheap to maintain; but the vassals were often a threat to the state, and neither they nor the kings could provide public safety. The Islamic *iqta* system was non-hereditary; this allowed greater state control but encouraged corruption.

- **Regulars** are soldiers as a profession, as in the Roman or Chinese empires, or today in the US. This eliminates the fuss of raising an army when you want to make war, but at the cost of maintaining the army in peacetime.

  You don't want it to occur to your soldiers that they've got guns and the civilians don't and that they could take power— a perennial problem in ancient Rome and the mid-20C Third World, and only a bit less so in imperial China. Sufficiently prosperous democracies with highly professionalized armies seem to avoid the problem. In premodern times canny rulers kept armies under civilian control and rotated their generals.

- **Mercenaries** fight for money, land, or citizenship. There have been periods when these were key resources— Alexander hired 50,000 of them, and the Swiss infantry were highly sought after in medieval Europe; the Pope's Swiss Guard is a remnant. There are always questions about their loyalty and reliability, so modern states prefer regulars.

- **Slaves**— *mamluks*— were the main military element in many Islamic states from the 9C, and persisted in some form till the 19C. Early mamluks were mostly Turkish, and raised to be strict Muslims. Their sons were not allowed to become mamluks; rather, new recruits were found in the Turkish lands. This system allowed the Arabs to avoid having to fight other Muslims; just as importantly, the Turkic mamluks had no local ties or allies and thus were loyal. Until they weren't; in the 1250s they took over power for themselves.

Army sizes vary immensely. Here's a few representative samples:

- The Roman army under Augustus: 250,000 total, across the empire.
- The Byzantine expeditionary force that recovered North Africa and Italy for the Eastern Empire: 15,000.
- Mongol army, at the death of Genghis Khan— 130,000 (including some allies)
- Medieval standing armies, 16C: a few hundred in peacetime; 15 to 30,000 in wartime.
- Sòng dynasty, 12C China: 1 million men, though this army was considered bloated and inefficient
- US, World War II: 12 million
- US, 2007: 1.37 million

Great battles

Military history is a slightly macabre affair; aficionados pore over neat diagrams which, after all, represent enormous numbers of violent deaths. Nonetheless it's valuable to learn what the generals are thinking. Let's look at some of the great battles of history.

Cannae, 216 BC

Carthage was the underdog in its second war with Rome; Rome expected to easily pick off its Spanish colony. Instead the Carthaginian general Hannibal advanced over the Alps and took the war to Italy, beating several Roman forces.

His masterpiece was the battle of Cannae. The Romans, with 75,000 troops and a 2-to-1 advantage in infantry, were drawn up in standard formation: infantry in the center, cavalry on the flanks. Hannibal placed his weaker allies in the center, thrust far forward to invite an attack; his best infantry units were on their flank, and cavalry farther out.

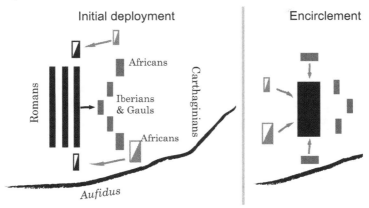

As the Romans advanced, the Carthaginians gave way, moving backwards. Hannibal sprung the trap by having his flanking infantry move forward, hitting the Romans' flanks on both sides.

Meanwhile the left half of the Carthaginian cavalry routed the Roman cavalry opposite them, rode *behind* the Roman army, and attacked the Roman left-side cavalry from behind. They chased the Roman cavalry away, then moved back to attack the trapped Roman army from behind.

50,000 Romans fell, there was no Roman army left, and southern Italy went over to Carthage.

Tyre, 332 BC

Sieges are the complement of battles; to conquer a nation its fortified cities must be taken. When he besieged Tyre, Alexander had already won two of the three land battles that bested the Persian Empire; but the Persian navy had not been defeated, and threatened his supply lines and even Greece. But rowed galleys cannot maintain themselves at sea for long; they would be defeated if he captured their ports, and Tyre was the chief of these.

It wouldn't be easy. Tyre stood on an island a thousand meters off the coast, was entirely surrounded by walls 45 m high, and had a strong garrison of 15,000. The usual expedients of mines, rams, and siege towers looked impossible, and starvation was out of the question as the city could be supplied by sea.

With typical bravado Alexander determined to alter the facts. He had a causeway built across the water, which remains to this day. The forward end of the work was protected by two enormous siege towers, themselves fighting platforms. The Tyrians sent a fireship against them and burned them down.

Ships from both sides fought nearby, but Alexander had the better of the battles. He mounted battering rams on his ships; finding that underwater blocks of stone kept them from reaching the walls, he mounted cranes on ships and hauled them up.

Finally, after seven months, the rams were able to make a breach in the south walls. Bridges were dropped from his ships and troops poured in. The result was a massacre (as frequently happened when a city was stormed).

Chìbì, AD 208

In the 3C, the Hàn empire had divided into Three Kingdoms (*Sànguó*). The warlord Cáo Cāo controlled the north, in the name of the Hàn; the southeast was the kingdom of Wú ruled by Sūn Quán, and the southwest was Shǔ Hàn, ruled by Liú Bèi, a remote relative of the Hàn.

To unify the country, Cáo Cāo had to take the middle Yangtze— modern Húběi province. He took a large army south, estimated at 220,000 men; the southern states, who formed an alliance, had only about 50,000.

Early battles favored Cáo Cāo; he captured the important naval base at Jiangling and gave Liú Bèi a drubbing at Changban. The warlord's forces, fatigued and suffering from a plague, sailed down the Yangtze to Chìbì (Red Cliffs). The ships were tied together, perhaps to reduce seasickness among the northern soldiers.

The warlord was approached by an enemy commander offering surrender. A squadron of defecting ships appeared; but the surrender was a ruse and the ships were filled with oil and kindling.

The sailors lit them on fire and escaped in small boats, letting the wind bear the fireships to Cáo Cāo's fleet, causing a conflagration.

The remnants of Cáo Cāo's army fled north, pursued and harrasssed by the allies. For half a century China would remain divided into Three Kingdoms.

The battle is a classic demonstration that numbers are not enough, even when technology is matched. Even apart from the ruse, Cáo Cāo was defeated by his own overconfidence, stretched supply lines, and unfamiliarity with marine warfare.

Chìbì is a major event in Luó Guànzhōng's 14C novel *The Romance of the Three Kingdoms* and remains a favorite in movies and games.

Hastings, AD 1066

This is one of the classic confrontations of infantry and cavalry. King Harold's English army was almost entirely infantry, wearing chainmail armor and wielding spears and battle axes (six feet long, a blow from these could take down a horse). Harold was a competent warrior; he had just defeated the king of Norway 200 miles north. The Norman army under Duke William was mixed: archers, infantry, and heavy cavalry armed with lances and swords. Neither army had more than 8000 men.

The English line formed along a ridge, and formed a shield wall that was able to resist the initial volley of arrows, a follow-on infantry charge, and a cavalry charge.

By accident or design, a cavalry division on the left fled away from the shield wall. The English were unable to resist the temptation: they broke ranks and rushed after the fleeing Normans. William was unhorsed and at first thought dead.

But he was alive, and rallied resistance and then a counter-attack. The English had lost cohesion, and many of the shield carriers were picked off; the Norman archers were also ordered to fire over the shield wall, devastating the farther ranks— Harold was killed by an arrow at this time. William's army attacked again, broke through the shield wall, and finished off the fragmented English.

The two take-home lessons: a determined infantry line can hold off a charge of the best cavalry— but it must be careful in pursuing retreating riders. The feigned retreat (also a favorite nomadic tactic) is an invitation to the infantry line to break, greatly increasing its vulnerability.

Ain Jalut, AD 1260

In the 13C the Mongols exploded out of their homelands, a threat to China, Europe, and the Middle East alike. They conquered Persia and Mesopotamia and seemed poised to conquer Syria, Palestine, and Egypt— once they had sorted out the matter of the succession; the Great Khan Möngke's death in 1259 required the local leader Hulagu's presence back in Mongolia. He left Mongol forces under the command of his Turkish general Kitbuga, 10 to 20,000 troops.

Egypt was ruled by the Mamluk sultan Qutuz. The Mamluks were themselves Turks, maintained as a slave army by the Egyptians, but had recently taken power for themselves. Qutuz had 20,000 men, of which half were Mamluk cavalry. The two sides met in Galilee, not far from Acre.

Qutuz, knowing the local terrain, hid the bulk of his forces in the highlands while baiting the Mongols with a smaller force under his commander Baibars. Baibars used typical nomadic tactics, advancing with his cavalry and feigning retreat several times. Eventually Kitbuga took the bait and pursued Baibars into the hills where Qutuz's forces emerged from hiding and attacked.

The Mongols fought fiercely on, but the tide turned when Qutuz rushed into battle calling "O Islam!"— appealing to the ideological unity of the Mamluks as against their religiously mixed enemies. The Mongols were forced to retreat, though Kitbuga fought to the death.

The battle checked the momentum of the Mongols; they were never able to do more than raiding west of Mesopotamia, while the Mamluks retained control of Syria and Palestine. Just as importantly, perhaps, it marked the ability of a sedentary state to field a cavalry strong and skilled enough to resist the nomadic armies using their own tactics.

Stalingrad, AD 1942

Stalingrad is perhaps the pinnacle of European all-out war, and arguably the turning point in the German-Soviet struggle.

In 1942 Hitler decided that he needed more oil, and made a drive for the Caucasus. The operation started well— the leading panzer division got halfway to Baku— but stalled as the Germans failed to take Stalingrad.

From August to November the Germans continued to pour troops into the city, fighting street to street and sometimes floor to floor within a building. This made little strategic sense; the city could simply be bypassed. But Hitler had a thing about willpower and wouldn't hear talk of retreat.

The Soviets, at first overwhelmed by German aircraft, built up their air forces till they could serve as an effective counter. In late November the Soviets attacked the weaker Romanian armies on either side of Stalingrad with mechanized units. Three days later the arms of the pincer met, trapping 22 German divisions (250,000 men) in the city. Hitler was not worried; he had supplied seven divisions in Demyansk by air the previous winter and proposed to do it again. But the logistics were much more daunting this time, and the Soviets inflicted heavy losses on the Luftwaffe. Not enough supplies were getting through.

In December the Soviets launched an even larger pincer movement, advancing from two points 300 miles apart. Hitler had to admit defeat; the armies in front of the city retreated, but those inside were lost. Total deaths in the campaign exceeded a million, one of the deadliest in history.

The large-scale pincer movement was a feature of World War II, enabled by mechanized troops and radio communications.

Fantasy war

You can have an earthlike planet with earthlike war. Or you can mix it up a bit— but follow the sorts of balances and limitations of actual war. Some general questions to ask about any element you add:

- What skills are required? Is this something all soldiers will adopt, and if not why not?
- Does it require special resources, and if so where do they come from and who controls them?
- What are the limitations?
- How is it countered?
- How does it interact with conventional elements?

Magic

Novelists don't always have to make a coherent, balanced system; video games do. In *Oblivion*, magic works like this:

- There are three basic types of damage: fire, shock, and frost. Some enemies are immune to one of these; there are also element-specific shield spells.
- Spells cost *magicka* to cast; this regenerates fairly quickly, but limits the rate of fire. Your total magicka depends on your skills; there is thus a tradeoff between swords and sorcery.
- Armor interferes with spellcasting, which means that magicians are vulnerable, and it's an option to go in and bash them with a sword. There are Shield spells, but as magicka is limited there is a tradeoff between offensive and defensive spellcasting.
- There are also spells specifically designed to interfere with spellcasting, such as Silence, Paralysis, and Drain Magicka.
- Spells to heal and rally and to fortify skills and attributes allow magicians to support other fighters.
- Spells can be permanently cast on armor or weapons, creating magic items with those properties. Magic weapons have an inherent charge and thus a limited number of uses. They can be recharged via a somewhat gruesome operation (it requires killing other creatures). Permanency has a huge unbalancing effect, so it's wise to put limits on it.

The net effect is that conventional fighting complements magic. An army would have a corps of battlemages, which can be used for both offensive and defensive purposes. Magic has limits, and can be countered either by traditional weaponry or by other magicians.

In Susanna Clarke's *Jonathan Strange and Mr Norrell*, the title magician Strange accompanies the Duke of Wellington on his campaign in Spain. Asked what would most help the army, the duke gives an answer which resonates with military history: good roads.

On Almea, one of the sapient species, the iliu, has the power to generate visions or images in other people's minds. This is normally used for communication and art, but it has military applications: enemies can be confused about where an iliu force is, or made to imagine forces that aren't there. Their main enemy, the ktuvoks, have a related mesmeric ability that allows them to enslave other sapients— though the iliu are immune to it.

The Force in the Star Wars universe is essentially magic (molest me not with talk about midichlorians); it doesn't transform warfare only because it's highly limited in numbers— fewer than one Jedi per planet, it seems— and in effects. Yoda can lift an entire X-wing, but there's no suggestion that he could pull the Death Star down from the sky with his mind. Jedi are thus something like elite commandoes, not something you're going to deploy in regiments of thousands.

Magic systems may have a metaphorical basis— they're associated with divinity, or mind, or life. This can produce narrative and military restrictions: e.g. if magic is tied to the gods, only holy men can use it in battle; if it's linked to femininity, the battlemages are women.

Novelists' magic systems have a tendency to get out of hand. I admire the inventiveness of J.K. Rowling's magic, but it seems to me to invent too many powers, like Marvel superheroes or D&D magic systems. They go down smoothly enough while we're reading, but I think that's because readers and writers forget all the inventions already made. Give your heroes too many powers and they become boringly invincible. For narrative balance the writers start to create absurd vulnerabilities (such as Superman's unhealthy reactions to bits of his home planet) or increasingly campy supervillains.

Again, the key to avoiding that path is restraint. One good idea is better than twenty. Take a lesson from s.f., which usually concentrates on exploring one idea at a time— teleportation, or time travel, or robots. Instead of creating long lists of spells, perhaps take **one** idea, such as—

- healing spells

- the dead can be revived and made into dull-witted but relentless soldiers

- magic can make a soldier invulnerable, but only for 10 seconds at a time

—and think out all the consequences.

Strange creatures

The example of the horse (p. 255) shows how much warfare can be transformed by a single suitable animal. Fantasy animals could make a similar impact.

Did you just think of dragons? You're not the first. But a large ridable bird or pterosaur would create a very distinctive form of aerial warfare. As with airplanes, the beasts could be used for communications, scouting, infiltration, skirmishing, or bombing. Walls would no longer secure a city— the only sure defense against a flying creature would be a cavern or building.

Again, think about limitations. Perhaps, like horses, the creatures only thrive in certain habitats. They should have limitations on how long or far they can fly. It's hardly fair to make them invulnerable; defenders would surely rain crossbows up at them, or launch their own flying creatures. Perhaps they can be confused by smoke, loud noises, or the smell of certain animals.

More ideas:

- Mole-like animals would be useful for mining city walls, or for reconnaissance.

- Our species hasn't had much luck militarizing predators, but perhaps others have done better. A lionlike mount could be terrifying on the battlefield; even more so a lionlike sapient.

- Sea creatures would be effective allies against ships. If they're large enough, they might serve as mounts or transports.

- An ogre or golem could serve some of the functions of a tank: a massive, highly destructive shock force. But perhaps they're easily confused, or have a tendency to run amok among their own lines.

Strange environments

Another approach is to create new environments. This has been discussed under alien species (p. 76), but it's worth reconsidering these from a military perspective.

For instance, a marine sapient has great inherent mobility— it doesn't need roads and isn't impeded by vegetation or mountains. (Venturing off the continental shelf where most sea life congregates might be risky, though, like a human being venturing into the desert.) It also adds a three-dimensional aspect to fighting; a common tactic would probably be to rise suddenly from the inky depths.

On the other hand, ranged attacks would be difficult, and metallurgy would be nearly impossible, to say nothing of gunpowder. Appendages for manipulation might be necessary for civilization, but it's hard to imagine them large enough to wield strong weapons without impeding swimming; most fighting might therefore come down to natural weapons— teeth, claws, tentacles. A battleground— battlepool?— would soon be choked by blood, reducing vision to a few feet and inviting marine scavengers.

An entirely aerial species, or a very small one, would similarly have its own distinctive advantages and disadvantages.

Future war

Nukes

As a future weapon nukes seem decidedly retro. Nuclear weapons haven't been used in battle for fifty years.

This is largely due to the overkill of the Cold War: in 1967 the US had over 30,000 warheads. A war fought on this scale wouldn't be a war; it'd be planetary suicide. For reference, the bomb at Hiroshima killed over 100,000 people, perhaps a quarter of the population; the blast was equivalent to 13 kilotons of TNT. An average modern warhead is 100 times as powerful.

Your typical rogue dictator has fairly rationally concluded that nukes are the best defense: Iraq was invaded, North Korea was not. As offensive use of nukes by a state would surely result in devastating retaliation, this might lead to a stasis where nuclear powers are safe from invasion, but they fight proxy wars among the nukeless.

That leaves non-state actors, the stuff of many a thriller and CIA briefing. It's hard to be sanguine; on the other hand it's hard to picture nuclear terrorism as very effective, as it would invite a furious response and certainly not lead to the perps' demands being met. (One million dollars, maybe; ending capitalism, no.)

It might be far more militarily useful to use nuclear weapons to generate an electromagnetic pulse (EMP); a single high-altitude detonation can disrupt electromagnetics for hundreds of miles. Live components are more vulnerable, so one countermeasure may simply be to keep spare parts on hand.

The story changes in interplanetary or interstellar war. If you don't have to live on your enemy's planet, you may be happy to blow it away. Counter-measures would include a screen of space fighters and hiding industrial facilities, perhaps in the asteroid belt.

Robots

Already in Iraq and Afghanistan we see an increasing use of unmanned drones, more than 10,000 of them. They can disable roadside bombs, provide an extra set of eyes, venture into areas unsafe for soldiers, shoot down incoming mortars, fly over enemy terrain and shoot missiles, even succor the wounded. Most can be controlled from halfway around the world— a way of economizing on expensive First World soldiers. They're also an increasingly effective counter to asymmetric insurgent tactics, and allow operating in areas such as northwestern Pakistan where outside troops would be highly unwelcome.

It's not hard to imagine future conflicts largely fought with drones and robots, in which case war would come down to a nation's industrial capacity.

Military robots obviously have no use for Asimov's Laws of Robotics. They're subservient to humans, though, right? P.W. Singer offers a sobering anecdote: in 1988 a cruiser patrolling the Persian Gulf spotted something in the air. The object was broadcasting radar and radio signals showing it to be a civilian flight. The cruiser's Aegis system, however— designed for projected war with the Soviets, not for observing in peacetime— insisted that it was an F-14 fighter. The crew trusted the computer system and authorized fire. But the computer was wrong; it was an civilian airliner, Iran Air Flight 655, and 290 people were killed.

Military technology triggers the invention of counter-technology, and then counter-counter-technology. The Iraqi insurgents have been improving their bombs and tactics, finding new ways to trigger them and to hide them from the robots or to jam their sensors; at least once they co-opted a captured robot.

The next level of technology may well be swarms of tiny robots— if one extra pair of eyes is good, a hundred or a thousand is better, and much harder to counter.

Lasers

Since the days of Buck Rogers at least, writers have been eager to see energy guns. The military agrees; in 2010 an aircraft-mounted laser successfully destroyed a ballistic missile travelling at 4000 mph.

Laser beams travel at the speed of light, have no recoil, and minimal divergence— the beam is narrow even at long distances. Laser sights make use of the latter property.

Unfortunately, lasers consume enormous amounts of energy and generate huge amounts of heat, making it difficult to create hand-held weapons. Plus, human tissue is mostly water and lasers do mostly heat damage; the physics makes this a bad combination. And if the target stays still and you do vaporize some tissue, the vapor will block the beam.

In the short run it's more practical to make weapons that dazzle or stun the enemy, or explode their rockets. Or stick with bullets, which use energy efficiently and do lots of damage.

Plasma or antimatter are even more speculative. They'll probably require enormous energy too.

Information

The World Wars were all about applying industrial technology to war, making armies and ships as massive and powerful as our dams, factories, and steamships. The next military revolution may be the application of information technology.

We're starting to see this in the Iraq war— e.g. the US often undertakes major actions at night, when its forces can use night goggles to see, and the insurgents can't.

In future wars, soldiers may have heads-up displays that show information about the enemy and the environment, personal AIs to offer advice and warnings, weapons that offer targeting assistance, and radio contact with buddies, robots, neighboring divisions, and command. War, in short might be like a video game, with live fire.

This is more of a novelty than it sounds; one of the universals of combat has been the fog of war. The individual combatant sees only a tiny fraction of the battle. In the gunpowder era the battleground was literally covered by fog, by persistent clouds of gunpowder. In WWI trench warfare, once a battalion climbed out of the trenches to advance into the no man's land, they were eerily cut off from all contact, even if they were only a thousand yards ahead. The fog only began to lift with the widespread use of radio technology in WWII.

It'll be interesting to see if the classic military hierarchy survives this change. Your typical cannon-fodder had to obey because he had little training but drill, and saw only a tiny portion of the battlefield. If every private is a highly trained expert and has the same information as the general, he can be a good deal more autonomous.

Unobtainium weapons

There's no need to restrict yourself to cutting-edge or foreseeable weapons; if you do you'd be like a Roman writer inventing really fancy swords. You'd might as well posit something impossible.

The same questions apply as to fantasy war (p. 271). Few weapons are devastating for long. Think about what happens when everyone has your weapon. What are its limitations; what are the counter-measures?

Alfred Bester is an excellent model for how to think things out. In *The Stars My Destination*, personal teleportation is possible, but only to precisely known and visualized locations; effective counters include total darkness and obscuring coordinates with mazes. The book is full of implications neatly drawn from the idea, such as homesteads out in the middle of nowhere and corporate tycoons who express their status by maintaining pre-teleport modes of transportation.

Quite a few s.f. themes have interesting applications to war:

- Teleportation: appear in ones and twos in enemy territory to infiltrate, or in thousands to invade

- Telepathy: track where all the insurgents are and what their intentions are. On the other hand, codes and surprise attacks become impossible

- Time travel: go back a week to disable the enemy's defenses before the war starts, or back a century to stop his rise to power

- Nanotechnology: flood the enemy's bodies and machines with microscopic invaders

- Matter duplicators: finally solve those pesky logistics problems; easily duplicate the enemy's more advanced weapons so long as they fit in the analyzer bin

Future cultures of war

Beyond the technology of war, think about future cultures of war. It's questionable whether the European idea of massed battling armies will continue to be useful. Large and comfortable nations have much to lose and little to gain by throwing themselves at each other.

Perhaps new conventions will develop for nearly symbolic combat between advanced nations. A nuclear tournament, for instance: set off some bombs in space to show who has the most effective weapons. Perhaps a corps of volunteers is placed at the detonation point to demonstrate that the will to sacrifice still exists. The side that demonstrates insufficient courage and firepower concedes the battle.

Asymmetric warfare can be expected to continue. In a 2002 set of war games preparatory to the Iraq war, Paul van Riper, the commander of the "Red" forces (those playing the enemy), used a series of simple evasions that discomfited the "Blue" troops planning a high-tech offensive. To avoid Blue's electronic eavesdroppers, he use motorcycle messengers; he sank massive Blue battleships with suicide bombers.

Saddam Hussein himself was not nearly so clever. But as the insurgency showed, though a high-tech military can easily occupy a lower-tech country, an insurgency can make it nearly ungovernable for years on end. Roadside bombs or suicide bombers are cheap, and require the occupier to stay in safe zones or venture out only in highly militarized units, making the occupation politically difficult.

This can also be thought of as a matter of military culture: the insurgents do not recognize the Western rule that an occupation definitively ends the war.

Space imperialism

That people will form interstellar empires and then have grand old battles is a hoary old s.f. tradition, and probably hooey.

Respecting Einstein

If you respect the speed of light— that is, you stick with science that's held up for more than a century— then interstellar states, empires, and wars are nearly impossible.

Space is really, really big. There's a nice sunlike star four light years away, but as we saw above (p. 40), comfortable stellar systems are likely to be rare— space is full of red dwarfs. And we're far from having anything that can come anywhere near lightspeed. A grand tour of the human colonies near Sol could take several lifetimes.

But suppose we have a workable STL drive. Are you really going to pack up a large fraction of your metals, use some unimaginable amount of your energy reserves to send them way out of communications range, and have them take on an enemy right next to his own industrial base?   Space imperialism is the mother of all quartermasters' nightmares.

And for what? Once we've got the nanoduplicators set up, what material goods could they send back that we don't have? Spices? You want to take a chance on alien plant species? Kudzu is bad enough.

Some people are convinced that we've messed Earth up so badly that we need to find a new planet. First, good luck convincing the rest of the planet to fund your departure. More importantly, the skills needed to start a new colony somewhere in space— long-term economic and political stability, sustainable industry, a light ecological footprint— are precisely those that are most lacking on Earth right now. *You've got to solve those anyway.* And once you do, you don't need a lifeboat.

S.f. empires are an unwarranted extrapolation from our Age of Navigation. But planets are not oceans. As Charlie Stross puts it, get back to me on space colonization once we've got burgeoning colonies in far easier environments, such as Antarctica and the bottom of the ocean.

This also explains why no aliens have ever, to our knowledge, taken over this prime bit of real estate. Anyone advanced enough to get here is advanced enough not to need the place as *Lebensraum*. Personally I suspect that galactic protocol is "hands off any planet with an ecosphere."

My own s.f. future, as used in *Against Peace and Freedom*, addresses these issues in this way:

- Human lifetimes are far longer— well over 600 years. This makes it practical to undertake several space journeys in one lifetime.

- Human colonies are linked in a loose confederation, the Incatena. The Incatena has some police powers— in effect, its agents have extraterritoriality— but has nowhere near the power needed to conquer a member planet. Its agents are free to use diplomacy and espionage, however.

- There's little trade in anything massive; instead, what's traded are ideas: databases, information and entertainment, franchises, patents.

Screw Einstein

OK, sigh, you want faster than light travel.

Interstellar war is still a difficult proposition, for the same reason that it's hard to take over a nation entirely using ships or aircraft. You're still sending out a lot of metal way away from home. You can only send a fraction of your industrial output, while the enemy has *an entire planet*. No matter how magic you make your supply lines, they're still longer than his.

Plus, you're attacking from space; though that gives you some advantages (e.g. you can nuke the planet at no risk to yourself), it also makes you highly visible and highly vulnerable— rather like a WWII aircraft carrier, an impressive feat of engineering that could be sunk by three torpedoes.

OK, think big— you have factories that take up entire planets, you can fuse metals out of gas giants, and every ship can use minimal energy to go directly anywhere in the galaxy from just outside planetary orbit. (You still want those lovely tracking shots of the spaceship approaching or leaving the planet.)

But you have to assume the enemy has the same technology, if not the same level of resources. So when your megafleet arrives, his can just *leave*. Space is big. Which of the hundred billion stars in the galaxy did they move to? If space travel and resources are cheap, there can hardly be choke points and fortifications.

As Arthur C. Clarke said, a sufficiently high technology is indistinguishable from magic. But that means that, like magic, it should be defined in a satisfying and plausible way. Magic that make a character omnipotent is uninteresting, since the character no longer has any needs or limits. By all means create superweapons and super-travel, but give them interesting costs and limitations.

The precise nature of the galactic society you come up with, and the kind of wars it fights, will depend on those costs and limits. For instance:

- *Spaceships are expensive enough for a group of private investors to build, and take a few months between stars.*

  Then you essentially have the age of sailing ships: spaceships can be maintained by corporations, colonies are distant but not unimaginably so, most wars will be local since only large states can assemble a fleet in one place.

This is similar to some of the universes created by Robert Heinlein... as a libertarian, he made sure to keep space affordable for private citizens.

- *FTL spaceships are huge investments only states can afford, and take a few weeks between stars.*

Now you have something like WWII and its battleships and aircraft carriers. A fleet of three spaceships is an enormous imposition of force (at least against another fleet, not necessarily a planet). Spaceships might have a squadron of STL fighters to deploy as protection, or to land on a planet. Decoys that imitate the radiation signature of a spaceship might be an important obstructive tactic.

This is largely the model of *Star Trek* or *Battlestar Galactica*.

- *Space travel is instantaneous, but only along particular wormholes.*

In effect a large set of worlds becomes closely interconnected— and can have wars not much more complex than those between planets of a single stellar system— but this may be only a small part of the galaxy; the rest remains nearly inaccessible.

This is the setup for the *Mass Effect* games.

- *Space can be directly travelled with little energy by teleportation, perhaps directly by individuals.*

In essence, all planets are connected, if only for foot traffic. The same sort of wars can be fought as within a planet; but you can't prevent the enemy from taking the war to your doorstep.

A variation: *only* biological entities can be teleported. That means you can't bring your space scooters, factories, or guns... though you could bring your war horses and attack wolves. (Might as well allow thin layers of dead animal or plant material, so people arrive with their clothes on, to say nothing of their hair and epidermis.)

- *Individuals can travel directly between planets— but only a select, trained few.*

Space travel becomes a form of tourism or very restricted trade. War is essentially limited to espionage, or to expensive conventional means.

One universe that follows this idea is *Le cycle de Cyann* by François Bourgeon and Claude Lacroix.

Making maps

One of the primary tools for visualizing your world is maps. In this chapter we'll go over how to make beautiful maps that make you want to go there.

See the Astronomy chapter (p. 47) for how to create the geological elements of the map: what continents should look like, where the rivers go, where mountains will appear. This chapter is about drawing the actual maps.

Methods

Methods: Paper

My first maps were on paper, generally made with pens and colored pencils. Also, we lived in a paper bag in the middle of the road and our Da killed us every morning.

Paper maps are hard to modify, hard to get right, and harder to show to the world. Nonetheless they may be an essential first step in creating a computer illustration. Most of us can draw better on paper than on the computer; if that's the case with you, draw your map and then scan it.

Given that, you don't need to worry too much about all the art school techniques— what paper to use, what brush or pen. You're basically doing a clean rendering that you'll finish up on the computer.

If you do want maps as permanent works of art— well, throw away the ballpoint pens and get to know your local art supply store. Calligraphic pens offer a sensuous thick black line; technical pens give a very black line of uniform thickness.

Uniform coloring is very hard to do. You may have luck with art markers. If you have patience, there are color films that you can cut into shapes with an X-acto knife.

Clean-up on the computer can be tedious, so for best results you want a nice thick line on white paper. If you have pencil sketch lines, erase them, or draw very lightly and ink the final line heavily, then turn up the contrast once it's scanned.

Methods: Computer

First: get a **drawing tablet**. Drawing with a mouse, to say nothing of the horrors that come with notebook computers, is like trying to wrangle a knife and fork with your feet. I use the cheapest Wacom tablets, which have hovered around $100 for years. Though if enough people buy this book I'd love to get a tablet-monitor. Those things are *sweet*.

Tablets are not only easier to use— you use a stylus, like a pen, rather than the mouse— but they're pressure-sensitive, which is essential for nice-looking lines and for airbrushing.

Second: forget all about Microsoft Paint. There's lots of great paint programs out there. For drawing I like **Photoshop**— though it's an annoyance that its brushes aren't sharp enough. Sometimes I use Painter for its better brushes; or I just use the Sharpen filter in Photoshop.

There's a low-end alternative, **Photoshop Elements**, which is perfectly adequate; I got it free with my Wacom tablet. Or use the free **Gimp**.

The hand-eye coordination takes a little getting used to. Or a lot. But you have an **Undo** button; use it often.

As a map largely consists of sharp lines and text, **Adobe Illustrator** is a natural for them. You can import a shaded bitmap for terrain. As Illustrator is vector-based, it supports scaling much better than Photoshop. Plus, you can edit the path point-by-point, a boon for drawing smooth curves.

There are programs specifically for making maps; I'll list some on the web resources page, http://www.zompist.com/resources/pck.html.

Layers

Photoshop (and similar programs) have a wonderful feature: **layers**. These are like a stack of transparent acetate cels you can draw on.

Here's a representation of the layers of a simple map of Arcél: text on top; then borders; then rivers and coastline; then terrain in grayscale; then the ocean.

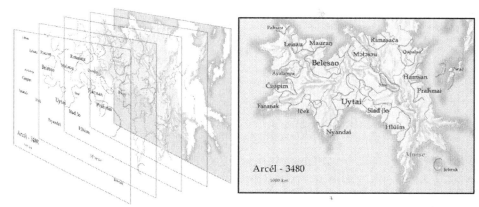

Layers don't conflict with each other, so you can move text around without messing up the image below, or draw the terrain without affecting your rivers and coastlines.

Best of all, you can create multiple maps with the same base: maps of political states, languages, resources, religions, sapient races, whatever. With transparent colors, these can all share the nice shaded terrain.

Overall tips

The first map you make, you're likely to be in a hurry, and draw big blobby shapes and nearly-straight rivers and mountain ranges. That's fine, but go back and **refine** it later. Natural shapes (including coastlines, rivers, and mountains) show a certain randomness— learn to cultivate a jiggly line to suggest detail.

Here's an example of a region of Almea, Nan, in an early and late form:

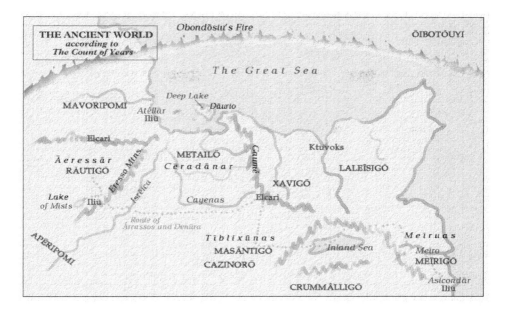

THE ANCIENT WORLD
according to
The Count of Years

Obondōsiu's Fire

ŌIBOTŌUYI

The Great Sea

MAVORIPOMI

Deep Lake

Dàurio

Atéllār
Iliū

Elcari

Ktuvoks

Āeressār
RĀUTIGŌ

Bresso Mtns.

METAILŌ
Cēradānar

Caumé

LALEĪSIGŌ

XAVIGŌ

Isrélca

Lake
of Mists

Iliū

Cayenas

Elcari

*Route of
Árrassos and Denūra*

Tiblixūnas

MASĀNTIGŌ

CAZINORŌ

Inland Sea

Meīruas

Meiro
MEĪRIGŌ

APERIPOMI

CRUMMĀLLIGŌ

Asicondār
Iliū

Plausible mountains

Here's a step-by-step guide to drawing a shaded relief layer.

We'd might as well look at what mountains actually look like. Here's a Landsat image of Madrid (the city is the white stain just right of center); the mountains are the Sierra de Guadarrama.

The problem is, this map is only about 200 km across. On the larger scales you're likely to be working with— entire countries or continents— mountains barely register. So what we're really after is a convincing illusion.

I'll illustrate with the northwestern portion of Arcél, a region 2000 km wide, ten times wider than the satellite image above, though it's only a portion of the continental map a few pages back.

Always draw at magnification— I used anything from 200% to 600%. You have a lot more control over your lines that way. (But frequently go back to 100% to see how it looks.)

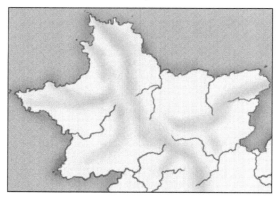

First, I used the airbrush tool (17-pixel width), in a gray a few shades darker than the neutral background, to draw the shaded sides of the mountains. Note that the mountains are basically parallel sets of long ridges, not the individual triangles you remember from Tolkien's maps.

Remember that you're drawing *half* of the mountain at this point, the shaded part. Which side is shaded? Pick a direction for the light (mine is the northwest) and be consistent. It may help to use a sketching layer to draw the continental divide— the highest points of the mountains. Shade the side of the mountains away from the light.

Don't overdo it... note that the river valleys are left flat. You can draw some low relief here in very light colors, but there's no real need.

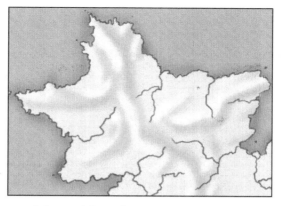

Now I used a white airbrush to draw the other side of the mountains. Again, remember where the light is coming from.

I've also gone back and added some smaller ridges (for instance, the spur that divides the two river basins that drain into the northern ocean).

For this whole process, by the way, I'm working with the terrain area selected. (The magic wand is useful for this.) That way I don't have to worry about drawing outside the continental area. (I don't draw over the rivers because they're on a separate layer.)

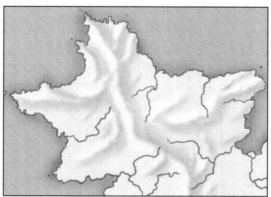

Now that the shading is more or less in the right place, I switched to a smaller airbrush (size 5 or 7) in a darker color, and sharpened up the top of the mountain ridges. I want the top ridge to be fairly sharp, but the bottoms to be fuzzy.

I've also taken the opportunity to make the ridges a little more random. Natural boundaries (coastlines, rivers, mountain ridges) are fractal, with plenty of detail at all levels.

In the northern peninsula, among other areas, I've made the minor ranges meet up with the main range, instead of running parallel to it. It looks nicer that way.

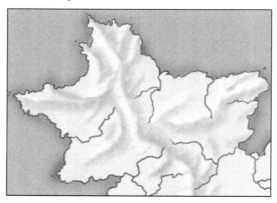

The mountains don't look bad now, and indeed if you use color overlays this is about all you'll see anyway. But to add some final detail, I used a smaller airbrush yet (3 pixels) and drew cross-shading: white lines on the shaded areas, dark lines on the bright areas.

Remember, Undo is your friend. Don't be afraid to draw some stuff just to see how it looks. If it doesn't look like you want it to, undo and try again.

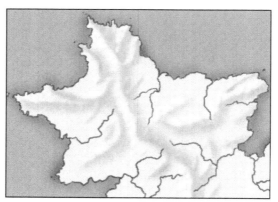

At this point I decided that the mountains were a little too dark and sharp-looking. So I used the blur tool to soften up the edges, and also applied a lightening filter. Now the mountains don't overwhelm the map.

Cheap mountains

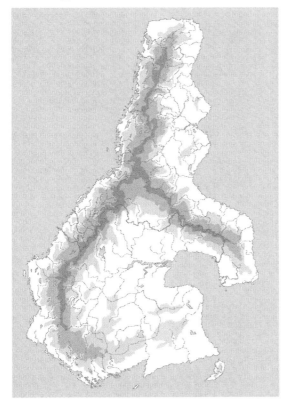

An alternative to shading the mountains is to draw a contour map. You don't have to go crazy with this— three levels of shading (plains; low mountains; high mountains) are about all you need.

Here's an example, a map of the island of Apoyin on Almea. I made it as a contour map because it was originally a set of D&D hex maps which only indicated two levels of terrain.

See also the map of Borneo on p. 63.

A CGI globe

Rectangular world maps will distort your world horribly. But they have one neat use: they can be used in a 3-D modelling program to create a globe.

You need a cylindrical projection for this— that is, a map whose height is half its width, with the latitudes equidistant, fortunately one of the easiest maps to mark out. (Contrast with the Mercator, where the latitude lines get farther apart closer to the poles.)

Load the map into your favorite 3-D modelling program (p. 342), create a sphere, and use your map to texture it:

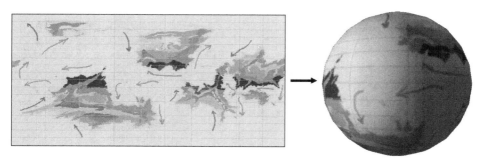

Within the program, you can rotate the globe to see what it looks like from various angles.

A sinusoidal map

There is no projection that represents a sphere on a flat surface without distortion— and the better ones require plenty of math and good technical drawing skills. A good compromise is the sinusoidal projection.

Let's start with one spear, 45° in width. (You can use any width, up to the entire circumference of the planet.) The globe will be made of eight of these spears (because 45° is 1/8 of the full 360°).

The drawing width is thus 1/8 of your drawing size. If the equator is 10" long (which will fit neatly onto a sheet of typing paper), the eight spears are 1.25" wide.

The spear's height is half the size of the equator, thus 5".

If you're using A4 paper, a spear width of 3.5 cm and height of 14 cm will work well.

Here's the clever bit. The sides of the spears aren't straight, but curved, and the curve obeys a simple rule: the width at any degree of latitude x is cos x times the width at the equator. Let's work that out for increments of 10° and a spear width of 1.25":

x	cos x	width
0°	1.0	1.25"
10°	.984	1.23"
20°	.940	1.17"
30°	.866	1.08"
40°	.766	.96"
50°	.643	.80"
60°	.500	.63"
70°	.342	.43"
80°	.174	.22"
90°	0	0"

In Illustrator, you can click with the Line tool selected and you'll get a dialog where you can enter the line width. You can also let Illustrator center the lines for you.

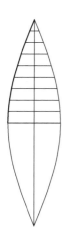

Now connect the edges of these lines with a smooth curve.

I used Adobe Illustrator, drawing the curve by eye, then lining up the anchor points with the latitude lines and smoothing out the curve.

This only needs to be done once; for the other segments the curve can be duplicated, moved, and reflected.

Duplicate this basic shape eight times, and you have this bristly little map of the world:

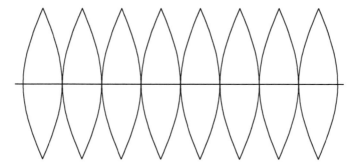

This map won't be very easy to read (it's hard for the eye to connect land masses across spears), but it minimizes distortion.

You can even make it into a physical globe— many commercial globes are made this way, in fact. Use a printout of the map. Carefully cut around the edges of the spears (leave them connected at the equator). Tape the edges and you have a little paper globe of your planet. Or make a map whose equator matches the circumference of a ball; then you can paste the spears on the ball, for a less delicate globe.

To show off your continents, you simply combine spears as needed:

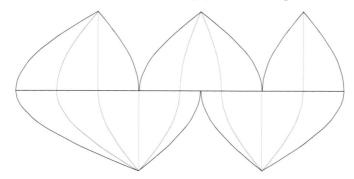

You can combine any number of spears— even half-spears, as in the fifth spear on the bottom. One longitude will always be straight and thus distortion-free; it need not be the one in the middle. For the bottom left lobe I made the longitude that passes through Verduria straight.

If you're drawing on the computer, drawing the combined lobes is easy: just take a half-spear and stretch it horizontally. The middle

Most of the map should be in **subdued colors**— at least halfway to white. Otherwise the text on the map won't be readable. You don't actually need a coastline at all if you color in the ocean, while shaded terrain means that mountain ranges don't need to be indicated with lines.

Use subdued and harmonious colors all over, in fact. Most amateur maps are way too garish. Instead of a white background, a light beige works well.

Color-code your text. I use red for country names, blue for water features, brown for mountains, black for cities. This can't be reproduced in a book, of course, but it makes a map much more readable.

Keep text small— just big enough to read. Use the same font for everything— nothing too fancy.

A little **airbrushing** can subtly emphasize certain features. I like a darker blue shade in the oceans near shore, as seen in the Arcél map above. If you're making a political map, select each colored region and airbrush a darker color along the edges; this creates a nice old-fashioned effect.

For a hand-drawn effect, explore some of the Photoshop brushes and tools. I like the **watercolor** brush, for instance, which I used in this schematic map from the *Count of Years*:

top lobe, for instance, is stretched 300%. (If you're drawing by hand, you'll have to re-measure.) Now you can draw the continents:

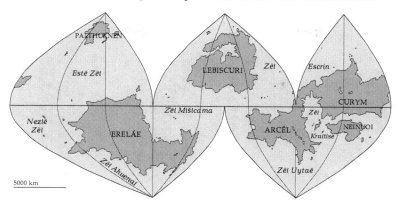

You can combine *all* the spears, if you like. The resulting map gets rid of the orange-slice appearance, but the left and right edges do end up pretty stretched out. (Note Palthuknen in the upper left.)

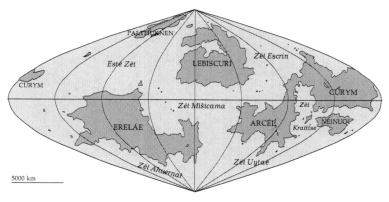

A city plan

A plan of your main **city** may be useful. The easiest method is to draw the walls, fill in the city area with one color, then draw lines on top of it for the streets.

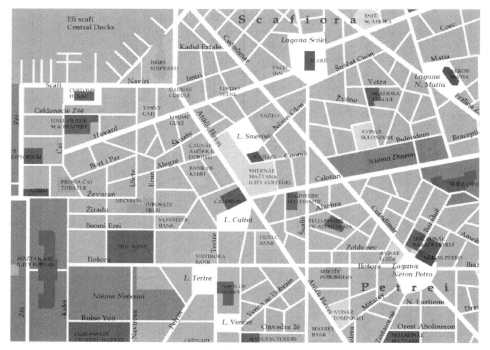

Above is part of the plan of Verduria city; since it's entirely made of geometric shapes and very text-heavy I used Adobe Illustrator rather than Photoshop.

What do you indicate on the city plan? I took the same approach as a guidebook: street names, parks, government buildings, cultural and recreational buildings, temples, palaces, and the top-tier taverns and stores.

Remember that premodern cities were tiny by modern standards. Ancient Nineveh, terror of ancient Mesopotamia, had a population of 30,000 and a size of 720 hectares or less than three square miles. Ancient Rome had about 250,000 residents, which would put it in the rank of Buffalo; medieval cities were only half of that. Verduria has about 600,000 residents, since it's at the start of the steam age.

Some cultures seem to like rectilinear cities, others don't. Seemingly formless cities may have developed out of smaller settlements and following natural features— rivers and streams, ridges and hills.

Whatever is most important to your people will get the most space and the grandest buildings. Roman cities were dominated by public works: forums, baths, theaters. The largest buildings in medieval cities were the churches; in modern cities, corporate offices.

City size correlates with the prevailing mode of transportation. Cesare Marchetti has pointed out that since ancient times people have preferred a commute of no more than one hour— meaning that the radius of a city for pedestrians is limited to about 5 kilometers. Trains, cars, teleportation, and rideable dragons all change the largest practical city size.

Illustrations

If all you do is write, you can skip this chapter. But there's nothing quite like pictures at showing what your world is like and how it differs from other worlds.

You can also skip it if you're a great artist already. It's aimed at the person who thinks they can't draw, or can cartoon but would like to do better.

How to draw better than you could

Methods

Keep your drawing simple. Beginning artists try to solve problems by adding lines. Spend your time instead making sure they're in the right place.

If you work on the computer, you'll really need that graphics tablet. If you don't have one, draw on paper and then scan.

We've already seen the use of **layers** on maps (p. 286). For figure drawing they have a number of uses:

- Put a simple colored background on the lowest layer. The color helps you choose detail colors that harmonize with the overall tone of the picture.

- Use a layer for sketching: draw roughly; then reduce the opacity to 50%. Add a new layer and draw more cleanly on that. Repeat if necessary. Once you've got the final drawing, hide or discard the sketch layers.

- Draw background objects or patterns on a layer above the background, below the figures. It's a lot easier to draw even a straight wall as a single object rather than drawing it in pieces behind the main character. All the more so if the background includes a tree or a desk.

- You can paste images onto a layer and use them as models for drawing.

- Use a separate layer for colors and shading, under your line drawing. This will produce a more even coloration, without having to get the drawing perfectly clean.

- Layers can be used for details— jewelry, beards, shiny patches— that you're not sure if you want or not. You can easily delete them.

- If your picture includes multiple objects, draw each on a separate layer— then you can easily move or resize them without messing anything else up.

Be prepared to **break habits**. You may have some facility with cartooning— you've drawn the same figures for years and have quick ways of drawing ears, eyes, hands, etc. These habits will get in the way of accurate figure drawing. Look at the models and retrain yourself to draw something more complicated but more accurate.

Proportion

If you only absorb one word from this chapter, make it this one: **proportion**. If a picture looks wrong, the proportions are probably off. *Don't try to fix it by adding shading or extra detail.* Get the proportions right in the sketch. If you've gone further, you *may* be able to save the drawing by selecting parts of it and resizing them.

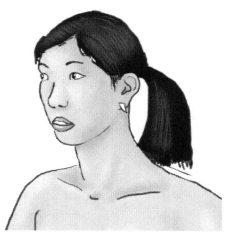

An example: this picture is well rendered, but it still looks bad— the proportions are off.

The girl's eyes are too high on her head and too far apart; her mouth is too low.

Also, her neck is too long, and her shoulders are too broad.

Here's the corrected version of the same picture.

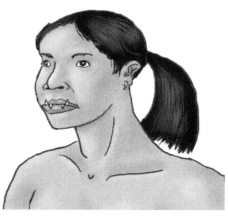

Or you can go the other way: purposely violate the rules to create aliens and monsters. For instance, a high eyeline, tiny eyes, a big nose, and a massive lower lip with overhanging teeth makes a good orc.

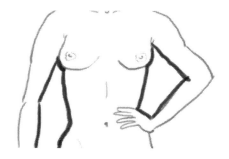

If you're copying a picture or drawing from life, be aware of **negative space**: the voids in the picture have a shape too, and they make excellent diagnostics of an error in proportion.

Even a sketchy drawing will look pretty good if the proportions are lifelike.

Zoom zoom zoom-a zoom

Do you find it hard to get control of the stylus? No problem. Just zoom in.

For instance, this hand needs work, but it's hard to do anything with it at this size.

But blow it up 400%, and it's a lot more tractable.

I've redrawn the hand and then shrunk it back to its proper size.

I always make a drawing much larger than its target size... the eventual shrinking will hide plenty of sins. While working on it, I zoom in as far as possible.

But go back frequently to regular size— in Photoshop this is a single keystroke (Windows ctrl-alt-0; Mac option-command-0). Don't waste your time making the zoomed-in part look fabulous if the details will just get lost at regular size.

Zooming, like shading, can't fix a drawing with bad proportions. If the hand is too small for the arm, it doesn't matter how well drawn it is.

A female face

Drawing pretty girls is a useful skill, and not an easy one. I've been working on it for about thirty years.

Let's start with the basics: a frontal view of the face..

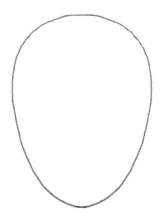

Draw an oval. For extra points, make it more egg-shaped, narrow end down.

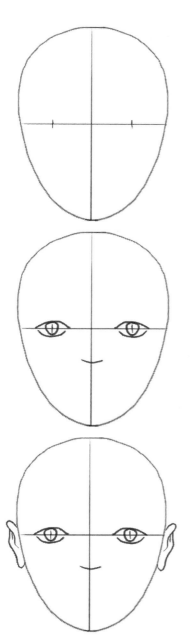

Now draw lines down the middle.

Divide the horizontal lines in half; we're going to put the eyes there. (Slightly inward would be more accurate.)

The eyes live on the middle line— not above them. They are little almond shapes, twice as long as they are high.

Draw a little curve for the nose, a little less than halfway to the chin.

The ears run from the top of the eyes to the bottom of the nose. Don't give the poor girl Dumbo ears; we're not seeing them from the side of the head.

If the ear shape scares you, a narrowed C shape will do. Or cover the ears with hair.

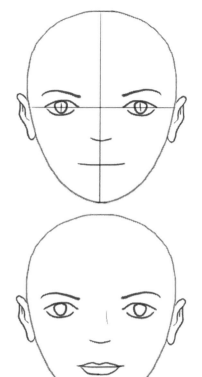

Eyebrows live pretty close to the eyes— about an eye-height above, in fact. They're thicker closer to the nose.

The mouth is closer to the nose than to the chin. The curve you draw here largely determines the expression, so get a line that satisfies you.

The top lip, with its double-bow shape, is only about 1/3 the total height. The bottom lip is half an ellipse.

If you draw an equilateral triangle with two corners at the edges of the eyes, the bottom of the triangle will touch the bottom of the lip.

You can erase the cross-hairs now.

There's a million hairstyles; here's a few simple examples:

The face and figure are timeless, but hair immediately brings in a sense of period. My favorite drawing book, Jack Hamm's *Drawing the Head & Figure*, has extremely '50s hairstyles.

Don't overdo the lines— we know it's hair, you don't have to draw every curl.

If you draw a jagged shape for the hair, remember that the jags can't cut into the outline of the head.

Getting things symmetrical can be tricky; on the computer you can cheat— duplicate the eye or ear and flip it horizontally.

Eyes

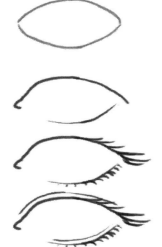

If you draw almonds for eyes you're ahead of many people who are under the impression that eyes are circles. But we can do better yet.

The eye bows in a bit toward the nose, and the corner is curved. The lower edge can be left out or lightly sketched.

Add some sweeping lashes to the side opposite the nose, and some much smaller lashes on the bottom edge.

In close-up only, add a line above for the eyelid and one below for the rim of the eye.

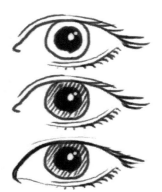

Add a big circle, and a smaller black one for the pupil. The highlights are actually reflections of the lights in the room.

Shade the iris. If you're drawing in color, the color of the iris may not be uniform.

For East Asians, draw a heavy dark curve along the top of the eye, curving down to hide the corner. Asians vary in how much the epicanthic fold covers.

The face in profile

The head in profile isn't egg shaped. Who knew?

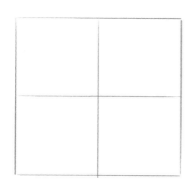

Start with a square, and divide it in four.

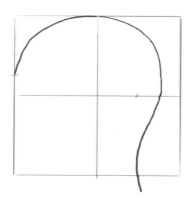

Mark a point ¼ of the way up the left top cell, and draw a smooth curve to the top of the head.

From there draw a smooth curve down; it hits the bottom of the cell ¼ of the way in.

The final curve is a bow shape, hitting halfway across the bottom of its cell.

These lines need not be perfect—they're usually covered by hair.

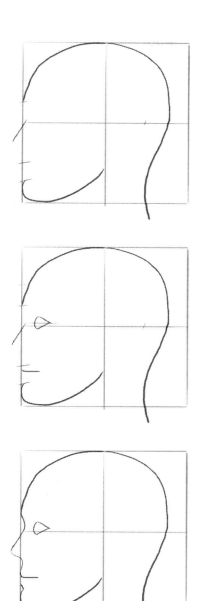

Draw the straight part of the nose, from just above the center line outward. It goes downward about ¼ of the cell.

The jaw is a smooth curve; it's ¼ of the way up the left of the cell and ½ of the way up the right.

The eye is a diamond shape on its side, a tad above the center line.

Draw the mouth a little bit below the center of of its cell, not very far inward.

Fill in the rest of the profile. It curves inward at the level of the eye, and again below the nose and under the mouth.

This is probably the hardest part to get right. Undo, or your eraser, is your friend.

The nose is a bit upturned, which helps it register as female.

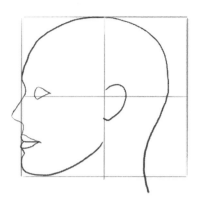

The lips form a sideways heart shape; the bottom lip is bigger.

The ear is a backwards C extending from the top of the eyes to the bottom of the nose.

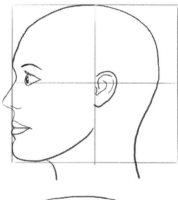

I've added the eyebrow, nostril, and details of the eye and ear.

The main line inside the ear is another C, opposite the main C of the ear. Just below that, and fitting inside it, is a a sort of extended V.

The front of the neck hits ½ of the way along the bottom of the cell.

Finally add hair. Don't start too close to the eyes.

Erase your guidelines so people think you can do without them.

Race

How you draw the eyes, nose, and lips will largely determine the apparent race of the character. These differences should be subtle—

our brains are highly sensitive to tiny facial details, so there's no need to exaggerate.

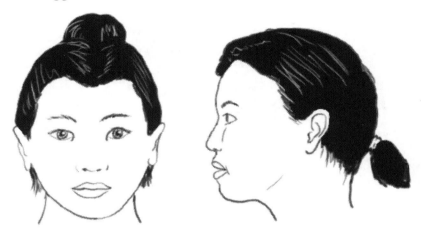

For an East Asian appearance, the main factor is the epicanthic fold, which hides one corner of the eye with a little curve. The eyes are not slits; they aren't slanted either.

The nose is often blunter and a little wider. The lips may be a bit more prominent.

In profile, the cheeks and mouth may be farther forward. Asian hair is normally quite straight.

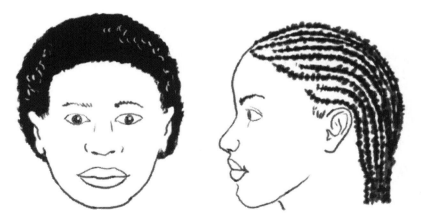

Africans are very varied— what Americans think of as "black" is more generally West African. Here the nose is wider, the lips larger, and the jaw is farther forward.

Natural African hair is frizzy; it can be straightened, but rarely ends up as fluffy as white folks' hair.

 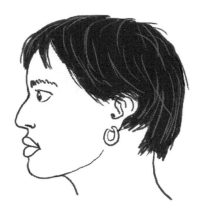

Hispanics aren't very uniform, but a prominent nose and bigger features will help. The nose can be a bit beaky. Try a mixture of European and Asian, or European and African.

Oblique views

Frontal and side views are boring; you want to know how to do oblique perspectives. Fine, but they're harder; don't say I didn't warn you.

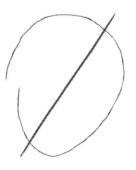

The head is more or less an egg shape, with an extension in the back.

The slash indicates the overall axis of the head; it may help you draw the egg shape.

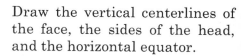

Draw the vertical centerlines of the face, the sides of the head, and the horizontal equator.

These are all half-ellipses. The line going up the face is a bit flattened.

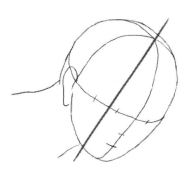

Divide the horizonal line into thirds. The eyes will live on the frontward of these marks.

The nose and mouth are marked out as when you're drawing the front view.

The ear is drawn back of the cross-hairs on the side, just as we did in the side view, but a little foreshortened.

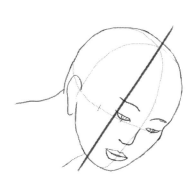

Eyes and mouth aren't straight; they follow the curve of the head.

The edge of the head bows inward at the eyes.

It's the nose that's most distinctive in this view; it's kind of a soft L shape.

The nose and the left eyebrow (the one on our right) form an extended smooth S-like curve.

I added hair and a few more details.

Her eyes are narrow because she's looking downward.

Sometimes you'll see the edge of the cheek bow inward toward the mouth.

A common mistake with three-quarter views is to draw the facial features too far back. There's a lot of space in between the eyes and the ears.

Male faces

Male faces are a lot more forgiving. Drawing girls, a line a few millimeters off may ruin the drawing; you may not even notice it drawing men.

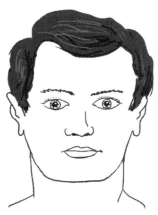

Follow the same basic procedure as for female faces, but note the differences: a squarer jaw, a wider neck, more emphasis on the nose.

The brow is a little lower as well.

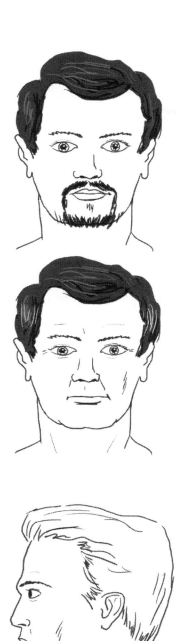

If you've mostly drawn girls, your first attempts at males may look too feminine. Easy solution: add a beard.

Adding more lines will make your character look older— but this may improve the portrait of a man.

I added lines around the eyes and forehead, creases by the side of the nose, and a suggestion of jowls and cleft chin.

Men have lips— go check!— but the picture often looks better if the top lip is removed and the bottom merely suggested with a heavy line.

For the profile, note the blockier brow, nose, and jaw and wider neck. The nose is less upturned, the upper lip straight.

Again, some extra lines look good on a man: beneath the eye, between nose and mouth, along the upper brow and the cheekbone.

A basic female body

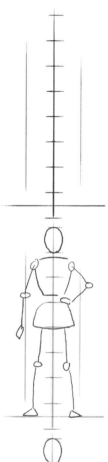

Figures are often measured in heads— after all, the person you're drawing is more likely to have a head than to be holding a ruler.

Hamm recommends 7½ heads— actually a tall frame; a petite girl may be only 6 heads tall. Some artists like to make their women 8 or 9 heads tall; I guess they're leg men.

Anyway, draw a line and mark it in eighths.

You may draw vertical lines a head away from the center— the body will lie well within these lines.

Draw a skeleton figure, following these guidelines:

Torso: a little less than 2 heads tall; shoulders are about ¾ of the way to the side vertical. Note the taper inward.

Hips taper the other way, and extend from head 3 to 4. They're wider than the shoulders.

The **knees** live at head 5½, the **feet** at 7½.

For the extended arm, the elbow is about at head 3, the hand reaches head 4½.

Some helpful landmarks:

• the **nipples** are one head down

• the **navel** is a head below that

• the **crotch** is one more head down

There's a stagger at the knee: the lower legs aren't on the same line as the thighs, they're shifted outward a bit.

Draw the outline of the body. The limbs are **not parallel**— they taper inward as you go down. The neck tapers outward.

The outside curve of the leg starts at the hips and extends to the top of the knee. The *inner* curve goes down farther, below the knee. That is, the bowed-in bit on the outside of the knee is higher than on the inside.

In relaxed position, the thumb is closer to the body and the elbow points away from us.

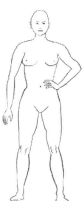

Get your lines in the right place, redrawing as necessary. When they look right, redraw the whole thing on a new layer to get a clean line. (And only then. A bad drawing isn't saved by re-inking.)

The knees are suggested by a couple parenthesis shapes.

You can draw the face as described above, without of course worrying about the tiny details.

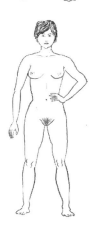

A few more details, and of course hair.

Get to know the shape of the clavicles and the depression in between.

At this angle, the feet form a kind of triangle.... they don't extend out sideways, as I drew them years ago in an otherwise fairly good picture of a flaid.

Male bodies

Adaptations for male bodies:

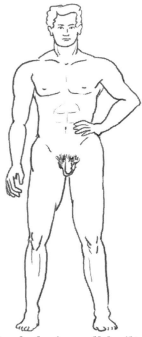

- This figure is eight heads tall. The knees are just above head 6.

- Shoulders wider than hips, as much as two heads wide.

- The neck is thicker, and the muscles on either side (the trapezius) are convex rather than concave.

- The deltoid is more prominent— there's always a curve at the top of the arm.

- Men have waists too, but they're not as indented.

- Without the breasts, it's easier to see how the chest muscles hang from the shoulders. Look at his left arm: the arm slots in under the pectoral muscle.

This dude is well-built but not a superhero. If you're drawing an ordinary shmo, the neck and shoulders will be closer to the female figure.

Shading

My favorite tool in Photoshop is the airbrush. It's amazing how much better a drawing looks when it's properly shaded.

Shaded sphere

Let's start with a very simple object— a sphere.

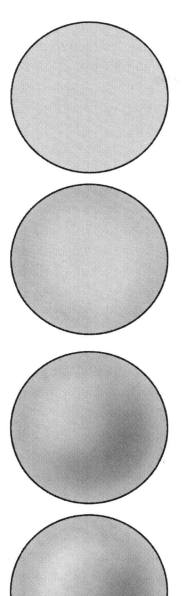

Draw a circle and color it in.

Select the colored area, so the rest of the drawing is restricted to the circle.

Take an airbrush a good fraction of the sphere's diameter— about 1/5 its size will do. Open the color dialog and select a somewhat darker version of the overall color.

Then draw around the circumference, so you get an even shading on all edges. If it's not quite even, add a few more light strokes.

Select an even darker shade. Then draw a sort of crescent moon shape well within your sphere, at an angle.

The idea here is that the darkest part of the sphere is well inside its boundaries— the edge nearest to it is actually lighter.

Now select a color *lighter* than the original shade. (The upper left of the sphere should still have that color, so you can use the eyedropper to get back to it.)

Draw another crescent moon shape, but smaller, on the opposite of the sphere from the dark one.

Select a yet lighter color, close to white. Use this to create a highlight (n the center of your crescent-shaped lighter area.

The exact nature of this last shiny spot will do a lot to suggest the surface material. For instance, use a smaller white airbrush to add a small, very bright highlight, and the sphere will look very shiny.

Experiment with Photoshop's filters. One of my favorite tricks is to use Noise and then Blur, which suggests a more textured material. (An example is the arch pictures on the back cover.) Pixelate / Crystallize suggests a lumpy surface, Brush Strokes / Spatter a rougher one.

The light here is coming from the top left. This may suffice for your first few years of drawing. Of course you can reverse it if the light is coming from the right. Other angles can be more complicated, but the basic principle is easy enough, innit? Areas facing the light are brighter, and throw shadows away from the light. The picture above is cleverly designed so that the angle of the light can be varied by rotating the book.

Shaded face

One you can do a sphere, you can do a face. Bodies are largely composed of overlapping squishy spheroids.

Do the shading on a separate layer, *below* your drawing. That way you can change it easily, and the shading won't spoil your drawing. Plus selecting an area won't be as fiddly— the lines of the drawing add a forgiveness factor.

First, select the area you want to shade.

I use the magic wand on the drawing, non-contiguous, and select the face *in the drawing layer*. The area probably won't reach to the edges. That's fine; use Select / Modify / Expand and expand the selection by 2 or 3 pixels. That'll probably do it, but there may be bits of the drawing that didn't get selected. Use the lasso to add them to the selection.

Move to the drawing layer and use the paint bucket to shade the whole face region with your basic skin color.

Do the same to color in the hair, lips, and clothes.

Now use the magic wand to select just the skin, so you can airbrush merrily away without affecting anything else.

Treat the face just like the sphere, and shade it the same way, ignoring the features.

The neck and the hair can be treated the same way.

Use a smaller, darker brush, and add shadows where something blocks the light: under the nose, chin, and ear; inside the ear; behind the clavicles.

The hair itself casts a shadow, so you can darken just under the hairline.

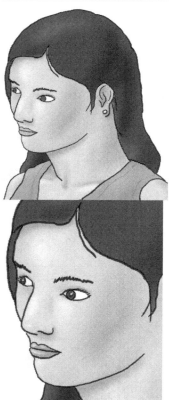

Add light and dark shading to the individual features: nose, forehead, arms, neck.

The cheeks bulge out slightly, so they get a highlight; you can also emphasize the cheekbones with some shading.

The lips are squashed spheres, so they get the usual dark shading toward the bottom, plus an irregular highlight.

For the pupils, use a drawing brush (not an airbrush); draw a solid black pupil, leaving a rim of iris; then add very small white highlights.

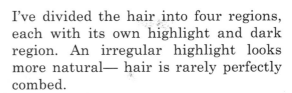

I've divided the hair into four regions, each with its own highlight and dark region. An irregular highlight looks more natural— hair is rarely perfectly combed.

Since this drawing is black and white, the eyebrows are part of the base drawing. In a color drawing, they should be the same color as the hair.

Switch to a drawing brush, and add dark lines over the highlights, and light lines on top of that.

Avoid the temptation to scribble. You want separate lines, nicely curved following the lines of the hairstyle.

Some straggling hairs at the edges help make it look like hair rather than a helmet.

If the face starts to look clownish, undo your last moves and switch to a smaller brush or a color closer to the original skin shade. Or just use a big airbrush set to the original color and swipe it over the whole face, which will reduce all the contrasts.

For a female face, if you go much beyond the above, she'll start to look old. For a **male**, signs of age tend to add dignity: fleshy jowls, a cleft in the chin, bags under the eyes.

Shaded body

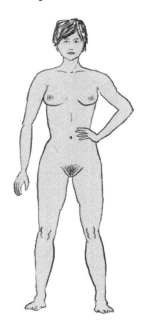

Now let's color in a full figure.

Again, start by applying a uniform base color. The easiest way to choose a color is to find a photograph and sample the skin color (you can't copyright a pixel).

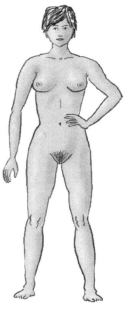

Apply the basic shading rules to each body part: head, arms, torso, breasts, legs: a darker shade on one side, a lighter one on the other.

The arms are thin enough that you can just lighten one side. With the legs, it looks better if the lighter area is within the leg rather than at the edge.

The armpits are a depressed area; also the area just behind the clavicles.

The top of the pelvis— the iliac crest— may be visible at the top of the hips.

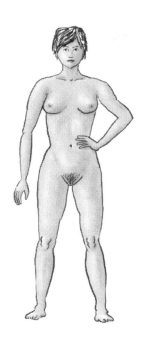

More details, added with a finer airbrush. Note the upside-down U of the rib cage.

Often bones are close to the surface and create visible lines. In the line sketch these are indicated with ink, but some of these have been removed since they are better indicated with shading.

In more complicated poses, the arms and legs are likely to shade other body parts.

Clothing

Unless your people are nudists, you're going to want to put clothes on them. See p. 169 for designing clothes.

Drawing fabric is a study in itself. Here's a picture of a towel draped over my desk lamp.

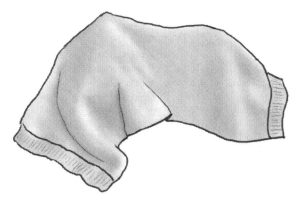

The main thing to notice is how the fabric drapes down from a protruding point (the top of the lamp). It'll do the same thing from parts of the body, usually bony points like shoulders, knees, and the iliac crest (the top of the pelvis).

The lamp has a snaky neck; the towel follows it but is stiff enough to extend past it on the right end.

Note the curtain folds in the middle; you will see these also in draped skirts.

When starting out, it's best to sketch the nude figure first, then add clothes. This will get the proportions right and prevent many errors.

Very tight clothes may approximate the lines of the body... just draw the edges and you've got a swimsuit or superhero outfit.

The drawing below is intended to demonstrate **common errors**.

- No reference to the underlying figure. This is an impossible pose! E.g. the waist and torso point in different directions, and the left foot doesn't fit the leg.

- No attempt at drapery. Cloth folds over itself, especially in areas like the armpit.

- Assuming that body features (the breasts and crotch) look the same in the clothed figure.

- The ends of sleeves and pants legs aren't straight once you put them on. They curve around the limb.

- In several areas (waist, left leg) the clothing is drawn *inside* the line of the body.

- Blouses and shirts usually billow out at the waist.

Sometimes you *want* a flatter, more naïve look— e.g. you're imitating older styles of art.

Here's the same outfit drawn from life.

- There will always be wrinkles at the armpit.

- Note the twist in the fabric on the left sleeve.

- Protrusions produce folds— that, rather than its curve, is what marks the bust here.

- The pants are of a bit stiffer material; they try to retain their cylindrical shape, producing distinctive crush folds at the knee and ankle.

If you use shading instead, you can get rid of most of the little lines:

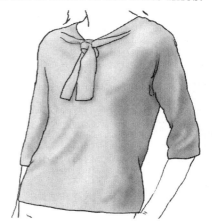

Another blouse. This one is tucked into the pants; note how the material bunches up at the waist.

The breasts produce folds, pointing at the nipple. The breasts are not well separated with most outfits.

The material wrinkles at the armpit and elbows, and bunches up just above the wrist.

About the simplest clothing item to draw is a skirt. The fabric largely heads straight down from the hips. The knees can produce folds as well. A lighter material, or more of it, will produce more folds. Note the squarish curtain folds at the bottom of the skirt.

Pants hide the line of the legs somewhat; they mostly drape down straight from the hips and knees.

The model here is extending her left knee forward, which makes the knee the focus of several folds.

The V-shape of the crotch disappears under clothes. Tight pants tend to have *horizontal* folds at the top.

Good books

Is that everything you need to know to draw figures? Oh god no. Everything looks different as soon as the pose changes. But you can get a whole book of hints: Jack Hamm's *Drawing the Head & Figure*.

Your friendly local bookstore will also have books full of photos, which are invaluable resources. A few I've used:

> John Cody, *Atlas of Foreshortening* (1984)
>
> Erik A. Ruby, *The Human Figure: A photographic reference for artists* (1974)
>
> Thomas Easley, *The Figure in Motion* (1986)
>
> Elte Shuppan, *Pose File*— a series of books published in the 1990s

The Internet is full of pictures, clothed and nude. Fashion catalogs are a great resource too. You can teach yourself a lot by using them as models. If you're going to publish your work, don't copy existing photos; I'll show you a great alternative in a moment.

Good models

You may or may not have a friend who will be willing to pose for you, but you do know at least one person: yourself.

It can take a long time to master full frontal drawing— and then it turns out people don't stay in that position, and each pose is a minefield of new things to learn. Once you're a fabulous artist, you may be able to execute complicated poses from memory. But till then, your best friend is a digital camera.

For instance, here's a panel from a comic of mine, and the photo I took for reference, just for the position of the arms and hands:

That's not a bad reference shot for drawing shirts, too.

A mirror can help too, but the camera is even better. Very likely it has a setting to take a picture on a timer, which allows you to use both hands. Or ask a friend to take the shot.

With some practice you can change sex... here's a panel of my character Fuschia Chang, and the photo I based it on. I could never get that pose right without a model.

3-D Modeling

Fantasy illustration is no longer limited to drawing and painting; you can now create three-dimensional renderings, and even wander around inside of them. The cover illustration includes part of such a rendering.

For me, this is most useful in representing architecture. In theory you can draw anything, and the top artists (such as the French BD artists François Schuiten, Moebius, François Bourgeon, and Jean-Claude Mézières) create jaw-dropping fantastic structures. But to draw even a couple of houses in proper perspective, to say nothing of adding cultural flavor, is a dismaying task.

By contrast it's a few seconds' work to make a building in a 3-D modeling program, duplicating it is a snap, and the program handles perspective, shadows, and even beautiful water reflections— see the example on the back cover.

The ease is deceptive, however; to make an attractive scene you'll still have to put in a lot of work.

I'll describe the basics of modeling, then list a few free modeling programs.

Prims

Whatever program you use, you'll be doing the same thing: creating simple 3-D shapes called **prims**, then shaping and distorting them.

For instance, walls are just stretched-out cubes. Or you can create a room by making a big cube, then hollowing it out. Doors and windows can be made by carving out a space for them, or by careful building: build the wall on either side, then a smaller piece on top between them (and one below, if it's a window).

Prims can be moved, stretched, rotated, and often more complicated operations can be performed— e.g. skewing a cube into a slanted shape, or drawing only part of a torus so you have a curved arc, or extruding a flat shape into a three-dimensional one along a curve.

Prims can be connected together in groups and manipulated as a unit.

The program doesn't care if prims interpenetrate. You can use this to cheat fancier shapes. For instance, a tool might be made with a hollow piece fitting round a shaft— you don't actually have to hollow the thing out.

Textures

Prims can be textured; that is, a picture is applied to the surface. Your modeling program likely comes with a bunch of textures— many varieties of stone, brick, dirt, carpet, etc. Thus with a few clicks a set of prims becomes a stone wall.

Good texturing separates the ugly, fake-looking model from the pros. Slapping on a few canned textures may create something workable, but all too often the textures clash luridly, the interfaces are sloppy (e.g. bricks don't look right at the edges), and the details are unconvincing.

If you do much modeling, you'll want more than the canned textures.

- Google Images is your friend. Try to use free or public domain images, unless you're making something entirely for your own use.

- Take pictures. You're probably surrounded by usable textures— a walk around town will give you hundreds, and best of all you can get multiple variations— e.g. a solid wall, a wall with window, a doorway, interesting architectural details.

- You can draw your own textures using Photoshop— or take photo images and manipulate them. Maybe those red bricks would look better in brown; or you can add in a picture of a window, even adding a drop shadow.

Seamless textures

Ideally you want a **seamless texture**— one that can be tiled without the edges being obvious. Let's go over how to do this in Photoshop.

First, here's a picture I took of a wall in town.

The image isn't rectilinear; this is easily fixed. Select the whole image, then Edit > Transform > Skew. Move the corners till the lines between the bricks are parallel to the edges of the picture.

Here you can see where I moved the corners— I expanded the window so I could move them outside the image itself.

Here's the image after skewing.

I increased the contrast, and also lightened or darkened some of the individual bricks, to add to the visual interest. (This sort of thing is less necessary if you're working in color.)

I've cropped the image along the lines of the mortar between the bricks, which will make the rest of the work easier.

Modelling programs prefer textures in powers of 2, so this would also be a good time to resize the image to something like 512x512 pixels.

Select Filter > Other > Offset; you'll get the dialog shown. Enter offsets half the size of the image. (E.g. if the image is 512x512, enter 256 for both offsets.)

Now you can see what the image looks like tiled. There are a number of problem areas.

Select the Clone Stamp tool and choose an airbrush— for this image I used a 17 pixel brush. Alt-click (Mac: option-click) in a suitable area of the image, and apply it in one of the glitchy areas, scrubbing over the border region.

Use Undo if you mess up.

Keep going till the image looks smooth. In this image, I worked on the bricks first, then the mortar lines between them.

If there are too many variations in texture and lightness, such that you can't find enough areas to clone from, use another, more uniform image.

Use Filter > Other > Offset and again enter values of half the image size into the horizonal and vertical offsets.

Now we're back to the original view, but the edges have been modified.

One brick had a staggered edge; I decided I didn't like that and fixed it with Clone Stamp.

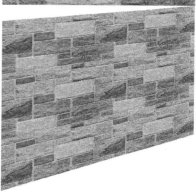

Now we've got a seamless texture that can be used to tile a wall of any shape.

With this image, the repetition is noticeable. If that bugs you, use a more uniform image, or a larger texture (more bricks would make the repeat stand out less).

Advanced texturing

The default texturing will apply a single texture to the entire prim. You can get a lot fancier than that, however.

Each surface can have its own texture. You can use this for variety (e.g. some walls have windows, some have none), or for non-uniform objects, like a fireplace with a wood mantel on top.

You can tile a seamless pattern on one or more surfaces; this looks far better than just stretching the image. The tiling can be different horizontally and vertically— e.g. a long brick wall might tile just once vertically, and many times horizontally.

The image can be cropped or offset. For instance, perhaps a wall texture has a baseboard at the bottom. But perhaps you have a partial wall up above somewhere. You can set a vertical offset so the baseboard doesn't appear.

Alpha textures

Here's a mind-blowing tip: textures can include **transparent areas**. So, instead of messing with prims to make a window, you can just create one or more transparent areas in your wall texture, apply the texture to a solid wall, and behold, you have windows you can see through!

You can use the same trick for doorways if they're just for show. It doesn't work for avatars though, since transparency only affects appearance— the prim is still solid. You can cheat sometimes, though— e.g. if a short wall is mostly doorway, you can make the entire prim non-physical.

Another application is to make irregularly shaped decals. For instance, you could create a circular clock, or a bloodstain, and apply it to a very thin prim in front of a wall. This sort of thing can add variety to the walls without creating a load of textures.

Generally this involves creating an **alpha channel** in Photoshop. Let's look at how to do this to create a railing.

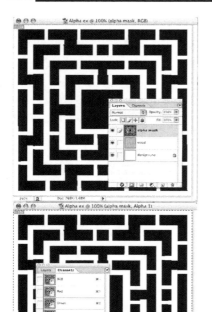

Create a layer for your alpha mask and fill the whole window with white. The idea here is that black areas are transparent; white areas are opaque; and grey is in between. That can be useful for semi-opaque windows, or special effects like a gauze curtain.

The screen cap shows the layer dialog over the artwork. Copy the contents of the alpha mask layer.

Select Channels in the Windows menu. You'll get the window shown. Don't worry about the color-oriented channels it lists.

Click the arrow above the list of channels and select New Channel... from the menu. Accept the defaults.

That gives you an all-black window. Paste in the contents of your alpha mask layer.

(You can draw directly in the alpha channel, but it's easier to have a layer corresponding to it, because it's easier to line it up with elements of the image.)

Go back to the layers window and select any layer to get the regular view back. Hide the alpha mask layer.

The image just shows a wood texture since that's what we want for the bars of the railing.

Save the image as a TGA file; make sure alpha channels are saved.

Here's the texture applied to a long rectangular prim in the modelling program, magically transparent.

The top of the railing gets a different, solid texture. Or you can add a second prim for the handrail, a little wider.

Prim or texture?

Often something can be handled either by adding prims, or by adding to the image.

It's easy to overdo the prims at first. E.g. you want a railing partway up the wall, or a set of pipes in your spaceship corridor; you add a bunch of prims. It looks great, and texturing is simple— e.g. a pipe just needs a generic metal texture.

However, it may end up a lot less work, and look just as good, if you add these details to the texture. It's remarkable how much character is added by a good texture. For instance, here's a simple spaceship corridor, with no textures and with fancy drawn ones:

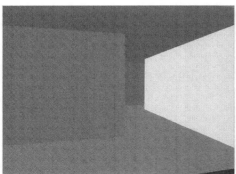

In general, use prims only where you need to get the lines right (e.g. you can see the edge of a building and it shouldn't be straight). If the model is to be traversable, judicious use of prims can increase the level of realism; e.g. a low wall will look better with a protruding cap.

Pay particular attention to transitions— e.g. wall to roof. Look at the nearest door: the wall doesn't just end at a particular spot; there's usually a protruding frame. That can make your modeled door look better too.

Say, this is starting to sound like a lot of work, isn't it? Well, yes. Creating an model for use as an illustration will take a few evenings— longer than drawing it, if you can draw architecture at all. But the learning curve is easier.

Meshes

Some things can't be nicely modeled with a few prims, however distorted. Instead they are modeled with **meshes**, three-dimensional surfaces composed of tiny polygons.

Character avatars are an obvious example; they're made from hundreds or thousands of polygons. It's quite an art to make such complicated figures— fortunately there are usually free figure meshes you can use if you need them. If you want to create your own tentacled owlbear, though, you're on your own.

Prims are actually very simple meshes— a cube has just six polygons. Circular prims (spheres, donuts, pipes) build the curved form out of multiple polygons. Something like a pipe can look surprisingly good with just six outside polygons— that is, its cross-section is really a hexagon, not a circle. A large column may not look good without several times that number.

An irregular surface, like **terrain**, can be created by subdividing a large simple prim— e.g. turning a single face into an array of 32 triangles— and then jiggling the vertices randomly. In combination with a good texture, it doesn't take a whole lot of vertices to make terrain look naturally irregular.

You could use the same technique to make a stone wall where the wall bulges out to match the texture. This is usually overkill, but it'll improve a wall that's supposed to look highly three-dimensional, but instead looks too much like a picture stretched over a flat surface.

In general, the more polygons, the more rendering time. If you actually want to move around in your world, you want to limit how fancy your models get.

Designing a building

How do you actually go about modeling a building?

It may help to draw a rough diagram of the floor plan. I find it easier to just lay it out using prims. If you're using a program that allows you to walk around in the model, go do so; it's the best way to see what the sizes really look like.

A huge square is a particularly unexciting design; try some of these instead. The interior rooms get more windows, and the designs create interesting exterior spaces as well— courtyards or gardens. Also see the section on Architecture (p. 175).

Once you have a design you like, roughly lay out the walls, exterior and interior. Vary the size of rooms— a mansion, for instance, might have a huge dining hall, a large kitchen, relatively large bedrooms, and small rooms for servants.

You probably need some corridors to get from room to room— the servants shouldn't have to get to their cubbyholes by tromping through milady's bedchamber. Rearrange the walls as necessary. To allow easy changes while you're working it out, it may be a good idea to make the walls non-physical so you don't have to add the doors yet.

If you have multiple floors, you need to leave room for stairs. Make sure you like the location, because they're going to be hard to move as you firm up the design, largely because they leave huge holes in the floor. The upper floors may be smaller, leaving nice balconies.

Once all the rooms look good, add the doors. Depending on the program you're using, this may be a matter of carving out the doorway, or rebuilding the walls (e.g. turning a straight wall into three pieces).

Roofs can be a pain. Flat roofs are easy but will make your building look like an office park. The traditional A-frame looks good, though it's tricky to make it work between wings. A barrel vault is pretty easy to make, though harder for elaborate floor plans. You can make also more elaborate shapes (e.g. a fancy pediment) as meshes.

Now add textures and details (such as door frames, columns, or larger corner posts). It may only be at this point that it's clear whether your building is a stone castle or a future space colony!

Some programs

These are just a few programs easily accessible for beginners. (Some of the high-end programs include Maya, 3ds Max, Softimage, and Lightwave 3D.)

I've only briefly used **Blender** and thus can't say much about it, but it's free and open source.

Garry's Mod is available cheap on Steam and allows creating an interactive environment with working contraptions. To create buildings you'll need **Hammer** (covered below) anyway.

Hammer is Valve's map editor; many other video games provide one too. The **Creation Kits** for *Fallout 3* and *Skyrim* are very powerful. The **Unity** game engine has a free version.

Second Life

Second Life is a virtual world created by Linden Lab, with a strong nod to the Metaverse described in Neal Stephenson's *Snow Crash*. From Stephenson, perhaps, it takes its relentless spatial metaphor: the entire world is one huge two-dimensional grid.

The grid is divided into "sims", each 256 m on a side— that's virtual meters, of course. Presently (2010) there are over 31,000 sims, for a total area of more than 2000 km². The content for all these sims is almost entirely generated by the users.

Access is free, but to do any serious building you'll need land, and that's where Linden makes its money. The smallest plots (512 m²), barely large enough for a house, cost about $5 a month— and as a background you'll have your neighbors' horrible constructions. You can build in the sky, however!

If you join the community, cheaper opportunities may occur— that is, you may be able to borrow someone else's land. I've created a castle, a couple spaceships and space colonies, a Chinese pavilion, and a steampunk airship, some on my own land and some on friends'. If you want a whole cityscape, Second Life will be very expensive.

Building is done within Second Life, using the Build dialog. Here's the dialog, with a freshly created prim. To create a prim, click the build button (A), then click in the world.

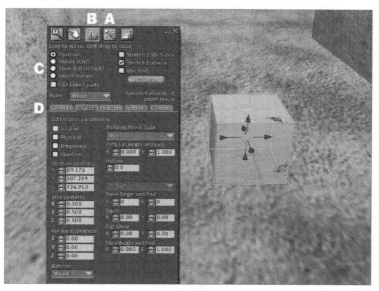

Now hit the edit button (B). Basic editing is done with the mouse; the radio buttons at (C) determine what you're doing (rotating, stretching, or moving). Click and drag the colored arrows on the object to affect it.

The tabs at (D) and the options below the tab menu allow you to do all sorts of things. Right-click on the object and pick Take a Copy to get a copy of the prim in your inventory; don't forget to rename it.

The interface is pretty intuitive— just play with the values and see what you get. If you get lost, there's a wiki available on the Second Life website.

On the plus side,

- You can learn to create a passable building in an afternoon, and there are good textures available for free in your inventory; many more can be cheaply purchased, or you can upload images.

- You can torture prims in interesting ways—add a twist, hollow them out, remove part of them— e.g. turn a sphere into a half-dome, or a cube into an L shape. Behind the scenes, what you're doing is defining simple meshes.

- You can link a set of prims into a single object, which can then be manipulated either as a unit, or piece by piece.

- You can move around in your build in real time. At the least you can choose the perfect spot to take a picture; at the extreme you can organize a roleplaying sim and go live in your world.

- Avatars, yours or your friends', are available as human figures. You can even design skins and clothes to directly represent your world.

- If you have access to Linden water, it's quite pretty, with realistic reflections.

- You can use Second Life's lighting model, even set the time of day. You can simulate a space environment, for instance, by building far up in the sky and setting the time to midnight. You can specify light sources and give items a nice glow effect.

- There's a huge market in clothes, furniture, plants, and all sorts of toys— including fantasy and s.f. variants. This can save a huge amount of time in decoration.

- You can import meshes (complex 3-D models), which can create some stunning effects. However, these must be created in another modeling program.

Some minuses:

- Prim counts are limited by your land size— e.g. a 512 m^2 plot comes with just 117 prims.

- There are some fiddly limitations on prim size— e.g. you normally can't create things larger than 10 m or smaller than 0.01 m. (You can acquire megaprims but they're not resizeable.)

- Applying textures is prim-oriented, though you can select multiple surfaces at once. This works best with simple textures or prims.

- There's no orthographic view available; this can make alignment more difficult. Instead of doing everything by eye, use the Build dialog to input set values— e.g. make all the walls 4.5 meters high and make sure they start at 11.25 meters.

- You can only edit terrain on land you own, and it's pretty low-res.

- You can't get less ambient light than the Midnight setting.

Second Life is great for creating an environment you can walk around in; but be aware of a subtle distortion created by the camera angle. Normally you see your avatar on screen, and the camera is a few feet above your head.

The problem is, you're likely to make walls look good by eye— and your eye is ten feet above the ground. As a result you're likely to overbuild. You'll make enormous buildings with 14-foot ceilings, and the avatars will look like dwarfs inside them.

If you scale the buildings to the avatars, however, you'll find that the camera is messed up— it can't fit in the same room as the avatar!

Compromise a bit— make the walls just high enough to allow the camera in. (Or use mouselook, which takes the perspective of your avatar.)

A newb mistake in Second Life is to build vast barn-like spaces. These are about as inviting as, well, barns, and they're hard to furnish. Think small! The max size prim— 10 meters on a side— makes a great room. To make an interesting house, don't tile your 10 meter prims; offset them.

Hammer

Hammer is the Valve map editor; it's used to make levels for *Half-Life 2, Team Fortress 2, Portal, Counter-Strike, Left 4 Dead*, and more. If you own any of these games, you can download Hammer for free— select "Source SDK" from your Library > Tools list.

Hammer looks more like most 3-D modeling programs: you start with four views, a 3-D render plus three orthogonal wireframe views.

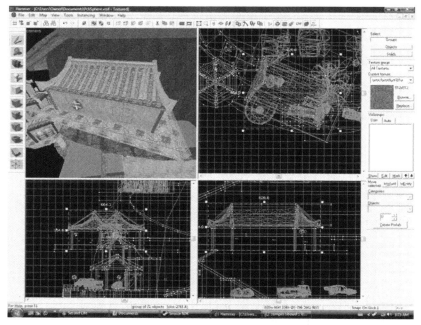

You create your map in Hammer, then compile it and run it using the target game.

A map consists of three types of things:

- "Brushes", Hammer's name for prims. This is your workhorse— your walls and terrain will be made of brushes. Each game comes with a set of textures, or you can use your own.

  Terrain is created using "displacements", brushes that have been subdivided into an array of triangles; the vertices are then moved to create an irregular surface. The Chinese roof seen in the screen cap above is a set of displacements.

- Models— imported MDL files. Basically these are fancy objects that it'd be hard or impossible to make with brushes. Each game comes with a bunch of canned models, and you can create and import your own. (An example is the ship in the front cover illustration.)

- Entities— basically things that tell the game how to behave. At the very least you need an info_player_start entity to tell the map where the player gets spawned, which you'll need to run the map. Entities are also used for all sorts of special effects— lighting, smoke, fog, fire— and of course to make maps work as levels within a game.

To make environments for fantasy/s.f. illustrations— such as the one on the cover— I've found it simplest to make Half-Life 2 Episode 2 maps. The only gameplay element you need is the spawn point, and since the player spawns by default with no weapons, there's no HUDs to obscure your view as you walk around the map.

You need to enclose the whole map in a huge hollow box, which you'll apply a sky texture to. Hammer gets very unhappy if there are "leaks" which would allow the player to see off into the infinite void.

Positives:

- You can make huge environments for free. No land fees or prim limits, as in Second Life.

- The maps are based on a grid, and brushes snap to the nearest point; the granularity is changed with the [ ] keys. This, plus the orthogonal views, makes aligning objects a lot easier.

- Since the games are first person, there's no distortion induced by the camera location. On the other hand, you need to refer to your spawn point (which is a simplified avatar), or import a character model, to get the scale right. (Dimensions are in "Hammer Units"; the player is about 83 units high, so a good minimum height for walls is 100.)

- There are great tools for applying textures across multiple objects. For instance, you can select a complex set of surfaces, then apply a texture across them all in one operation; no need to manually adjust the textures at boundaries.

- You have immense control over lighting (and the lighting effects are quite good). Light sources include a bright diffuse light (i.e. the sun), point sources, and flickering lights suitable for candles or fires.

- You can put water where you want it. (One limitation, though: water doesn't reflect models, only brushes.)

- You can carve out doors from a wall— much easier than building the wall in pieces.

Negatives:

- It's not as user-friendly as Second Life. You have to get used to the orthogonal views, and things like adding water or lights can take some careful reading of the wiki pages.

- To get water and reflective surfaces working right, you need to add an env_cubemap entity, compile and run the map, open the console, and run buildcubemaps.

- The compile process can get bogged down. The compile dialog has some options that make some operations faster or skip them entirely; use them if the compilation is taking too long.

  What's actually happening is that the compiler is calculating visibility and lighting ahead of time, to save time when actually playing the game. (If something isn't visible to the player, you don't want to waste time rendering it.) There are all sorts of advanced tricks to optimize the map to save on compiling and rendering time— look them up if you really need to. (The quick 'n dirty version: if you can see everything at once, compiling and rendering will take a hit. If you've played Valve games, note how you're usually in a building or a small street where you can't see the whole map.)

- Adding character models is possible but not simple, though you might get away with using the game's models from a distance. You can always keep your architectural rendering separate from your character portraits.

- The playable area of a map is about a half-mile square, though this can be supplemented by a 'skybox' for distant objects you can see but not get to. If you want really expansive scenery, the *Skyrim* Creation Kit may be a better bet.

Hammer basics

Here's how to make your first map. Use HL2:Ep2 as the game.

1. File > New to create a blank map.
2. Click the name of the top left view (it should say **camera**); select 3-D Textured.
3. Select the Block tool (the cube) from the toolbar. Draw a square in the top right view. (This is your overhead view.) In one of the lower views, extend it vertically by dragging the white squares.
4. Hit Enter; this creates your first brush. It's a floor.
5. Select the Entity tool (the little peg). The Object field in the lower right should read info_player_start. Click in the 3-D view to place the player spawn on top of the floor; it'll be a blocky green figure.
6. Move to the Object field and type light instead. Now click in the 3-D view to place your light.
7. Select File > Run Map.

Hammer will compile the map and run HL2:Ep2 loading your map. You'll be on the floor you created, lit by your light, and can walk around. When you're bored, hit Esc and quit the game to return to Hammer.

The sky will be crazy, so you need to create a **skybox**. (The method below is deprecated for making game levels, but it's fine for making architectural vistas.)

1. Select the Block tool and create a really large box around your original one. Zoom the view back using the mouse wheel so you can make it immense— it's going to enclose the whole map.
2. Use one of the lower views to make sure it's huge upward and downward as well.
3. The info bar on the upper right shows the current teture. Hit the Browse button. In the dialog that comes up, type tools in the Filter field; this will change what textures are visible. Double-click on the sky-blue tools/toolsskybox texture to select it and leave the dialog.
4. Hit Enter to create the brush.
5. Select Tools > Make Hollow and accept the default.

Run the map again; now you have a nice sky.

You can import a large number of premade **models**.

1. Change the Object field to **prop_static**.
2. Select the Entity tool and click in the 3-D view.
3. Press Alt-Enter to bring up the properties dialog. Move to the World Model field. Then hit the Browse button.
4. Browse through the available models. You can look through each directory, or enter a filter (like **box** or **tree** or **handrail**) to narrow the selection.
5. Hit OK, then Apply. Your model is now visible in your map.

Hammer definitely doesn't hold your hand. Here's some **tips** that may not be obvious:

- Hold the *spacebar* and move the mouse to move the camera within a view (whether 2-D or 3-D).

- It's easiest to select objects by clicking within the 3-D view. It works in the other views too, but you have to click exactly on the lines of the wireframes.

- Ctrl-click to select multiple objects.

- Hold shift while dragging the mouse to duplicate an item.

- If you have an object selected in the 3-D view, Ctrl-E will center the other three views on that object. (If you have an object selected in a 2-D view, Shift-Ctrl-E will center the 3-D view on it.)

For more tips and tutorials, Google for **Valve Developer Community**.

Autodesk Softimage Mod Tool

This is a free version of the professional 3-D modeling program Audodesk Softimage; it was formerly known as XSI Mod Tool. You can use it to create models— basically, sets of complicated meshes.

There is a free add-on available to allow the Mod Tool to export models for Hammer, and models can also be exported to Second Life.

If Hammer is a bit advanced, Mod Tool is downright arcane. There's an extensive manual included, and there are online tutorials.

Further reading

Christopher **Alexander** et al., *A Pattern Language* (1977)

> An exploration of the design patterns of the "timeless way of building", principles for humane and beautiful architecture.

Philippe **Ariès** and Georges **Duby**, eds., *A History of Private Life* (1987)

> A multi-volume anthology on private life, or as we'd probably say, everyday life, from Roman to Victorian times. A treasure trove of information; worth it for the introductory essay on classical Roman life alone.

Neil **Comins**, *What if the moon didn't exist?* (1993)

> *What if the earth had two moons?* (2010)

> An astronomer's exploration of what would happen under various physical scenarios: no moon, a smaller earth, a bigger sun, etc. Much better than just guessing!

Liza **Dalby**, *Geisha* (1983)

> Not just a book about the history and habits of geisha, but an admirable exercise in participant observation. Her *Kimono* is a great follow-up.

Jared **Diamond**, *Guns, Germs, and Steel: The Fates of Human Societies* (1998)

> Why did Europeans, rather than any other culture, take over the world? A century ago the usual answer was racist: white Europeans are better. That's just know-nothingism; but till recently it was hard to come up with a better explanation. Diamond has done so, quite convincingly, using principles you can rip off for your conworld.

Jared **Diamond**, *Collapse: How Societies Choose to Fail or Succeed* (2005)

Here Diamond focuses on cultures that failed: the Easter Islanders who chopped down all the island's trees; the failed Norse colonies on Greenland; the collapse of the Maya, and more. A sobering rebuke to naive optimism that we'll always solve our problems: it really is possible for a society to destroy itself.

Dougal **Dixon**, *After Man: A Zoology of the Future* (1981)

A delightful book which painlessly introduces evolutionary biology by imagining what evolution might come up with given another 50 million years: rats evolved into mighty predators, penguins taking on the role of the whales, an island where all the main niches are filled by bats...

John King **Fairbank**, The Great Chinese Revolution 1800-1985 (1987)

Everyone should read at least one book on China; this is a good choice. Though focused on the last two centuries, it covers a much broader ground, and Fairbanks has an eye for the arresting sensory detail.

Jean **Gimpel**, *The Medieval Machine: The Industrial Revolution of the Middle Ages* (1976)

What Tolkien never told you... the Middle Ages were highly mechanically oriented, a blossoming of development in milling, clockmaking, mining, and more, all preparing the way for the explosive transformations of the Renaissance.

Jack **Hamm**, *Drawing the Head & Figure* (1963)

The book that taught me to draw. You can start from nothing, and yet there's a plethora of information for the advanced student.

Marvin **Harris**, *Cows, Pigs, Wars, and Witches: The Riddles of Culture* (1974)

A whirlwind tour of the puzzles of material culture. The title names some of them: why Hindus love their cows, why Jews and Muslims hate pigs, why people fight, why people persecuted witches. And there's more: cargo cults, messiahs, potlatch.

Marvin **Harris**, *Cultural Materialism: The Struggle for a Science of Culture* (1979)

> The advanced course after you've read the previous volume. Lots more about how material factors affect culture, though there's a bit too much railing against alternative theories.

Herodotus, *The History* (-5C)

> An entertaining and wide-ranging view of all the cultures known to the Greeks, building up to a history of the war with Persia. Herodotus's own biases and assumptions are part of what makes the book fascinating.

Jane **Jacobs**, *The Economy of Cities* (1970)

Cities and the Wealth of Nations (1984)

> Two books which do nothing less than demolish and rebuild macroeconomics. Jacobs thinks economics went wrong with Adam Smith, who built his analysis around nations rather than cities. Cities are the engine of economic progress, and if you don't have healthy cities, you're hosed.

Archer **Jones**, *The Art of War in the Western World* (1987)

> A survey of war from ancient times to the 20C, with plenty of useful detail and attention to strategy and tactics. Really, every other page I was taking notes.

Olivia **Judson**, *Dr. Tatiana's Sex Advice to All Creation* (2002)

> A witty tour of sexual behavior in nature. Gimmicky in tone— it's framed as complaints and questions about sex from animals— it's nonetheless great science, and a treasury of models for interesting aliens.

John **Keegan**, *A History of Warfare* (1993)

> Really a theoretical analysis of war: the types of war culture, the limitations on warmaking, the key military inventions, the impasse created by Clausewitz. An excellent resource, as

Keegan is very interested in the same thing as writers: what it's like to be on the battlefield.

Bernard **Lewis**, *The Middle East: A Brief History of the Last 2,000 Years* (1995)

Despite the title, it's basically a history of the Islamic Middle East, from its origins through its heady heyday to its current dilemmas. Again, a great choice for the one book on Islam you should read.

C.S. **Lewis**, *The Discarded Image: An introduction to medieval and Renaissance literature* (1964)

A masterly exposition of the medieval worldview— the order of the cosmos, the components of the body, the tripartite soul, and how everything relates to God. Full of surprises for anyone whose understanding of the Middle Ages derives from pop culture.

Alison **Lurie**, *The Language of Clothes* (1981)

A witty introduction to the history of fashion and what clothes tell about us.

Scott **McCloud**, *Making Comics* (2006)

The bits on storytelling are good, but I've included it here for the amazing section on facial expressions.

Colin **McEvedy**, *The New Penguin Atlas of Ancient History* (2002), etc.

As discussed in the Historical Atlas section (p. 105). There's a sequence of four volumes devoted to Europe, plus volumes for North America, Africa, and the Pacific Rim. Great for getting the big picture, and enlivened by McEvedy's dry wit and lapidary character portraits.

Jack **Miles**, *God: A Biography* (1995)

If you want to understand religion, this is a great place to start. It's a reading of the Old Testament with fresh eyes, seeing what's there without theological presuppositions.

F.W. **Mote**, *Imperial China 900-1800* (1999)

> Westerners are often pitifully ignorant of Chinese history, but how do you catch up? This book will take you a long way there. As a bonus, Mote examines the Central Asian nomads in unusual detail.

Claudia **Müller**, *The Costume Timeline: 5000 Years of Fashion History* (1992)

> A huge fold-out book showing 800 color pictures of costumes from around the world— a great reference for designing your own clothing.

James F. **O'Gorman**, *ABC of Architecture* (1998)

> A short explanation of the basics of architecture, focussing on the Vitruvian trinity of utility, structure, and beauty.

Mark **Rosenfelder**, *The Language Construction Kit* (2010)

> *Advanced Language Construction* (2012)

> The companions to this volume; everything you need to know about creating languages and writing systems.

Bernard **Rudofsky**, *The Unfashionable Human Body* (1971)

> An amusing survey of the most user-hostile features of clothing through the ages. Clothing designers seem to have some strange ideas about what the human body looks like.

Index

Made in the USA
San Bernardino, CA
08 February 2016